Charleston in the 20th Century

By

Tom Dunham

ISBN: 0-7596-7990-8

This book is printed on acid free paper.

1stBooks - rev. 1/30/02

Cover: Kanawha Boulevard and part of downtown about 1968. At this date, Charleston's first urban renewal project had demolished all buildings from Capitol Street to the Courthouse at bottom of the photograph. On the first lot at Capitol Street, construction had not yet begun for the Charleston National Bank. On the second lot, work had started on the Holiday Inn. To the right is the boat dock, also serving as a parking lot. Haddad Riverfront Park world later replace it.

Table of Contents

Charleston in 1900

At the opening of the Twentieth Century, Charleston, West Virginia's uninterrupted capitol since 1885 had a growing population of 11,099, of which about twenty percent were Negro. As is the case with many states, West Virginia's capitol was not the state's largest city. Wheeling with a 1900 population of over 38,000 was West Virginia's most populous city. Both Huntington and Parkersburg each with nearly 12,000 individuals were larger than Charleston.[1] However, Charleston's 11,000 individuals provided the economic strength to support four banks, a local and long distance telephone company, one hospital, thirty one physicians, sixty lawyers, a paid police and fire department, and a well organized city government.

Charleston's economy also provided its residents with a choice among nineteen restaurants and thirty-four taverns.[2] The most upscale of the taverns was George Beller's Saloon located at 812 Kanawha Street. It featured a large wood carved bar and expensive furnishings. In business at the same address from 1890 until 1914, it was a favorite among many of the city's well healed.

Choices were, however, were more limited regarding cultural and educational outlets. But the Burlew Opera House, two newspapers, and bookstore helped fill the void. The Burlew, located in the second block of Capitol Street from the Kanawha River, had opened on 1891. A native New Yorker, Noyes S. Burlew, who came to Charleston in the 1870's and built a hardware business into one of the state's largest, funded the opera house. It was a large imposing building with a seating capacity of 1500.[3] Its forty-one by sixty-five feet stage was ample for live performances, the first for the new century being" The Bachelor's Honeymoon." But the Burlew's most popular 1900 production was "The Little Minister," which had earlier in the year ran for over 300 performances in New York City. In Charleston it did nearly as well, running from April until September. By the end of the first decade, the Burlew was still viable closing out the Spring 1910 season with nine productions.[4] Most of these were musicals lasting less than a week. The Burlew would last for another decade. In 1920 it was demolished to make room for a retail business.

Charleston's bookstore in 1900 would enjoy more longevity than the Burlew. The Capitol Book Store operated by the S. Spencer Moore Company had been selling books from its Capitol Street location between Quarrier and Virginia streets since 1890. In the early part of the century, the company sold school textbooks for all grades through high school. Always marketing other items in addition to books including wallpaper, stationary, and office furniture, the Moore Company became one of Charleston's most stable businesses lasting until 1987.[5]

Reading interest was partially satisfied by Charleston's two daily newspapers, the Charleston Daily Gazette and the Daily Mail Tribune. The older Gazette with offices at 305 Kanawha Street had been a daily since 1887. In January 1907, the name was changed to the Charleston Gazette. By either name, it was a Democratic paper, and it did not waver in subsequent years. Before the turn of the century, the Daily Mail Tribune had undergone many ownership and name changes. Later in 1900, the word "Daily was dropped from the name, and in June 1901, the paper became the Daily Mail. Calling itself the "Official Paper of the State Capitol," it was in 1900 published from offices at 79 Capital Street. As steady as the Gazette in political orientation, it was Republican at the outset and kept that posture throughout the century. Other than their political leaning, both papers were similar. The Gazette's page size was slightly larger, but both published eight pages daily with no photographs and small headlines except when one of their political favorites was elected. Cost for both was three cents per issue or four dollars per year by subscription.[6]

Although there were no photographs, both papers in 1900 carried numerous display ads with line drawings, a relief to the reader from the imposing mass of type characteristic of many of the pages. Both papers carried the passenger railroad and packet steamer schedules and rates. Neither paper had a sports page, but the Gazette and not the Mail Tribune reported the major league baseball scores. Although both papers carried medical advertisements promising cures for everything from cancer to drunkenness, the reader of medical self help would do better with the Mail Tribune.

Charleston's public school system had been organized in 1864. It was in 1900 as mandated by state law a segregated system. The first notable superintendent was George S. Laidley, who was appointed by the nine-member board in 1878. Except for the years 1881 to 1883, he held the position until 1922. The oldest white schools in 1900 were Mercer and Union schools, both east of the Elk River. Mercer, located on Washington Street, was built in 1889 while Union School opened three years later on State (later Lee) Street. On the West Side, Lincoln School at Maryland Avenue was the oldest as the century opened, having been built in 1898. These three schools provided instruction through the eighth grade. Charleston High School for white students was completed in 1903 on Quarrier Street.

Hotel Ruffner, Charleston's longest lasting hotel, serving guest from 1885 to 1970.

The "colored schools" as they were then known, were Garnet School for the lower grades, which had opened in 1889, and Garnet High School built in 1910. Both schools were located on the same lot on Jacob Street in the East End. As Charleston's population doubled by 1910, several more schools both white and colored were built later in the first decade. From the beginning to the end of the decade, the number of students grew from 2000 to 4900 and teachers from forty-seven to 137.[7]

A significant post secondary institution began in Charleston in 1906 when William S.Mason founded the Mason School of Music and Fine Arts. Mason, in his early thirties when he opened the school on Quarrier Street near Brooks, was an accomplished violinist having been trained in New York, France, and Germany. Mason headed the institution until his death in 1941. In 1936 Mason School became Mason College and began conferring the Bachelor of Science degree. The Mason College would last until 1958 when it was absorbed by Morris Harvey College.[8]

Charleston did not have a public library in 1900. That was not to come until 1909 when it was founded by the Woman's Kanawha Literary Club. When first organized the library had no public funding, being maintained by subscriptions and entertainments. Like the public schools, the library was also segregated. According to Laidley, it "is a free public library to which every white citizen of Charleston is welcome." For its first two years, it was located in two rooms of the YMCA building at Charleston and State streets near the Governor's residence. After 1911 the library, never with a building of its own, would move numerous times through the decade.[9]

Charleston's churches in 1900 like the public schools and the library were also segregated, but it was segregation by custom not by state law as were the schools. The most numerous denominations serving the white congregations were the Presbyterian and the Methodist each with seven churches. In addition there were four Baptist churches, three Episcopalian, one Lutheran, one Catholic, and one Christian church. There were also two synagogues. The Second Baptist Church at McCormick and Sage streets, the Simpson Methodist Episcopal at Quarrier and Dickinson streets, and the First Baptist Church on Washington Street served the colored congregations.[10]

Some of these church buildings still serve their congregations. Among the most architecturally significant is the Kanawha Presbyterian Church, which opened in 1885 on Virginia Street. St John's Episcopal Church at Quarrier and Broad streets was completed in 1890 and the Catholic Sacred Heart Church opened at Virginia and Broad streets in 1895.

The Reform Jewish community built the Temple Bene Jeshurum in 1894 on Virginia Street near Brooks, which served them until 1960 when the Temple Israel was completed on Kanawha Blvd. The Orthodox Jews in 1900 were holding services in a Court Street building that the congregation had purchased for $100 in 1895. The members remained there until 1908 when they purchased for $14,500 the former State Street Methodist Church, which served them for over forty years. In April 1950, the Orthodox community dedicated the B'nai Jacob Synagogue at Virginia and Elizabeth Streets.[11]

Business development

Although telephones in Charleston can be traced to 1880, formal organization of telephone service did begin until 1895 when a group of business interests formed the Charleston Home Telephone Company with a plant on Kanawha Street at Hale Street to service its 500 telephones. Long distance service to Montgomery was established the following year, and by 1897 plans were laid to connect Charleston with Parkersburg, Wheeling, and Pittsburgh. Business steadily grew, and in 1906 the company constructed its own building on Hale Street in order to better serve its some 1200 telephone subscribers. In 1911, the Southern Bell Telephone and Telegraph Company absorbed the local company with its 3000 telephones. By 1917, statewide organization had arrived, and in that year the Chesapeake and Potomac Telephone Company had taken over Charleston's telephone service. [12]

By 1900 the Charleston Natural Gas Company was supplying the city with gas lighting and homes with cooking fuel. The company was organized in 1892 and the following year began installing pipelines in the city. Like many young businesses at the time, many re-organizations were occurring. By 1905 the company was known as the United States Natural Gas Company, which in turn became the United Fuel Gas Company. Coal was viewed as the gas company's chief competitor at least in the area of home cooking. A newspaper ad in 1900 made the following pitch for gas cooking.

> If you burn coal, your cook will fill your house with dread. Your wife will wish she
> Had never wed. And you will wish you were dead. If you burn gas, your cook will
> Stay; your wife will be gay and you will say, "why didn't I burn natural gas before.[13]

Under the name "United Fuel," the company would last for several decades. In 1913 the company constructed a new three-story building at Quarrier and Dunbar streets and in 1928 added four additional stories. United Fuel remained at Quarrier Street until 1957 when it moved across the river to South Ruffner.

Electricity had existed in Charleston since 1887. An inventor named Otto Michaelson supplied the technical know-how and clothing merchant Philip Frankenburger the seed money to form the Kanawha Electric Light Company with a plant on Alterson Street just west of the downtown. At first the company's only product was street lighting, supplementing the gas streetlights that were first installed in 1871. In 1891 the electric company merged with a small gas company to form the Charleston Gas and Electric Company. Two years later the company installed a direct current generator at the Alterson plant, and it was ready to move beyond street lighting into electric motors. The Kanawha Valley Bank took advantage of this development in 1895 by installing an elevator in its year old building.

After the electric company began to grid the city, the Charleston Traction Company wasted little time modernizing its public transit system. Streetcar tracks had been laid in 1890 and since then Charleston residents rode mule drawn streetcars. When the mules gave way to the electric streetcars in 1894, there was just one transit route in the East End. Known later as the inner loop, the cars departed at Capitol Street, travelling east along Virginia Street to Brooks, then north to Smith Street, and west back to Capitol. This route benefited passengers wanting to board a Kanawha and Michigan railroad car at the Smith Street station. When the streetcars became electrified, a middle loop was added that extended farther east along Virginia Street to Ruffner, across to Washington Street and back to Capitol. In 1903 an outer loop took passengers yet farther east to Duffy Street still using Virginia and Washington streets. The West Side also enjoyed streetcar service. Its first tracks were laid along Tennessee Street and Bigley Avenue. In 1906, service was extended to Edgewood Park and later streetcars ran all the way to the Kelly Axe Handle Plant at Patrick Street.[14]

By the end of the decade, the traction company had twelve miles of tracks within the city and the number of cars had increased from six to twenty-four. The company's car barns were located on Virginia Street near Tennessee, site of the later Goodwill Industries. In 1910 the Charleston Interurban Railroad Company absorbed the local traction company and began to extend service east to St Albans and west to Cabin Creek. By 1912 the assessed valuation of the company was $625,000.[15]

Charleston was served by three railroads as the century opened. The oldest was the Chesapeake and Ohio, which entered Charleston from Virginia in 1873 and extended west to Huntington, Cincinnati, and beyond. The railroad officials laid the tracks on the south side of the Kanawha, and until a bridge was completed some eighteen years later, passengers from Charleston had to reach the train by river ferry. With a dining car and Pullman sleeping car, the C&O train departed Charleston eight times daily, four eastbound and four westbound. Complementing the C&O was the Kanawha and Michigan Railroad that entered

Charleston from Columbus in 1884. Its tracks extended east and west on the north side of the city, and to the bane of later motorists, intersected major streets on both the east and West Side of Charleston. After reaching Charleston, the K&M continued east to Gauley Bridge where its tracks crossed the Kanawha and connected with the C&O. One could take this line daily to Cincinnati, Columbus, Toledo, and Detroit. The third railroad laid its tracks to Charleston along the Elk River in 1890. In the mid-1890's, the Charleston, Clendenin, and Sutton Railway was purchased by Henry Gassaway Davis, who renamed it the Coal and Coke Railroad and extended the tracks to Elkins. By 1917, the railroad was in the hands of the Baltimore and Ohio.[16]

As convenient as railroad service appeared to be in 1900, Charleston residents were not limited to rail travel, for paddlewheel steamers regularly plied the Kanawha and the Ohio rivers. In 1898 the U.S. Corps of Engineers completed its quarter century endeavor of constructing a system of dams and locks along the Kanawha. Covering the span from the headwaters at the Gauley to the Ohio River the locks gave the Kanawha a navigable depth of six feet and afforded a cheap means of transportation to river travelers.[17] Several steamers departed Charleston. The Green Line Steamer Company operated two steamers. The Greenland, carrying both passengers and freight between Charleston and Pittsburgh departed each Monday. One-way fare was five dollars. In 1903 the Green Line put a new Greenland, equipped with telephones and electric fans, into service. The company's second steamer, the Evergreen, running between Charleston and Winfield in Putnam County, had a six-day per week round trip between the two cities. To get to Pittsburgh travelers did not have to rely on the Monday Greenland departure, for there were other steamers departing on other days. The steamer, Kanawha, for example departed each Friday destined for Pittsburgh.[18]

Serving the many rail and boat passengers into Charleston were eleven hotels in the first years of the new century. These were located in the downtown area along Kanawha, Capitol, and Summers streets. The two most prestigious at the time were the Ruffner and the Kanawha. The Ruffner, located on Kanawha Street at Hale Street facing the river, had been open since 1885. Originally built with five floors, two more were added in 1903 giving the hotel 175 guestrooms and a dining room. The Ruffner would be the most long lasting hotel in Charleston history, serving guests until 1970.[19]

The other first class hotel, according to contemporaries, was the Kanawha. Located at Summers and Virginia streets with its entrance on the north side away from the river, it opened in 1902 with seven stories. According to the contemporary chronicler, Laidley, it was West Virginia's largest hotel with 200 guestrooms. The Kanawha was one of the first buildings in Charleston with elevators, having been built with two. Other prominent hotels in 1900 were the two-dollar per night St Albert on Kanawha Street and the one-dollar per night Washburn on Capitol Street.

Travelers and residents alike were served by four banks in 1900. Charleston's oldest bank at the time was the Kanawha Valley Bank. Established in 1867 and located at the northwest corner of Kanawha and Capitol streets, the bank worked from two unimpressive buildings until 1894 when it completed a distinguished structure at the same location. Four stories high and set off with a turret over the main entrance, this building enhanced by a 1911 renovation, served the bank until 1929 when it moved to the north end of Capitol Street. The 1894 building survived until 1963 when it was demolished.

First in longevity among the remaining three banks was the Charleston National Bank located at 45 Capitol Street. It was established in 1884 and by 1900 its $300,000 of capital made it the largest of Charleston's banks. A third bank, the Citizens National Bank, located at Capitol and Quarrier streets had begun operations in 1890. With capital of $100,000, the Kanawha National Bank was the smallest of Charleston's banks in 1900. It too was located on Capitol Street. By the end of the first decade, the doubling of Charleston's population had resulted in the addition of six more banks. The ten banks now had a combined capital of $2,000,000 and deposits of $7,000,000.[20]

Wholesaling and Manufacturing

As a commercial city in 1900, contemporary observers have stressed Charleston's importance as a wholesale distribution center. In his 1898 book, Charleston and Its Resources, J.C. Tipton who was manager of the Mail-Tribune company, characterized Charleston as a mercantile city with ample distribution facilities. Tipton no doubt had in mind Charleston's three railroads and the Kanawha River shipping. At the time of his writing wholesale businesses numbered forty-six with annual receipts of $6.5 million. The investment in these businesses amounted to about $1.7 million. This book as was characteristic of the period depicts Charleston in glowing terms. In typical hyperbole, Tipton wrote that Charleston merchants in the past twenty years have "built up a jobbing trade and met the strongest competition both from the east and west, and in every line of goods came out a winner…." By the end of decade, a survey completed by the Charleston Chamber of Commerce called Charleston one the most important wholesale centers between Richmond and Cincinnati. In the distribution of such commodities as groceries, dry goods, shoes, feed and furniture, Charleston merchants, according to the Chamber grossed about $15 million per year.[21]

The largest wholesale business in Charleston at the turn of the century was Lewis, Hubbard & Company. Beginning in 1881 the grocery wholesaler grew steadily and in 1898 the partners built a large, five-story warehouse at Hale and

Quarrier Streets. Offices remained at 321 Virginia Street, a building still in use overlooking the South Side bridge ramp. In the same year, Lewis and Hubbard spun off another business from the firm by creating the Charleston Grain and Feed Company with offices at the same location. Because of growing business to the east, the company in 1900 established a branch in Roncerverte. According to the Chamber of Commerce, Lewis and Hubbard had annual monetary receipts totaling several millions. Another successful grocery jobber was the Ruffner Bros Company located at 306 Kanawha Street. Like Lewis and Hubbard, the partners shipped to many out of state locations. Other wholesalers in 1900 were James Laidley and Wholesale Produce.[22]

There were also four hardware wholesalers in Charleston. Noyes E. Burlew had established Burlew Hardware in 1876 and by 1900 Burlew had a large wholesale as well as a retail business. Located at 284 Kanawha Street, the wholesaler shipped such items as doors, windows, floor tiles, grates and other building supplies. Like Burlew, Goshorn & Company enjoyed retail as well as a wholesale business. Located in the same block as Burlew at 246 Kanawha Street, Goshorn had the largest floor space in Charleston selling such large items as wagons, wheelbarrows, and mine supplies. Goshorn also carried a full line of fishing supplies, guns, and ammunition. The other two hardware wholesalers were Charleston Hardware Company on Capitol Street and Lovell C. Gates on Kanawha Street.

Marketing a wide variety of lines was the D.A. Brawley Company. Brawley shipped heating and cooking stoves, tin ware, glass and china, table cutlery, and ice boxes. Lowenstein and Sons located on Capitol Street also marketed many lines, but was known as a manufacturer of saddles and harness equipment. One of the largest businesses in Charleston, Lowenstein employed about fifty men in the early part of the century.

The Kanawha Drug Company was one of the newer businesses in the city. Organized in 1901 and located in the first block of Summers Street off Kanawha, this firm in its first year was shipping as far as 150 miles from Charleston. On Virginia Street near Capitol the Payne Shoe Company from its four-story building was manufacturing, selling, and shipping shoes to the southern and western states. The Payne Company manufactured a full line of men, women, and children's shoes. Other wholesalers included those in such lines as dry goods, meat, and furniture. Lumber was much in demand at this time, and four companies milled and shipped timber.[23]

Although the value of manufacturing was not in league with Charleston's wholesale business, it was nevertheless significant. The West Virginia State Gazetteer for 1900 refers to Charleston as the state's third city in size and commercial importance. We have seen that in population Charleston was fourth behind Wheeling, Huntington, and Parkersburg. Moreover, Charleston in 1900 also lagged behind these three cities in manufacturing production. According to the U.S. Census, Charleston's manufacturing value in 1899 was just over $1.2 million well behind state leading Wheeling whose manufacturing production totaled over $15 million. Huntington and Parkersburg more than doubled Charleston, each with over $3.0 million of manufacturing production. By 1909 Charleston's manufacturing value was still fourth statewide at $ 3.2 million, but showed the greatest percentage gain. Wheeling still led the state in manufacturing with over $27 million. The census narrative pointed out that Charleston's gain was due to increased output in its flourmills, gristmills, foundries, and sawmills. The number of Charleston's manufacturing plants varied between forty-eight and sixteen-three in the century's first decade while Huntington's highest number was sixteen-seven and Parkersburg's seventy-five. Wheeling had 176 manufacturing plants in 1909. In number of wage earners in these plants, Charleston had between 686 and 951 during the decade. Huntington reached 3156 manufacturing employees and Parkersburg employed as many as 1495. Wheeling's plants in 1909 employed 7809. [24]

However, a 1910 Charleston Chamber of Commerce survey reported that the Capitol City employed some 2600 manufacturing workers. The discrepancy was due to the Chamber survey counting the Kelly Axe Manufacturing Company, which lay just over the city boundary on the west side of Patrick Street along the Kanawha River. Later this would be part of Charleston. The Kelly Company was the area's largest employer with about 1200 workers. Kelly had relocated to Charleston from Indiana in 1904 and occupied about twenty-five acres along the river. It manufactured axes, scythes, hatches, and handles. Differing from the U.S. Census, the Chamber reported that Charleston's other manufacturing plants employed about 1400 workers.

Charleston of course had many manufacturing plants older that Kelly. One of the oldest was Ward Engineering Works, which began operations in 1872 on the north side of the Kanawha next to the C&O Station. The company, started by Charles Ward an engineer from England, manufactured water tube boilers, marine engines, tow boats, and tug boats. The company employed forty to fifty men. Ward died in 1915, and his son Ed assumed control of the company. Also in production since the 1870's was the Kanawha Woolen Mills located at Virginia and Clendenin streets just west of the downtown. The company with seventy-five employees at the turn of the century manufactured flannels, jeans, blankets, and yard goods.

Opening in 1891, the Ohio Valley Furniture Company concentrated on dining room furniture. Located in the East End near the Kanawha and Michigan Railroad, this plant in the early part of the century had over $200,000 in annual sales with 150 employees. The Kanawha Brick Company also got started before the new century. With two plants, one on the West Side and the other above

Charleston on the south side of the Kanawha, the company turned out 50,000 bricks per day.

Two companies in particular served the growing coal industry. The South Side Foundry and Machine Works was first established in 1870 and reorganized in 1899. It manufactured mine cars, mine equipment, and smoke stacks from its plant on the south side of the Kanawha west of the C&O Station. By 1910 the foundry employed about 100 workers. The Kanawha Mine Car Company produced lumber supplies as well as mine cars. It opened in 1902 and soon employed about fifty-five workers.

Like the Mine Car Company, many of Charleston's businesses were established during the first decade. Opening in 1902 The Charleston Manufacturing Company turned out work shirts and overalls from its West Side, Charleston Street plant. Soon it employed 125 workers who in addition to production also shipped goods to states south and west of West Virginia. Established the same year, the Gill Manufacturing Company produced kitchen cabinets and other household furniture.

In the same business line was the Morgan Lumber and Manufacturing Company. Opening in 1910 with offices on Columbia Avenue (later Kanawha Blvd) and mills on Pennsylvania Avenue, Morgan produced desks, stair casings, and office furniture. In its second year of business, Morgan had sales of over $200,000 and employed over sixty workers. Also on the West Side on Virginia Avenue near the Elk River was the Vulcan Iron Works. Since 1900 the company had been doing general forge and foundry work with about twenty-five workers.

Near the Elk and just north of the downtown in a district that would later be known as the Triangle Area were two manufacturing businesses both opening in 1907. The Elk Milling Company on Bullitt Street produced feed and meal and also wholesaled flour and produce. The Kanawha Brewing Company grew out of the Charleston Brewing Company established in 1903. With forty employees at its Bullitt Street plant it could produce 50,000 barrels of beer annually.[25]

Retail

Much of Charleston's ample retail facilities were concentrated in the downtown, an area defined by Capitol, Summers, Kanawha, and Virginia streets. Kanawha Street in 1900 and for nearly four more decades had retail outlets on the river side as well as the north side of the street. Businesses were especially concentrated in the area where the street intersected with Summers, Capitol, and Hale streets. The downtown was a motley collection of stores. Even large ticket items as Steinway pianos could be purchased on Capitol Street.Several clothiers and smaller versions of department stores dotted the area. One of the principal clothiers was Frankenburger and Company, which had been selling men and boys clothing since 1860. Its latest location was on Kanawha Street at Summers. Other prominent haberdasheries were Schwabe and May, Wertheimer, Philadelphia One Price, and tailors E.A. Boone and Howten & Baird all located on Capitol Street. Beginning business in 1880, Schwabe and May proved to be the most durable of the downtown businesses. Finishing out the 19th Century and the 20th, it is currently in its third century. Another successful and long-lasting retailer was the Woodrum Outfitting Company, specializing in home furnishings. In 1906 C.E. and John Woodrum opened their business at 502 Virginia Street. Successful from the beginning, the partners moved to larger quarters two blocks away on Virginia Street the following year. In 1916 they built a new and permanent store at 602 Virginia Street, where the business was to remain for over fifty years.[26]

Christmas season of 1900 may not have been as commercial as later in the century, but Charleston retailers with heavy advertising gave the season a commercial flair. Both daily newspapers in December carried large, display advertising of the many merchants. Grand Rapids Furniture store on Capitol Street in repeated ads reminded shoppers of the declining days until Christmas. Goldberg and Strauss daily pitched its clothing line while the Loeb Shoe Company also daily touted its shoes. Sterrett Brothers, marketing carpets and curtains, was another repeated advertiser. Pringle and Company, selling home furnishings, ran frequent large display ads throughout the season. All these merchants were located downtown. Pre-Christmas sales were common. G.T. Barlow, located on Court Street, advertised twenty percent off on rocking chairs. And bookseller, S. Spencer Moore, offered discounts not only on books, but on toys and calendars as well.[27]

A standard West Virginia history text characterized Charleston in the early years of the 20th Century, as a "quite, rustic Southern town whose repose was disturbed only by the arrival and departure of numerous trains...."[28] This description connotes a lethargic town without verve or energy. But the pace of business activity renders such a description inaccurate. Actually Charleston was a bustling city—building and growing within its boundaries and expanding outward. From 1900 Charleston's population had doubled to more than 22,000 by 1910, and in the decade city boundaries had expanded westward and across the Kanawha. Retail outlets can provide a gauge of the growing activities. Grocers increased in the first decade from seventy-four to 135, druggists from eleven to seventeen, hardware stores from eight to ten, jewelers from seven to ten, and clothing stores from eight to twenty-five. Significantly the number of building contractors jumped from three to thirty-four in the decade. Business listings in the 1901 City Directory took up thirty-seven pages, but the 1911 Directory needed eighty-two pages to list all of Charleston's businesses.

As the century opened, Charleston was devoid of outlying suburbs, and most business owners lived near the central city and walked or road a horse to work. Clothing merchant Philip Frankenburger lived at 415 Virginia Street and his colleague Isadore Schwabe lived nearby at 436 Virginia Street. A few lived farther out east along the river. John Q. Dickinson, President of the Kanawha Valley Bank, lived at 1330 Kanawha Street and shoe storeowner, Charles Payne, resided at 1120 Kanawha Street. But proximity to their work did not make business any easier. There was no lock on any given market and competition was keen. Charleston residents in their shopping had many choices, forcing merchants to advertise heavily and offer quality merchandise. As the new century opened, Charleston was very much a middle class, commercial, and retail city, not a "quite and rustic" town.[29]

Charleston's government

Unlike Charleston's 1900 economy that was vibrant, bustling, and growing, the city's government was neither energetic nor forward looking. It had no planning department or any governmental structure that looked to the future. Such a body would not emerge until the late 1930's. Charleston's early 20th Century governments touched the lives of most residents lightly if at all. Social programs or any legislation concerning citizen rights were unheard of. The city government played largely a caretaker role, involved almost wholly in what later generations would call the infrastructure—streets, sewers, and building construction.

A detailed city budget for 1900 is not extant, but some statistics are available. In September 1900, the Council set the property tax levy at $1.25 per $100 of assessed valuation. Other than fines and fees, the property tax was the city government'sole means of support. Since the property assessment was just over $3.9 million, the city would have about $49,000 in revenue for the fiscal year. As an aid in helping the Council set the levy, the Treasurer reported that city would need $40,000 for general revenue expenses (this would include salaries), $37,000 for unpaid bills, $2500 for bonded debt, and $1118 for other debt. This is obviously more that what the levy would raise. The balance would come from special assessments for street improvements. As was characteristic of many cities of the time, Charleston paid for street paving and other street improvements by assessing property owners whose property fronted the section of the street being paved. For 1900 Council reported that about $50,000 was due the city from street and sewer assessments.[30]

The limited scope of city government can be gleaned by the budgetary funds in use in 1900. These were a street and drainage fund, a light and gas fund, and a water fund. Other than the police and fire fund, these funds were the only ones dealing with actual, substantive duties of the city. For accounting reasons the city used a sinking fund for control of bonds, a contingency fund, and a salary fund. A report in October 1900 concerning salaries showed the Mayor's monthly salary at $83, recorder $75, Treasurer $33, the entire fire department $420 and the police department $650.[31]

In 1900 Charleston was governed by a Charter enacted by the West Virginia Legislature in 1899. The Home Rule Amendment would not become part of the state constitution until 1936, and until that time the state legislature wrote the charters for all municipalities having a population over 2000. Though legislative lobbying occurred, neither the city councils nor the voters had a formal role in the charter process. The 1899 Charter perpetuated the Mayor-Council form of government first established by the Virginia Legislature in 1861. In 1900 the elected city administrators were the Mayor, Treasurer, Recorder (later Clerk), Assessor and the City Sergeant (tax collector), all serving two-year terms. The Mayor appointed a City Engineer and a Solicitor. The City Council consisted of fourteen members, two from each of the seven wards. Council elections were held annually. A 1901 amendment to the charter created the office of Police Judge to be filled by a two year Council appointment.[32]

Charleston was protected in 1900 by a paid eleven-man police force under a chief. In the same year the city employed thirteen firemen and a chief. In no sense could the police and fire departments be called professional, for the Council appointed all employees of both departments on the basis of political party. In the city elections of March 1900 the Democrats were turned out. The Republican Council with a ten to four majority began firing the Democrats and hiring Republican police and firemen. Within a month of the election, the new Council had appointed a new Fire Chief and six firemen. The Gazette made a point of mentioning that one of new firemen was "colored." The new firemen quickly gained experience, for monthly reports to Council usually indicated between five and fourteen fires per month.[33]

A charter amendment in 1903 mandated a re-assessment of property in that year and every fifth year thereafter. Although street paving had been provided for by the Virginia Legislature as early as 1833, it was not until the 1899 Charter that the city had to bid the paving contracts through newspaper advertisements.

Aside from the inevitable taxation, running afoul of the law, or unfortunate enough to need the fire department, residents principally came into contact with their government in the area of building construction. Permission to construct a house or building required a permit from the Council. However, in 1900 this appears to have been an easy task. In the absence of a zoning ordinance there was little objective criteria on which to deny a citizen petition for a building permit. The Council minutes for 1900 indicate many permit requests and all appeared to be granted. In January 1900, for example, Council granted building permits for the construction of a stable on Broad Street and for a blacksmith shop on Virginia Street.[34]

Council in 1900 also served as a conduit for businessmen wanting to sell liquor. Liquor permits were granted or denied by he County Court, but individuals first had to obtain permission from the Council to make application to the County. In the early years of the century, Council licensed a Wharf Master. For a fee of $425 in 1900 this individual controlled the city boat dock, making a living by levying docking fees.[35]

In 1907 the legislature enacted a new charter for Charleston. This charter was significant because it abolished the Mayor-Council form and established a three member Board of Affairs, each one elected for a two-year term from one of the three new districts defined by the Charter. The Board was the purchasing agent for the city and would pay all accounts. It had meaningful power through its ability to veto Council ordinances. Other elected officials under the charter were a Mayor, a Recorder, and a Treasurer each elected for two years. The ten wards were retained with two members from each ward. Meeting twice each month, Council members could not be paid.

In this national period of progressivism, the legislature in an attempt to create a non-partisan city government enacted a new Charter just two years later. The 1909 Charter retained the Board of Affairs, but increased the membership to four, each one to administer one of the four departments created by the charter. These were Finance, Public Safety, Police, and Streets. A separate elected Mayor was abolished in favor of the Board of Affairs member who received the highest number of votes becoming Mayor. As a body the Board appointed the Fire Chief, Auditor, and Health Commissioner. The Mayor alone named the Police Chief, Street Commissioner, City Attorney, and Police Judge. All appointments whether by the Board or the Mayor required Council confirmation. The new charter retained the ten wards but now four members were to be elected from each ward and no more than two could be elected from the same party. Thus the Council would have twenty Democrats and twenty Republicans. This brand of non-partisanism extended to the police and fire departments. Police and firemen were now hired so that each department had an equal number of employees from each political party.[36] This form of government would take the city half way through the next decade when the legislature would again draft a new charter.

Prelude to the Twenties

During the period of the First World War, specifically about 1915, industry in the Kanawha Valley began to cast a larger shadow. Far larger manufacturing plants than the Charleston area had experienced began to appear. The importance of coal, oil, and gas now became evident, and Charleston being the trade center of this activity became known as COG City. Employment in these industries continued to grow in the years preceding the Twenties and into the decade. By 1923 the area's seven oil and gas plants surveyed by the Charleston Chamber of Commerce employed nearly 1000 individuals. United Fuel Gas Company employed about one-half the total and the oil refinery to the east at Cabin Creek employed another 200.[1]

In part attracted to the area by the cheap supply of natural gas, the glass industry became a significant manufacturing force in Charleston during World War I when the Libby Owens Company and the Owens Bottle Company began operations in Kanawha City (not yet a part of Charleston). Though these operations were the largest, they were not the first glass companies in the Kanawha Valley. The Banner Window Glass Company in South Charleston, the Dunkirk Glass Company and the Dunbar Flint Glass Company both in Dunbar, and the Whittemore Glass Company all pre-date the First World War. Libby-Owens built the first units of its operations in 1916 at the east end of MacCorkle Avenue in Kanawha City, and by 1923 it had an eighteen-unit plant producing sheet glass for a worldwide market. Later it purchased the Dunkirk Glass Company and the Whittlemore Glass Company. By 1923 Libby-Owens employed about 700 men and women. It remained a Charleston fixture until 1980 when it closed, and its site became the Kanawha Mall. Owens Bottle Company opened in 1917 across the street from the sheet glass plant. By 1923 employment had reached about 500. In 1929, it merged with the national Owens-Illinois Company. It is interesting to note that when the Twenty-First Amendment repealing prohibition was ratified, Owens bottle business saw a sharp increase. The Charleston plant would last until 1964 when it permanently closed.[2]

During the war years, the chemical industry largely concentrated in South Charleston along the Kanawha began to make its imprint in Charleston and the Kanawha Valley. In 1915 the Rollins Chemical Company and the Warner Klipstein Company opened plants in South Charleston to produce chlorine and alkaloid products for the war effort. The following year Union Carbine Company began operations up the Elk at Clendenin. Following these enterprises the federal government built an ordinance plant along route 60 in South Charleston producing armor plates and gun forgings for navy ships. It closed in 1922 and re-opened in 1939 for the next war. Farther west along the Kanawha, the federal government gave birth to the town of Nitro by constructing an explosive plant and thousands of housing units for the workers. Opening in 1917, the plant closed just eleven months later, but the town was to last.

In the Twenties consolidation in the chemical industry began and some of the older names disappeared. Rollins Chemical in 1923 was purchased by Barium Reduction Corporation, which in turn was absorbed by Union Carbide after its move from Clendenin to South Charleston. Warner Klipstein in 1925 became Westvaco Chlorine Products Corporation.[3] In 1926 a survey by the Chamber of Commerce showed thirteen chemical plants in the Valley having a total investment of over $24 million and employing over 2500. Unlike the small manufacturing plants at the turn of the century, these newer companies measured employment in the hundreds. The five electrical plants employed nearly 1100 with an investment of over $12 million; and the three steel plants including the Naval Ordinance Plant employed about 2500.[4]

As new style manufacturing made it impact, local and regional transportation continue to grow. We saw that in 1910 the Charleston Traction Company was absorbed by the interurban, a development that allowed passengers to travel conveniently east and west of the city. Service had been extended west to St Albans in 1912. But eastbound service had to wait on a bridge across the Kanawha. This occurred in 1915 when the Charleston Interurban Railroad Company built the Kanawha City Bridge. Constructed to carry the sixty-ton streetcars, the $150,000 bridge also served automobile traffic. The company, however, levied a toll on all vehicles, which remained until 1928 when the city of Charleston purchased the bridge. The Charleston Daily Mail hailed the July 2 bridge opening, predicting that 50,000 people as far east as Montgomery would now have access to Charleston resulting in increased business that would be measured in the hundreds of thousands of dollars. Within a month of the bridge opening, service was extended to Malden and by September to Marmet. Montgomery would see service within months. But immediately after the July opening streetcars were running every twenty minutes east along MacCorkle Avenue. By 1918 the interurban had a monthly payroll of $12,000 for its 300 employees[5].

New Buildings

While industry was growing in the World War I period, Charleston was being aesthetically improved by the construction of many historically significant buildings that were to last into the next century. The eight-story Terminal Building was completed in 1910 at the northeast corner of Kanawha and Capitol streets. Always a busy intersection at the head of downtown, the popular Philadelphia One Price Store had been in business at this site since the turn of the century. The building it occupied was demolished to make way for the new building. Constructed of brick, the Terminal Building is distinguished by its curved corner on the southeast side and by its terra cotta parapet. As the Terminal Building opened the Alterson Stephenson Building just across Kanawha Street was a work in progress. Opening in 1911, it was noted for its height—at fourteen floors it was Charleston's tallest building. It was designed by Washington D.C. architect, Clarence Harding, who gave the front a Beaux-Arts look with ornamental details of animal heads, garlands, and urns. The original builders sold the skyscraper just two years later, and for many years the Union Trust Bank occupied it. When the bank moved out, it became known as the Union Building. In the building's first years, a popular restaurant was located on the top floor.

In June 1915 the present Security Building opened as headquarters of the Kanawha National Bank. Located at the northeast corner of Capitol and Virginia streets, the bank had been in business at this location since 1893. The bank razed its old building in 1913 in order construct a more modern facility. A Charleston architectural survey stated that the building represented the early 20th century movement away from the Victorian to the Classical style. The Kanawha National Bank would use its building for just fifteen years, becoming a victim of consolidation in 1930. The Security Bank and Trust Company on the West Side purchased the building, and when it occupied it in March 1931, the building henceforth was known as the Security Building. Another distinguished downtown bank building housed the Kanawha Banking and Trust Company. No longer a bank, but being renovated for other uses, the building was completed in 1918 on the west side of Capitol Street just north of Virginia Street. It is notable for its twelve stories with a three-story base.

Although originally built in 1897, the Masonic Building on Virginia Street at Hale was extensively renovated between 1914 and 1916. Constructed of brick with four floors, the first floor of the building was in its early years used by various wholesale distributors while Masons used the upper floors. Then in July 1914 the building was severely damaged by lighting and fire. In redesigning both the inside and outside of the building, Charleston architect H. Rus Warne added a fifth floor and included a sheath of white terra cotta over the entire structure. The building was ready for use in April 1916.[6]

Adding to Charleston's already impressive church architecture was the First Presbyterian Church building that was completed in June 1915. The church, located at the corner of Virginia and Broad streets, is just a block east of the older Kanawha Presbyterian Church whose building was completed in 1886. Designed by Weber-Warner-Atkins, First Presbyterian's building is distinguished by its six column Roman exterior topped by a fifty-two feet diameter dome of Byzantine character.[7]

During the second decade and into the Twenties the social scene among Charleston's affluent was growing, and the Gazette and Daily Mail began to expand its coverage of the dances, teas, parties, and programs of the well healed. By 1919, the Daily Mail carried a page called "Social and Personal" in which the social events were reported. The Gazette's equivalent page was called "Society." These pages, however, were not eye-catching, as they were not at this date embellished with photographs of the events' personalities. Much of the social life took place at the Edgewood Country Club, which developed from the Glenwood Athletic Club chartered in 1898. When the country club was organized in the first years of the century, its members purchased several acres at the top of the recently platted Edgewood subdivision, which was to become one of Charleston's finest addresses. In November 1907 the members, through the Edgewood Building Association, completed its $125,000 clubhouse and in 1911 extensively remodeled it to better suit the growing social life. To complete the story of the clubhouse, it was consumed by fire in the early morning hours of December 27, 1935, ending the holiday events for that season. But about ten months later the members had completed a new clubhouse at the same spacious site. Opening day was Halloween 1936.[8]

In September 1920 the autumnal social season began with a Cotillion Club dance at the Elks Club. The date of September 7 was set to allow members time to return from Summer resorts. The Club's first of the month dances would continued through the following Spring. During the Christmas season of the same year dances and parties were in full swing. One of the season's highlights was the Edgewood Country Club dance for members only. For the December 23 event, the Club brought in an orchestra from Cincinnati. A midnight buffet was served, and dancing continued into the early morning hours.[9]

Government

In 1915 the Legislature enacted a new Charter for Charleston marking a significant change in city government. After eight years the Board of Affairs was abolished and the form of government basically reverted to what it had been prior to 1907. Two Councilmen from each ward was re-established. The term of office was set at four years with one-half being elected biennially. The Mayor would continue to serve two years but with greater appointive power than previously. Under the Charter the Mayor would appoint the police and fire chief, all policemen (not firemen), the city solicitor, the building inspector, the engineer, and the health commissioner. None of these appointments required Council confirmation. For the first time a city Charter created the office of Manager. This office as well as that of Municipal Judge was also under the Mayor's appointive power, but for these offices Council had to confirm the appointments. The

Charter also changed the title of City Recorder to City Clerk who was now appointed by Council. Previously the voters elected the Recorder.

In this period of nationwide progressivism the Charter established this movement's principle of direct democracy by granting citizens the right of initiative, referendum, and recall. The initiative permitted ten percent of the voters by petition to send its own ordinance to Council while the referendum allowed citizens by special election to reject an ordinance. A petition signed by fifteen percent of the voters would start the election process. Twenty-five percent of the voters by petition would set up an election in which an official could be recalled or removed from office.

To finish up the Charter housekeeping prior to the Twenties, we need to mention the 1919 Charter. Breaking a tradition dating to 1875 this Charter increased the Mayor's term from two to four years. The voting wards were increased from ten to fifteen with the West Side going from three to six and east of the Elk from six to eight. One ward still remained south of the Kanawha. The Charter kept the Council size at twenty by mandating just one Council member per ward and requiring five members to be elected at large.[10]

The Twenties

Buoyed by continued population growth, Charleston gained economic strength in both business and government during the Twenties. The growing population also supported the city's expanding cultural life. From a population of 39,608 in 1920, the city grew to 60,408 by 1930. According the1930 federal census, Wheeling had just 250 more individuals than did Charleston, while Parkersburg lagged far behind with a population of less than 30000. Huntington in 1930 was the state's largest city with a population of 75,000.[1] Charleston's population growth was not uniform throughout the city. The upper East End showed the strongest surge. On the south side of the Kanawha, both South Ruffner and Kanawha City were annexed during the Twenties, increasing the city's area by over fifty percent. These South Side areas along with the older South Hills area just across the river from downtown showed noticeable population growth in the Twenties. The West Side north of Charleston (later Washington) Street also contributed to the city's population growth. On the other hand, the population of Charleston's central area remained relatively flat during the decade.[2] In 1920 Blacks made up 11.4 percent of the city's population. At the end of the Twenties, the figure for Blacks was 11.2 percent. Foreign born in 1920 made up less than two percent of Charleston's population. Public school statistics also illustrate Charleston's 1920's growth. Student enrollment in 1925 had more than doubled since 1910 to 9527 while the number of teachers had increased in the same period from 137 to 326. In 1925 Charleston had twenty-five public school buildings.[3]

Charleston had opened the century as a wholesale distribution center, a role it continued to play into the Twenties. A Charleston Chamber of Commerce study in 1926 put the value of the city's wholesale business at $ 49,243,313,[4] a significant jump from the thirteen million the wholesalers did in 1904. Many of the same wholesale houses that were open in 1900 were still prospering by 1920. Lewis, Hubbert, & Co was located on Morris Street while Ruffner Bros was still wholesaling groceries from Kanawha Street. Brown Bros had been reorganized since 1900 and was in 1920 operating as Brown Milling and Produce from facilities on Broad Street near the railroad tracks. The Kanawha Drug Co. was still wholesaling, but by 1920 had moved from Summers to Virginia Street. The Burlew Hardware on Quarrier Street and the Charleston Hardware on Virginia Street were still going concerns while Payne Shoe Store still operated from its Virginia Street building. No longer in business by 1920 was Lowenstein and Sons, but time had passed by its saddle and horse equipment business.[5]

By the 1920's, towns and communities to the east and west of Charleston along the Kanawha River had developed to the extent that the Charleston

Chamber of Commerce had begun to compile economic data on a region wide basis and releasing combined statistics for Charleston and its neighbors. Near the end of the decade in 1929, wholesale employees in the Charleston area numbered 2327 with an annual payroll of $ 4,572,000. Volume of sales in this year totaled $ 77,313,000 up from just over forty-three million in 1921.

Entering the Twenties, Charleston's manufacturing volume was still a distant second to its wholesale trade. Within the city proper, the number of workers engaged in manufacturing remained well behind that of Huntington and Wheeling. Based on U.S. census data, Charleston's manufacturing wage earners increased from 951 in 1909 to 2259 by 1919, of which 282 of these employees were women. Huntington's manufacturing workers, on the other hand, numbered about 6500 in 1919 while Wheeling's plants employed over 8600 workers.[6] But if we consider what the Chamber of Commerce was now calling the Charleston Manufacturing District, a different picture emerges. This district encompassed the area from Nitro on the West to Belle about ten miles east of Charleston. A 1922 Chamber study of this district showed employment in manufacturing to be 9847 yielding an annual payroll of over 9.6 million dollars. Annual production value was over $16 million.[7]

Retail

To satisfy the needs of a growing population during the Twenties, Charleston downtown retail trade grew noticeably, not only in sales volume but also by expansion into adjoining streets, thereby physically enlarging the downtown shopping area. One of the new retail areas was Quarrier Street. At this time Quarrier Street existed only to the east and not to the west of Capitol Street. In November 1923, the Gazette carried a front-page promotion article calling Quarrier St the "Fifth Avenue of Charleston." Formerly a residential street, the old homes had now been displaced by business concerns and by 1923 commercial activity extended all the way from Capitol Street east to Broad Street. Along his shopping strip were clothing stores, a bookstore, hotels, a theatre, a drug store, grocers, a jewelry store, and at Broad Street a professional building. The merchants numbering about 100 had by 1923 formed a business association, having the goal of keeping the street viable. They began to install better street lighting, more business signs, and more decorations. Property values reflected the increased popularity of the street. In 1904 a front foot of Quarrier Street property sold for $50. By 1918 the price had jumped to $600, and by 1923 the same front foot would cost a buyer between $2000 and $2500.[8]

Capitol Street also experienced commercial expansion during the Twenties. Until 1921, however, the street could not grow commercially west of Lee Street just three blocks from the Kanawha. But with the burning of the State Capitol and decision to move it and the Governor's residence to the East End, business entrepreneurs were free to expand. The first retail venture was The Diamond which, when it opened in early 1927, became Charleston's premier department store. As they developed in the large eastern cities in the last quarter of the 19th Century, department stores became unique institutions. These stores with their mass merchandising were able to satisfy the mass consumption tastes of the growing middle class. They succeeded because entrepreneurs recognized that middle class women were increasingly controlling home and family purchases. Attempting to make the stores attractive to women, the merchandisers gave them a grand look, designed with plush carpeting, rotundas, chandeliers, and expensive counters. The management hired designers who put up spacious displays that tended to educate the shoppers in their purchases. They also offered cafeterias, lunch counters, bridal and beauty shops, reading rooms and even nurseries. Most sales positions went to women. During the Christmas season, city and rural residents alike came to downtown to view the department store's Christmas lights and colorful widow displays.[9]

Charleston was home to several department stores by 1920, notably A.W. Cox, Coyle & Richardson, and O.J. Morrison. Entrepreneur Morrison was already operating stores in Ripley and Spencer when he opened his Charleston store in 1910 in a rented building on Capitol Street. After this building was destroyed by fire the night of October 29,1920, Morrison purchased the Burlew Theatre on the opposite side of Capitol. Before the year ended, Morrison except for some of the walls had demolished the theatre and had started construction of a new four-story department store that was open for business on March 25, 1921. Bucking the custom of other merchants, Morrison did not have bargain days or sales. Morrison claimed that his prices were low all year because he purchased inventory direct from factories and operated on a low margin of profit.[10]

But it was The Diamond that reflected the values of the large eastern department stores. The Diamond's genesis can be traced to 1906, but as a department store it began in 1917 when owner Wehrle Geary moved his former shoe store to 209 Capitol Street and branched into other lines. Later he teamed with A.W. Cox of Cox's Department Store, and they built The Diamond at the former Capitol site, occupying the corner of Capitol and Washington streets. Opening February 12,1927, The Diamond, as a Gazette writer phrased it "was the retail star of the Charleston shopping season, the year around crown jewel of the bustling downtown shopping district."[11] In line with the older eastern stores, The Diamond offered lavish displays and Christmas lights. A lunch counter occupied part of the first floor and a cafeteria took part of the fifth floor. The emporium also offered a beauty shop, a bridal shop, women's restrooms, and expensive furnishings.[12] From its original five floors, The Diamond prospered during the Thirties and beyond. It went through three expansions, in 1941, 1948, and 1965.

But in May 1984, The Diamond closed forever, the victim of another retailing phenomenon, the enclosed mall. As The Diamond and other retailers closed out the Twenties, retail sales for greater Charleston amounted to nearly forty-three million dollars, and the retail payroll for 1929 came to over five million dollars for the nearly 3700 retail employees.

Several other businesses followed The Diamond to Capitol Street's north end. Most notable were the Daniel Boone Hotel and the Kanawha Valley Bank, both opening in 1929. The bank was not a new institution but, as we saw in the first chapter, had been located at the head of Capitol since 1894. It had now abandoned its old building for a new twenty-story structure that opened in September 1929. Some years later the C&P Telephone Company opened its building on Lee Street just around the corner from the Kanawha Valley Bank. Then in 1947 Stone & Thomas Department Store opened on Lee Street beside C&P Telephone.

Still a third downtown street that boomed during the Twenties was Summers Street, one block west of Capitol Street. Summers Street would have several decades of life as a bustling and energetic street before it turned into a dull and lifeless area following urban renewal of the Sixties and Seventies. Already in the Twenties, two motion picture theatres had located there as well as seven billiard halls, a fish market, and a dry cleaning business. Many individuals had reason to be on Summers Street given the wide variety of its enterprises. By the early Thirties, Summers was home to two hotels, two jewelry stores, a hardware store, a fruit and produce stand, one dentist, a department store, several confectioneries, five barber shops, a drug store and a woolen mill.[13]

As Quarrier, Capitol, and Summers streets were growing as business locations, Charleston's first street, Kanawha, had been declining. Many former Kanawha Street business had moved to other downtown locations. Perhaps the most prominent was Frankenbergers a men and boys clothing store which in 1915 moved from Kanawha and Summers streets to the second block of Capitol Street. Kanawha Street merchants made an attempt in the early Twenties to return the street to a prime business location. As some businesses moved out, the street began looking a little frayed. Starting in late 1923, Many merchants began to repair and clean up their stores. The business association had plans to establish a community bank, a first rate hotel, motion picture theatre, miniature parks and gardens.[14] Little came of the effort, and some thirteen years would pass until Kanawha Street would undergo not just a business rejuvenation but a transformation that would forever change the character of the street.

Throughout the Twenties, Charleston housed over thirty hotels. In 1922 the Chamber of Commerce ranked ten of these with a total of 1421 rooms as first class. The Ruffner and the Kanawha hotels still held the most prestige, but the Holly Hotel on Quarrier Street, built in 1913 and the Fleetwood on Capitol Street were also in the upper tier. In 1929 Charleston got its landmark hotel, the Daniel Boone. The force behind the Boone was Wehrle Geary, part owner of The Diamond. After the state's temporary Capitol burned in 1927, Geary purchased two tracts of land where it had been located on the west side of Capitol Street at Washington. Geary wanted a locally owned downtown hotel with banquet and conference space capable of handling large conventions. His dreams became a reality on February 1, 1929 when the $1,250,000 Boone opened with 251 rooms. The opening was a major Charleston event with ceremonies lasting three days. Governor Morgan, Mayor Wertz, a U.S. Senator, and three former Governors took part.[15]

The Boone purred through the depression years of the early and mid Thirties and in February 1936 opened up a new ten-story addition on the northwest corner of the building. The Boone now had three penthouse apartments and another eighty-nine rooms. Still another addition in 1949 gave the hotel a total of 465 rooms, making it the largest non-resort hotel in the state. Along with the 1949 addition a new ballroom was added and improvements in lighting, ventilation, and to the kitchen were made. By 1947 air conditioning had been installed in all hotel guestrooms.

Lifestyle Changes

The Twenties was the first decade that saw significant residential movement into new housing developments in Charleston's surrounding hillsides. Suburbs were of course not new in the Twenties. Early in the century, streetcar lines allowed many individuals to pioneer suburban living. After 1906 when Edgewood was developed, Charleston had its own streetcar suburb. But by the Twenties, the rapid growth of private car ownership led to an organized development of suburbia. Early in the Twenties, seven of Charleston's many realtors were specializing in suburban property. By the middle of the decade, realtors in the Spring were sponsoring Better Homes Week and taking out full page Gazette ads promoting home sites in the outlying areas. One such site that later grew into a prominent area was Fort Hill on the south side of the Kanawha overlooking what later was the interstate bridge. Platted by the Fort Hill Realty Company, the promoters took out a full page Sunday Gazette ad in May 1926 advertising home lots of a "restrictive nature" with paved streets, sewer, city water, gas, electric, and telephone service.[16]

The following year, the Loudin Heights Company had platted 400 acres on the south side of the Kanawha and also began advertising restrictive lots for "high class homes." The area west of Charleston also became a favorite development site. Realtors in 1923 were selling restrictive lots in the Elmwood area, fifteen minutes from Charleston on a paved road and streetcar line. The ads further promised city water, sewer, and sidewalks. Even farther west was High Lawn development located on the Kanawha just east of St Albans; a forty-minute ride on the interurban said the ad of the C. J. Pearson Company.[17]

An Outer Loop streetcar in the late 1920's. These cars running along Virginia Street to the East End, would make their last run in October 1937.

The Twenties were characterized in part by the growing popularity of motion pictures, and ample theatres were built during the decade. Charleston's first run theatres were the Virginian, the Capitol, and the Kearse. This was the period of the studio system in Hollywood, and it was typical of a given theatre to concentrate on the productions of one or two studios. The Virginian, for example, showed principally Warner Bros movies. The Capitol was the MGM theatre while Paramount and 20th Century Fox sent their productions to the Kearse. The oldest of these theatres was the Virginian. Located at 703 State (later Lee) Street, it was built in 1914 and remodeled in 1922. The Capitol on Summers Street opened the day after Christmas in 1921, and the Kearse, also on Summers, the largest of the downtown theatres opened in 1922. With seats for 2000, Kearse movie patrons were entertained prior to the feature by an Austin pipe organ and occasionally by a sixteen-piece orchestra. The Kearse's large stage could also accommodate live productions. Still in the downtown, but a notch below the other three was the 1000 seat Rialto theatre that opened in October 1917 on Quarrier Street. On the same level as the Rialto was the Strand theatre on State Street just a block from the Virginian. Neighborhood theatres also dotted the city. By 1925 Charleston had twenty-five movie theatres.[18]

Although not as popular as motion pictures, Charleston residents had enjoyed live theatre much longer. The Burlew Opera House, as we have seen, had nearly a three-decade run. When commercial theatre at the Burlew ended in 1920, the gap was soon filled by the Kanawha Players of Charleston, a little theatre troupe that grew out of the Drama League of America, a national organization promoting theatre as art. Beginning without a permanent stage, the Players gave its first performance in November 1922 at the Charleston High School. The troupe presented three one act plays charging seventy-five cents admission. From the start, the Players were a combination of local and professional talent, and for much of its history has had a paid professional director. Its first director was Rose Fortier, a faculty member of Charleston's Mason School of Music and Fine Arts. For many years music was an integral part of the players productions, and William Mason, founder of the Mason School, stepped in as music director.

Toward the end of 1925, the Players secured a permanent theatre when it leased the vacant Methodist Church at Washington and Dickinson streets. With seating for 300, this site was home until 1936 when the building was destroyed by fire. But the Players persevered staging plays of Shaw, Chekov, O'Neill, and Tennessee Williams. After some seventeen years of performing at such Charleston sites as the Shriners Mosque, the clubhouse of the Woman's Club of Charleston, Municipal Auditorium, and Morris Harvey College, the Players secured a permanent stage in early 1959 when the Civic Center Theatre was completed.[19]

The beginning of the symphony orchestra in Charleston is fuzzy due to lack of documents prior to 1939. A background article in the Gazette gave credit to Charleston musician William S. Mason as the founder of the symphony in 1919. An unpublished 1947 article by Charleston symphony conductor Antonio Modarelli traced the origins to 1910 when Mason was conducting concerts. But Modarelli pointed out that prior to 1939 symphony performances were irregular due to various disbandments and subsequent reorganizations. There is no record that in these early years that the symphony had a governing board or steady management. Modarelli puts the modern symphony's birth in 1939 when the Charleston Symphony Orchestra was organized by William Wiant, who became its first conductor and C. R. Adams who served as chairman of the Charleston Civic Orchestra Association. Unlike in the Mason era, the orchestra beginning in 1939 had a governing and an executive board. From this date, the orchestra enjoyed an organizationally if not a financially stable basis. Unable to afford professional musicians, the management recruited talented individuals with day jobs from the community. The were paid one dollar per rehearsal and five dollars per concert. The first season five concerts were given to audiences of 700 to 800. However in 1942 Wiant entered the armed services. The board then asked Wheeling Symphony conductor Antonio Modarelli to step in as guest conductor while he remained resident conductor at the more established Wheeling Symphony formed in 1928.[20]

In the early 1940's, some Union Carbide executives whose interests extended beyond chemistry came up with a unique proposal to recruit musicians for the orchestra. Henceforth the company would advertise for chemical engineers who were also symphony musicians. The management agreed to give hiring preference to applicants with the ability to perform under Modarelli. Carbide's unique employment ads caught the eye of Readers' Digest, which published a 1947 article on the subject. By 1947 Modarelli had agreed to serve as resident conductor. With the Carbide musicians and Modarelli at the helm, the orchestra began to grow. During the war years, the symphony gave radio concerts each Sunday, and by the late Forties, it was performing fifteen concerts per season for a membership of over 3000.[21]

As music and the theatre were making positive strides in the Twenties, the Charleston Board of Education which at this time was governing the public library made a decision that would insure the library's second class status for the rest of the century. We have seen that when the library was founded in 1909, it spent its first two years in the YMCA building. It continued with shared quarters and a peripatetic life as it stumbled into the Twenties. After leaving the YMCA building, the library moved into the old Presbyterian Church manse on Quarrier Street near Hale Street In 1914, the library was at 1006 Virginia Street where it remained for a year in a street level store front with the YWCA overhead.

Beginning in 1915 and for the next six years, the library was located in another storefront at Kanawha and McFarland streets. In 1921 the library now with 10,000 volumes found shelter in the barracks like Red Cross building on the south side of Kanawha Street between Capitol and Summers streets. While there it appeared as if the library picture might brighten.[22]

In 1923, a wealthy oilman, A.E. Humphreys, offered $100,000 for a new site if matched by other citizens. In about a year $156,000, had been raised, of which $50,000 came from the Rotary Club. Humphreys then made his pledge with 3000 shares of his company's oil stock, which resulted in more than $100,000. With its newfound wealth, a library commission, a body created by the Board of Education to search for a building site, had in 1925 purchased a lot on Kanawha Street just west of Bradford Street. Some opposition developed to this location because it was too far from downtown. About this same time a Charleston business group had purchased the Capitol annex on Lee Street so that the state government could proceed with the first wing of the new Capitol. Shortly thereafter, the business group apparently feeling it had made a bad investment engaged the Board of Education in negotiations. The conversations between the business group and the Board of Education are not extant, but the result was an agreement by the library to purchase the annex from the businessmen. The previous decision to construct a new building on the library's own lot on Kanawha Street was abandoned in favor of another used building designed for another purpose. The Board agreed to pay $400,000 for the former annex, $150,000 down with the remaining 250,000 to be paid in installments. Under the contract with the State, the library would be allowed to use the second floor only of the three-story building. The state department of archives and history would occupy the third floor for several years. Then beginning in May 1935 and for the next twelve years the library would have Morris Harvey College as an upstairs neighbor. Various tenants occupied the first floor, notably the Supreme Court of Appeals, the Red Cross, and the West Virginia Medical Association. For over two decades, the library was known as the Charleston Public Library. This name, however, did not mean that the city Council exclusively funded the library. It did not. Two years after its founding, the Board of Education raised a levy for library financing. In 1933, when the state adopted the county unit system for boards of education, the library became the Kanawha County Public Library. After 1937, the board of education no longer had any governing functions over the library.[23]

Carrying the library saga forward, the governing board kept the library in the annex building for forty years when it once again moved into used quarters that another government agency no longer wanted. When the library moved into the post office building on Kanawha Street in 1966 from which it would enter the next century, the building's unfunctional design and later cramped space, as library services expanded, would insure that Charleston's library community would be less that adequately served. But at least the library had a building to itself.

Kanawha Street, Capitol to Summers streets, about 1920, before the Boulevard project. Two buildings still remain: theTerminal Building with rounded corner on left side of street and Union Building, across the street. The partially seen one story building on the right is the Red Cross location.

City government in the Twenties

Republican William S. Wertz, who had previously served as the elected Police Judge, was Charleston's Mayor during most of the Twenties, having been first elected in 1923 and re-elected to another four year term in 1927. Campaigning in early 1923, Wertz advocated street improvements and park expansion. For their part, the Democrats in this age of prohibition attempted to portray Wertz as a "wet." In a full-page advertisement in the Daily Mail a few days before the April election, the Democratic City Committee addressed the women voters, assuring them that Wertz supported an "open town" and an "open Sunday." Such ads were of no help to the Democrats, for Wertz and the Republicans coasted to victory. Wertz's margin was 10,618 to 8375. If the attempted "wet" label directed at Wertz was effective anywhere, it may have been in the Triangle District near the downtown, where it was thought prohibition violations occurred. But it was a reverse effect. Wertz swept the Triangle 547 to forty-five. All of the twenty Council seats were open in 1923; the Republicans captured eighteen of them.[24]

Wertz proved to be an energetic Mayor and a city booster. Toward the end of his first term, he authored a book entitled "Charleston, City with a Future." In the book, Wertz wrote that "Charleston is growing very rapidly to become one of the great industrial centers of the United States, and the future in an industrial way is now assured."[25] He went on the catalog Charleston's future as a focal point of coal, gas, timber, and glass.

In spite of Wertz's apparent interest in Charleston's industrial base, his two administrations were characterized by an almost constant absorption with Charleston's streets. Meeting twice each month with Wertz presiding, the City Council directed most of its attention to various aspects of the city streets—street paving, street extensions, street assessments, sewers, and bridges.[26] If Wertz and the Council were consumed with Charleston's streets and traffic, they very well may have been reflecting public opinion, if an unscientific survey by the Daily Mail is any guide. Answers to the public survey dwelled principally on street traffic with suggestions for one way streets, new traffic laws, better enforcement of traffic regulations, and the closing of Capitol Street to motor vehicles.[27]

Wertz wasted little time acting on his campaign pledges. Taking office in April, he by year's end had a $ 1.5 million bond issue on the ballot. Of this total, $480,000 was earmarked for land purchases for new streets. Another $480,000 was for street improvements, $200,000 for an Elk River bridge, $100,000 for park land, $190,000 for sewer construction, and $50,000 for a city market. However to Wertz's dismay, anti-tax citizens formed a Citizens Taxpayer League to oppose the bond issue. On election day, December 20, the League prevailed as voters rejected the bond issue 5559 to 4463.[28]

Wertz bounced back from this defeat and initiated an active street paving program throughout 1924. A total of eight and one-half miles of streets were paved at a cost of $678,000,making it the largest street paving program in six years. Street paving continued at a rapid pace during Wertz's first term. In 1925 over $211,000 was spent on paving.[29]

As it was at the beginning of the century, street improvements were still being financed by special assessments against the property owners whose property fronted the street. The process was clear. The street department would present Council with a list of streets needing paved. This was publicized along with the names of the affected property owners, allowing them the chance to appear before Council. As might be imaged, many citizens not wanting to be assessed protested the paving.

Such protest fell on deaf ears, for once the list of streets were published, Council's mind was set. The Council minutes during the Wertz administration showed paving assessments ranged from $76 to $500. Thus the $678,000 spent on paving in 1924 came directly from the pockets of property owners. The street department budget in 1924 was just $78,000; most of this marked for salaries and wages.[30]

In addition to street paving, Wertz also in 1924 made a three-quarter mile extension of Piedmont Street, a major east-west street on the northwest side of the city. This extension took the street nearly to the Kanawha City bridge. Wertz's plan was to connect Piedmont Street to Route 60, thereby providing another way in and out of the city. At present Kanawha Street provided the only link to Route 60 for eastbound drivers. Once the link was made in 1926, it was hoped that traffic on Kanawha Street would be alleviated.

The Wertz administration attached such importance to street improvements that when a single additional block of Washington Street was opened in October 1923, it was cause for celebration. The new section extended from Summers Street west and linked up with the rest of the street, then called Lovell, which ran to and crossed the Elk River. Along the extended street, the Mayor held a ribbon cutting ceremony followed by a performance by the recently created municipal band, fire works, and street dance. [31]

After the Capitol was destroyed by fire and plans were made to relocate it and Governor's residence to the East End, the current administration knew that eventually the three sections of Washington Street would extend through the former Capitol grounds to form one continuous street from the East to the West Side. However, the street had three names: Charleston Street west of the Elk, Lovell Street between downtown and the Elk, and Washington Street in the East End. A street re-naming committee from the previous administration had proposed re-naming the entire span Lincoln Street. The Wertz administration supported this proposed change. When the Woman's Club of Charleston learned of this, it immediately opposed the name change. Appearing before Council in the Fall of 1923, the Club argued that the connection between the country's first President, who once owned land along the Kanawha near Charleston, and the capitol city should continue by virtue of the street name. The Club's views prevailed and the administration dropped the proposed Lincoln name change.[32]

After failing two years earlier, Wertz again took up the issue of a bridge across the Elk at Spring Street. This time he vastly scaled back his request, asking for bonding authority of $145,000 designated for the bridge only. With no organized opposition, the voters approved in December 1925, and the next month work began on the bridge, which was completed by year's end 1926.[33]

Railroad crossings, however, were a more intractable problem for Wertz than bridges. When the K&M Railroad laid its tracks in the 1890's no thought was given to the fact that these tracks would be at the same grade level with intersecting city streets. Surprisingly, these intersections as Wertz assumed office numbered over twenty. Now well into the automobile age, these tracks created havoc as drivers waited in long lines while trains passed in front of them. Compounding the traffic congestion at the intersections were the re-occurring accidents and injuries because neither gates nor warning lights were located at the crossings to keep pedestrians and drivers off the tracks in the face on on-coming trains. The Wertz administration had been in negotiations with railroad officials and in January 1926 an agreement was reached. Council passed an ordinance mandating that the New York Central who now owned the tracks either construct gates or signal lights at certain crossings. The railroad agreed to signal lights and at its next meeting in February, Council designated seven streets that would have the lights. These included among others Ruffner, Elizabeth, and Broad on the East End and Virginia and Charleston on the West Side.[34]

The ideal solution to the railroad crossings would have been to change the grade levels, but for the numerous crossings throughout the city, the cost would be prohibitive. However, across the Kanawha, the city administration did reach such an agreement with the C&O Railroad officials who at no cost to the city agreed to build a viaduct at Ferry Crossing. It was completed during 1927.[35]

Wertz wanted a second term in order to continue his work on Charleston's streets. During the Spring 1927 campaign, Wertz cited his record with city streets, pointing out that during the past four years more streets were paved than in any previous administration. He also took credit for holding streetcar fares to six cents, and for successful negotiations with the railroads. Yet it was not an easy election for Wertz, winning by just 245 votes out of the 22,000 cast. In the Council races, the Republicans gave up four seats, but claimed 14 to six majority.[36]

Although street paving continued into 1928 and 1929, Wertz by 1929 had bigger plans. In October 1929 he proposed to Council a $1.3 million street widening project to be financed by a bond issue. He wanted Lee and Summers streets widened from thirty to thirty-six feet, Charleston Street west of Patrick from twenty-six to thirty-two feet, and the rest of Charleston Street widened to thirty-five feet. Hale and Capitol streets were also on the list with Capitol being widened from thirty to forty feet. As part of the project, Dunbar Street would be extended from Quarrier to Lee Street, Dickinson Street extended to Virginia, and Alterson Street just west of the downtown extended to State Street. Determined to do more with railroad crossings both east and west of the Elk, Wertz would have designated $500,000 to change intersection grades. Throughout the city there were now twenty-seven railroad intersections at grade level. Of these only Florida Street on the West Side had an underpass.[37]

The Gazette reported that Wertz had not previously discussed the proposal with the Council and hearing it for the first time, the members were taken back by the scale of the proposal. But Wertz argued that the city's current debt was $1.6 million, making it low relatively to the $5.0 million allowed by state law.[38]

From the viewpoint of a traffic engineer, Wertz's proposals for street widening, street extensions, and railroad underpasses were needed. Traffic congestion on Charleston streets was becoming legend. Never designed or laid out for the geometric increase in private automobile ownership, the city streets were overloaded. By 1930 vehicle registrations in Kanawha County were over 24,000. Prior to 1930 County registrations are not available, but statewide West Virginia vehicle registrations soared from 5100 in 1913 to over 80,000 in 1920 and to over 266,000 by 1930.[39] Using the same percentage increase, Kanawha County's registrations would have jumped from 500 in 1913 to 8000 in 1920 and increasing to 24,000 by 1930. Spin-off businesses serving the automobile industry also showed large increases. Auto repair shops within Charleston increased from twenty-six in 1920 to sixty-three in 1935, and gasoline filling stations grew from sixteen in 1925 to thirty-seven in 1930. In 1920 there were fifteen car dealerships in Charleston; by 1925 there were thirty-three.[40] Yet in spite of the need for the bond issue, the Council found the scale and expense of it overwhelming, and it never appeared on the ballot.

Wertz's failure to persuade Council to place his street widening proposal on the ballot marked the end of his major initiatives in street improvements. But before leaving office, he would lay claim to two other successes, both occurring in 1930. These were the opening of Wertz Field, Charleston's first airport and the completion of the Patrick Street Bridge. After a more than two year construction period, the bridge over the Kanawha connecting South Charleston with Charleston was opened on May 3, 1930. Although all vehicular traffic was permitted, work continued for another six weeks on the approaches and the lighting. Charleston and Loudin District voters made the bridge financially possible by passing a $1.2 million bond issue in 1928, $900,000 of which was for the Patrick Street Bridge. The balance was used for the purchase of the Kanawha City Bridge from the Traction Company. This purchase brought to an end the tolls that motorists had paid since 1915. No ceremony took place for the bridge opening, although one was planned when all construction was completed.[41]

Ceremonies were, however, lavish at the dedication of Wertz Field. Located nine miles west of Charleston at Institute, the city leased the field to West Virginia Airways, a group of Charleston businessmen. The dedication took place on Friday July 4 with thousands in attendance. Mayor Wertz made opening remarks calling the opening of the airport one of the three great historical events in Charleston history, the other two being the receiving of the charter in 1794 and the legislative act making Charleston the state Capitol. Festivities continued through the weekend and included flyovers and honoring of pilots.[42]

Saturday evening a banquet per ticket only was held at the Daniel Boone Hotel. The airport, however, would last just twelve years. In 1942 the federal government took the property for a synthetic rubber plant.

Growth of government

By the Twenties, the cost of Charleston's government had grown about tenfold. We saw that the levy raised $49,000 in 1900. By 1923, Wertz's first year as Mayor, the levy raised $520,000, which would pay for all operations of the city excluding special assessments for street improvements. Salaries in 1923 appeared modest. The Mayor and Manager were paid $4500 per year, the Police Chief $3300, the Fire Chief $3000, the Health Commissioner, who was a medical doctor, $4000, and the Clerk $2400. Salaries barely increased during the Twenties.[43] By 1929 the Mayor received $5000 per year, but the Manager and Health Commissioner were still at their 1923 salaries. Council members were paid $100 per year during the Twenties.[44]

Charleston still had a caretaker, limited government during the Twenties, and city functions were largely what they were in 1900. Budget categories in 1927, for example, were remarkably similar to the spending categories in 1900. The bulk of the expenditures in 1927 went for police, fire, streets, engineering, and health.[45] Thus the tenfold growth of the city budget between these years was not due to new functions of government, but to increased personnel carrying out the same role of the city. For example, the increased population and larger urban area necessitated more police and firemen. Whereas in 1905 the city employed nineteen policemen, by 1927 a chief, a captain, two lieutenants, three sergeants, and thirty-three patrolmen made up the police force. In the fire department, the rate of increase was even higher, jumping from thirteen firemen in 1900 to fifty-two by 1925. In 1927 the police department budget was just over $126,000, the fire department's was $96,000, the engineering department's budget was nearly

$30,000, and the street department received over $62,000. Administration was a growing expense. By this date all department heads had assistants. Salaries were $46,600 while other administrative expenses were over $98,000.[46]

The city in the Twenties was able to garner revenue between $500,000 and $600,000 without extortionate taxes because of the growing housing and commercial building stock. We saw that in 1900, the property assessment was $3.9 million. In 1927 the assessment on all property had soared to over $105 million.[47] The property levy in 1927 was sixty-five cents per $100 of assessed property. Although most of the levy was for general revenue items, Council always had specific use for a portion of the levy. In 1927 fifteen of the sixty-five cents was for debt retirement. Something new beginning with the first Wertz administration was funding for the newly created municipal band, which was allotted one-half cents of the levy.[48]

The Thirties

Charleston like the state and the nation endured economic pain during the Great Depression of the early Thirties. Retail sales in the area began to plummet after 1929. In the Charleston area, including the small municipalities to the east and west of the city along the Kanawha, sales fell from over $ 42 million in 1929 to $23 million in 1933. Wholesale trade showed a similar trend. In the same period sales declined from $77 million to $39 million. The number of employees losing their jobs was drastic. In retail nearly 1700 of a 1929 high of 3695 workers were let go, while in wholesale over 1000 employees lost their jobs between 1929 and 1933.[1]

Manufacturing took a similar hit. In Kanawha County there were counting coal miners nearly 15000 employees in 1929. Two years later over 5000 of them were out of work as the number of plants declined from 296 to 234. Some old manufacturing names in Charleston did not survive these years. Ward Engineering Works, maker of boats and boilers on the north side of the Kanawha, ceased business in 1931. The Kanawha Woolen Mills, one of the oldest factories in the Charleston Industrial District, and the Charleston Manufacturing Company could not maintain profitability and closed. The area's largest employer, Kelly Axe Handle, survived but in a truncated form. In the early Thirties, Kelly consolidated with American Fork and Hoe of Cleveland and with a Dunkirk, New York concern. This economy move reduced Kelly's employment from 1200 in pre-depression times to 560 in 1936.[2]

In the industrial district, however, the coal miners bore the brunt of the unemployment. From 1929 to 1932, the number of miners declined from 7030 to 4356. Moreover, the decreased number of miners were working only one, two, or three days per week during the early Thirties. Coal tonnage in the district fell from seven tons in 1929 to 4.3 tons by 1932.[3]

Within Charleston, private construction slowed to a craw in the early Thirties. In 1922, the boom year of the decade, the city issued over 1100 building permits with a monetary value of $4.1 million. In 1925 when business slumped nationwide, Charleston still granted 574 building permits with a value of $2.3 million. By 1929 permits were back to 809. But by 1931 the city issued just 385 permits having a value of nearly $879,000. The downward spiral continued, and in 1933 the value of private construction was just $266, 500.[4]

But not all was grim. Some industries grew during the depression. The chemical plants in South Charleston buffered business decline elsewhere. Carbine and Carbon Chemical expanded each year between 1926 and 1936 and became the largest plant in the industrial district. In 1929 the plant employed 350 and the following year, employment had jumped to 850. By 1936, it had over

2800 on the payroll. Westvaco Chlorine Products Company grew from 350 employees in 1929 to 450 in 1933 and to 600 in 1936. Similarly DuPont's employment grew from 400 in 1929 to 650 in 1939 and to over 2000 in 1936. Looking at the entire chemical industry in the industrial area, employment in 1929 was just over 2500. In 1936 the figure was over 7400.[5]

The two glass plants in Kanawha City held their own during the Depression. In 1929 the Ford Motor Company acquired an interest in Libby-Owens and name became Libby-Owens Ford. New units to the plant followed in 1930. Across the street, the Owens Bottle Company merged in April 1929 with Illinois Glass giving the new corporation an asset value of over $100 million nationwide.[6]

Charleston's banks came through the Depression in good order. Only one bank failed, the Charleston Trust Company, a small bank on the West Side. It ceased business in 1933, paying depositors three cents on the dollar. In 1929 other banks began to strengthen themselves through consolidation. The Charleston National Bank absorbed three banks—Citizens National Bank, Union Trust Company, and the State Bank and Trust Company. Not yet finished, Charleston National Bank in November 1930 brought the Kanawha National Bank into its growing system. The Charleston National Bank now was the state's largest bank, and with deposits of $15 million and resources of $19 million, it was the largest bank between Richmond and Cincinnati. Three days after ceasing as an entity, the Kanawha National Bank sold its fifteen year old stately building at Capitol and Virginia streets to Security Bank and Trust Company located on the West Side. This bank moved into its new quarters in February 1931, and its building was henceforth known as the Security Building.[7] In 1933, the city's oldest bank, the Kanawha Valley Bank, absorbed the Capitol City Bank, and the same year, the National Bank of Commerce took over the Peoples Exchange Bank.[8]

Turning from business enterprise to Charleston's society scene one finds that the routine of life among Charleston's affluent was largely unaffected by the economic depression. The social life of the city's well healed was in the Twenties a round of dances, teas, parties, and benefits and this carried on uninterrupted into the Thirties. Both the Gazette and the Daily Mail in their editions highlighted society in a special section. Although society functions continued throughout the year, the Spring and Christmas seasons were especially active. The Edgewood Country Club and the Kanawha Country Club held an annual pre-Christmas and New Year's Eve dance. The Pioneer Club sponsored two holiday dances—one at the Woman's Clubhouse on Virginia Street and the other at the Daniel Boone Hotel. [9]The Junior League also enhanced the social whirl; the League's biggest event was the Spring Ball. In April 1931 the Ball featured a gay Nineties theme. For this the Edgewood was given a brass rail tavern ambiance while League members attended in Nineties style costume.[10] Numerous parties and teas given in the many wealthy homes in the East End always preceded the dances and balls. The Music Department of the Woman' Club was active at this time, sponsoring concerts and bringing in performers of professional status. The Club's Spring concert in 1931 held in its two-year-old Clubhouse featured arias by a mezzo-soprano. Lectures were also a featured activity. In January 1933, the Woman's Club held a bridge luncheon followed by a lecture on bridge. In the same week, the Club members heard a lecture on the sonata afterwhich music department members performed choral works.[11]

Many Charlestonians traveled to Huntington in the Spring to attend that city's Beaux-Arts Ball. In 1931 the Huntington sponors extended invitations to the Junior League of Charleston and to the Kanawha Players.[12] Charleston in these years had a chapter of the National Society of Colonial Dames. Its annual meeting in 1931 was held in the Spring at the YWCA building on Quarrier Street.

Many members of the society clubs had children attending out of state colleges. During the Christmas holidays, they returned to town from such private institutions as Swarthmore in Pennsylvania, Hollis College and Sweet Briar College both in Virginia, Goucher College in Baltimore, Agnes Scott College in Georgia, and Gulf Park College in Mississippi. The students took part in their parents' dances and parties and also found time to attend functions given by their own set.[13]

City government

Unlike Charleston's society set, the Depression had a profound effect on the city government. Mayor Wertz continued with an active street paving program through 1930, but by this time the city began to incur financial reverses. Property taxes and street assessments were increasingly not being paid. By 1933 there was over $100,000 in delinquent taxes owed to the city.[14] Mayor Wertz chose not to seek a third term. In April 1931 another Republican R.P. DeVan was elected Mayor and would serve through the major part of the depression. DeVan experienced the pain of decreased city revenue, budget cutbacks, salary reductions and layoffs. During the new Mayor's first year, firemen were dismissed. In 1932 the police department had to layoff ten patrolmen. The Council met in special session in the Fall of 1932 to deal with the budget crisis. In that year city employees suffered salary reductions of ten to twenty percent. The following year Council was forced to cut administrative salaries. The Mayor's annual salary was reduced from $4500 to $4000, the Manager's from $3600 to 3200, the Clerk's from $2295 to $1147, and the Health Commissioner's from $3200 to $3040. The Engineer dodged the axe in 1933 and continued to receive $3200 for the year. The Police Chief and Municipal Judge also held on to their salaries of $3100 and $2700, but the Fire Chief took a $50 reduction to $2500. However, in 1934 the Police Chief and Engineer took a $400 cut.[15]

The Tax Limitation Amendment, which became part of the state Constitution in 1932, was responsible for some of the revenue loss. This amendment limited the amount of tax that a municipality could levy against property owners. Dividing property into five classes and setting a maximum levy on each class, the amendment had the effect of reducing Charleston's revenue by about $100,000 per year.[16] The amendment, however, allowed a municipality to exceed the mandated levy limit by a voter approved excess levy. By 1934 the DeVan administration was showing a $95,000 budget deficit. Consequently under the authority of the recent amendment, the Council in October 1934 placed a special excess levy before the voters.

Although the voters overwhelmingly passed the proposed levy by a margin of 7893 to 3813, the amendment required an affirmative vote of sixty percent of the qualified voters. Since over 30,000 were registered to vote, the number voting for approval was far short of sixty percent. The city argued that the amendment meant sixty percent of those voting not registered. The city's position prevailed, and the DeVan administration got some financial breathing space. The excess levy would last for three years, giving the city about $110,000 in 1934 and just over $196,000 the following two years.[17]

Before the DeVan administration left office in 1935, the federal New Deal program aiming to combat the nationwide depression was well underway. Of particular interest to Charleston were the Works Progress Administration (WPA) and the Public Works Administration (PWA). DeVan made several funding requests to Washington under these programs. They were for street improvements, bridges, and a rail and river terminal at the mouth of the Elk River. But it was not until the following Dawson administration that the federal funds began to impact Charleston. D. Boone Dawson, who had been Municipal Court Judge in the DeVan administration, secured the Republican nomination for Mayor. In a race that saw the Democratic nominee, Hornor Davis II, resign in the midst of the campaign and then a few days later withdraw his resignation, Dawson won by a margin of 14917 to 12485. Republicans continued to dominate Council, capturing fifteen of the twenty Council seats.[18] The Dawson mayoralty represented the fifth straight Republican administration.

The Dawson Record

Within months, after assuming office, Dawson got a taste of the same financial problems that DeVan had faced the previous four years. Dawson's first budget being prepared in August 1935 showed expenses exceeding revenue by over $100,000 and this was counting revenue from the 1934 special levy that would yield about $177,000, $20,000 less than originally calculated. The regular levy would give the city $353,000. This figure added with the special levy and $100,000 in miscellaneous fees yielded revenue of $630,000. But projected expenditures were $751,000. The Council's historic practice of piling bond issue upon bond issue was beginning to drain the city. The new administration was paying for bond issues passed in 1905, 1907, and 1908 as well as on the many passed in the next two decades. For the 1935-36 fiscal year, the city owed $120,000 in bond interest.[19]

Like DeVan in 1934, Dawson saw no alternative other than increased taxes. Dawson's approach, however, was not another levy, but a gross sales tax. As drafted this was a tax of one-tenth of one percent on gross sales of all retail businesses in Charleston. For wholesale businesses the rate was one-twentieth of one percent of sales. The tax, lasting for two years, would provide the city coffers with about $100,000 each year. Unlike the property tax levy, the sales tax did not require voter approval. Council unanimously approved the tax in August 1935 retroactive to July.[20] With the budget in order, Dawson wasted no time in securing federal New Deal money for the city, and this meant large construction projects.

In terms of city sponsored building projects, Dawson could lay claim as Charleston's most successful Mayor. Serving twelve years until 1947, Dawson had a remarkable record of seeing all twelve of his administration's capital improvement bond issues passed. Yet his success as a builder could not have been achieved without the Roosevelt administration's New Deal programs. Combining local bond issues with federal funds Dawson was able to build a new South Side bridge, a civic auditorium, an incinerator, new fire stations, the Lee Street bridge, the downtown deep sewer project, and the largest of them all, the Kanawha riverfront project.

The year following Dawson's election, work began on the new South Side bridge across the Kanawha that connected the downtown with South Hills. The original bridge had served the city since 1891, but it was now too small and growing unsafe for the vehicle traffic currently using it. The bridge would cost future taxpayers $330,000 over the twenty-five year bonded debt. The New Deal WPA funded $240,000 of the cost.[21] The old bridge was closed in August 1936 as work progressed on the new structure that including the razing of two buildings at Virginia and Kanawha streets to allow for longer and wider approaches. Until the new bridge opened in 1937, the city provided ferry service at fifteen minutes intervals across the river.[22]

The incinerator plant was also under construction in 1936 and opened on January 4, 1937. Of the $150,000 total cost, WPA funded forty-five percent of it. Henceforth the Kanawha and Elk rivers would now be spared much of Charleston's waste. The Dawson administration wanted the operation to pay for itself and was not hesitant about using its legislative authority to eliminate competition from the many self employed pushcart men who plied the streets and alleys picking up garbage from paying customers. An ordinance passed just prior to the plant opening prohibited the pushcart method of garbage collection.[23] With competition eliminated, the city had little difficulty collecting the five-dollar monthly fee from private residents and ten dollars from business owners.

Of all Dawson's achievements, his mark as Mayor was principally made with the Kanawha riverfront project. The deep sewer project may have been more needed and certainly more healthful, but sewers go largely unappreciated until they backup. Thus his laurels would come from the riverfront. Within the administration, the project began in August 1935 when Dawson submitted a funding application to the WPA in the amount of $1,653,000. The largest amount—$700,000—was for widening Kanawha Street, riverfront improvements, demolition of structures and, essential to the success of the plan, a bridge across the mouth of the Elk. The project would cover the entire length of the street and riverbank from Patrick Street to the Kanawha City bridge, a distance of 4.7 miles. Dawson wanted no piecemeal solutions; it would be done in one swath.

The $1.6 million application included $175,000 for a civic auditorium, $100,000 for widening and paving MacCorkle Avenue on the south side of the Kanawha, $380,000 for other street widening and paving, $50,000 to extend Bradford Street north to Lewis Street, and smaller amounts for swimming pools, playgrounds, and park access. Approval of the application hinged on a local match of $800,000. Undeterred that this would be the third bond issue in three years, Dawson forged ahead, and after a year of planning, Council placed it on the ballot for a December, 29, 1936 vote.

It would be unfair to imply that the Dawson administration was the first to consider Kanawha Street improvements. For all the fanfare it would later receive, Dawson riverfront plan was in essence a street widening project that included a bridge across the Elk, that is to say it was a traffic solution. Traffic solutions were a consideration of every administration since automobiles began to crowd Charleston's streets. The idea of an Elk River bridge in order to continue Kanawha Street was not new in 1935. The previous DeVan administration had discussed it and before that Mayor Wertz had proposed widening Kanawha Street—though not to the width it later became—and extending it by an Elk River bridge. But as we have seen his 1929 bond issue that would have funded the project failed (however the bridge funding had been removed from the bond issue ordinance). Wertz it seems was a decade too early. Charleston's voters and the Council were not ready to spend so lavishly when there was no federal help. By the time Dawson's even larger proposal was made, Charleston was hurting economically, the New Deal was in full swing, and it was easier for voters to approve knowing that the federal government would be helping with a large portion of the cost.

The Dawson administration did not take the 1936 bond issue for granted. Although the WPA application was for many projects, the administration structured the bond issue so that voters could focus just on the riverfront project and the civic auditorium. Therefore the $800,000 to be raised was divided into $550,000 for the riverfront and $250,000 for the auditorium. Each was to be voted on separately. Dawson campaigned hard for a favorable vote while the business community also worked for passage. Two days before the election, the Charleston Chamber of Commerce took out a large Gazette display ad urging passage, and in the same issue a group of Charleston businessmen bought a separate ad advocating support for the issue. Dawson need not have worried. Unlike with Wertz in the past decade, there was no organized opposition, and the riverfront project passed 11547 to 406. Auditorium support was nearly as great with an approval of 11127 to 764.[24]

The administration wasted little time selecting an auditorium site. After considering locations at Kanawha and Clendenin streets and Capitol Street at Fry, the site committee in January 1937 settled on a lot at Virginia and Truslow streets, which could be purchased for $40,000. Construction was started before the year's end, and the municipal auditorium, as it was to be called, opened in September 1939. Seating 3500, large concerts would no longer have to be held at Charleston High School.[25]

A river view of downtown showing unsightly buildings on the south side of Kanawha Street. Such views provided ammunition to those who favored the 1930,s riverfront project, which would demolish all buildings on the river side except the Union Building at right side of photo.

Riverfront project

In spite of the large voter approval for the riverfront proposal, the project had many critics. Many of the complaints centered on the destruction of the upper east end of Kanawha Street. At Bradford Street, the commercial area ended and the affluent residential area with grand and spacious homes began. Throughout the 20th Century state architectural historian Rodney Collins stated "… richer professional people started to build larger homes and what you had was a parade of the grandest houses in southern West Virginia. In many places houses lined both sides of the street."[26] Some of these houses had been built earlier in the century by Charleston's most prominent citizens, as banker John Q. Dickinson, shoe merchant Charles Payne, hardware owner, Noyes Burlew, and furniture manufacturer Curtis Dawley. One of the great qualities of the street, according to Collins, "were the American elm trees which arched over the street and nearly connected, forming almost a bowler."[27] Not only did many residents lose their 100-year-old trees, but also they saw their property condemned by the city. Many homeowners, however, were able to save their houses by having them moved by barge across the river to Kanawha City. As the four lanes were coming into focus on the East End, criticism was voiced that the street would become little more than a speedway.

In the downtown area, there were pleasant memories of the street. Harry Brawley, whose family owned a hardware store on Kanawha Street, recalled the World War I era in a Goldenseal article. Impressed with the bustle and camaraderie of the street, he wrote: On Saturday night, "it was almost a weekly Mardi Gras with the noise most intense in the 500 and 600 blocks. This was the area between Court and Summers streets where buildings on the two sides of Front Street (Kanawha Street) formed a canyon 30 or 40 feet high…" Almost always there was something going on at the levee … Showboats were often there during the warm months and there might be cargo or passenger boats loading or unloading." [28]

Those who wanted to escape the Saturday night crowd could walk to the Ruffner Hotel, have dinner, and relax on the front porch that faced the river. Or one could go to the Union Building, the fourteen-story structure that looked down Capitol Street from its river edge site, and enjoy its roof top restaurant.

However, some areas of the street were seedy. In the downtown area, the river side of Kanawha Street was characterized by cheap hotels and dilapidated stores and houses. On some of the back porches, residents hung old clothes. Cheap houseboats were also docked in the area. All this gave a tacky look from the river. Many people supported the project in order to eliminate the slum look along the river.[29]

Armed with its overwhelming vote, the Dawson administration moved ahead with the project that would forever alter the character of Charleston's first street. The city purchased over 250 pieces of property, taking all structures on the riverside of the street except one. Included in the demolition were three restaurants, two hotels, a food market, the C&O ticket office, an office building, the Chamber of Commerce, the Western Union office, and two pawnshops.[30] The Union Building constructed in 1911 survived. It appeared that it was too expensive to demolish. Consideration was given to routing the eastbound lanes on the riverside of the building, but that would be too costly. In the end it was decided to curve the widened street around the building. Farther east many homes were located on the riverside of Kanawha Street. Between Morris and Bradford streets, there were eight homes that had to be moved or demolished.

The riverfront project progressed through 1937 and continued into 1938, giving employment to some 2000 individuals. Unskilled laborers earned fifty-five to seventy-five cents per hour, but those in skilled trades were paid about double the lower rate. A powder man earned $1.10 per hour, crane operators and boilermakers earned $1.25, and brickman earned $1.50 per hour. But now the city needed additional funds to extend the work to the upper east end so that the street could be connected to state route sixty. In addition to the riverfront, the Mayor's plans for the city included four new fire stations, a downtown sewer system, widening and paving streets on the West Side, and a new bridge over the Elk to connect Lee with Fayette Street. All of this of course meant yet another bond issue to put before the voters. The New Deal PWA would fund forty-five percent of all five projects—riverfront, fire stations, bridge, sewer system, and street paving. Dawson did not let the voters forget that a favorable vote would bind them to just fifty-five percent of the cost. On September 19, 1938 all five projects passed by nearly a seven to one margin,[31] and Charleston taxpayers were indebted for another two million dollars. Of the $3.5 million total cost, $100,000 was designated for the fire stations, $159,000 for the sewer system, and $250,000 for the Lee Street bridge. However, the Supreme Court of Appeals invalidated the election on the grounds that the Council ordinance was not specific as to the allocation of funds. The Council scheduled a new election on December 16, 1938. The voters as if to smite the court for its unwanted interference again passed all five projects, this time by a margin of thirty-one to one.[32]

The riverfront project was more than widening Kanawha Street and Columbia Blvd (the pre-bridge name of the street along the river on the West Side) to four and in some places six lanes and connecting them with a bridge. The project also reconstructed the riverbank along the entire length from Patrick Street to the Kanawha City Bridge. A process known as riprapping built up and stabilized the riverbank with large stones. Some sections needed foundation work. The bank was landscaped and two walkways added, one at street level and the other at the bottom of the first bank still well above the river level. When it was completed, the new thoroughfare was 4.7 miles in length and sixty feet wide. Some of the material used included 660 tons of asphalt for paving and 269,200 square feet of concrete. In addition, 938,000 cubic yards of the river had been dredged for fill along the riverbank.[33] For something that took so much time, so much material, and so much money it was not surprising that the praise was lavish. Typical was the statement of the Chamber of Commerce: the project "has changed the entire personality of the city and given it a riverfront which is the admiration of commentators throughout the nation."[34]

But when completed, the new thoroughfare had not formally been renamed. Many people wanted to call it Kanawha Parkway, even though as the Daily Mail pointed out, there was not a park within ten miles. By usage it was a "boulevard." The official documents and the plate on the bridge called it a "boulevard." The recent telephone directory gave addresses along the thoroughfare as "Kanawha Boulevard." But not until May 1941 did Council formally name it as such. In spite of all the fanfare the riverfront project caused, there was never a formal dedication or ceremony. Unlike Mayor Wertz who the previous decade organized an all day ceremony when one block of one street was opened, Dawson organized nothing to celebrate Charleston's biggest construction project ever.

East End of Kanawha Blvd in the 1940's, a few years after completion. Note on the river side, the narrow part for pedestrian use.

Improved economy

During Dawson's first term in the late Thirties, Charleston's economy began an ascent. The city's private construction, which at its low point in 1933 had a value of just $266,000, had by 1935 climbed to a value of over $1.3 million on 1312 building permits. In that year 119 houses and apartments were built compared to only eighteen in 1933. By 1937 construction value was over $2.4, and 192 houses were built. Most of the new home construction in 1937 was in South Hills, Edgewood, Kanawha City, and South Ruffner, largely Charleston's more affluent areas. The Daily Mail reported that "bricklayers, carpenters, architects, contractors, and building supply dealers have been on the run since last March in an effort to keep up with demand."[35]

In addition to private homes, many of the city's businesses were making capital improvements. In 1937 Woodrum's Home Outfitting Company on Virginia Street invested $118,000 in an addition. The Fleetwood Hotel on Capitol Street spent $50,000 to repair fire damage. Preiser Chemical Company on West Washington Street made a $26,000 improvement to its laboratory and warehouse. In January 1937 Greyhound opened a new $100,000 terminal on Summers Street.[36] In addition to construction projects, the city's ten banks were showing greater deposits. From a low of $37 million in 1931, Charleston's bank deposits rose to $44 million in 1934 and to $50.3 million by June 1936.[37] Improved business conditions prompted the opening of a new Ford dealership, the Elk Motor Sales, on Virginia Street West in December 1934.

But it was not just homeowners and businesses that were spending more. Retail sales showed that the public at large had more to spend. For 1940 retail sales within Charleston totaled $43,839,000. This marked the first time that sales exceeded those of 1929. Charleston consumers were more profligate in their spending habits than their counterparts in larger Huntington who spent just over $31 million in 1940. In the five years beginning in 1935, Charleston retail sales rose by $10 million.[38]

In the improving economy, Charleston's newspapers were enjoying a growing circulation. In a New Year's Day ad in 1937, the Gazette congratulated itself on its fiftieth birthday and for achieving for the first time a weekly circulation of over 50,000. In part the paper attributed the increased circulation to its reflection of the views of liberal, progressive West Virginians and to its practice of "criticizing constructively and denouncing fearlessly…."[39]

City salaries that had been cut during the early Thirties were boosted back up in 1936. In August the Council restored the salaries of the Mayor, Manager, Clerk, and Fire Chief to their pre 1932 level of $4500, $3600, $2295, and $2550 respectively. The Police Chief whose salary was $3120 before the reduction was set at $3000. Council members in 1936 began to pay themselves $200 per year.

Laid off employees began to be hired back. In addition to the Police Chief, the police department in 1936 had eighty men in uniform, an increase of thirteen patrolmen since 1933. The number of firemen including the chief increased from fifty-eight in 1933 to seventy in 1936. Due to the Tax Limitation Amendment, the assessed property value had grown slowly, from $108.8 million in 1933 to $111.6 million in 1936.[40]

Kanawha Boulevard about 1940. This view is from Hale Street looking west toward Capitol Street. At this time, Kanawha Boulevard was still a busy shopping area. Urban renewal later razed much of the area (see cover photograph).

Post Riverfront

Dawson's first term was one of major accomplishments and in his re-election bid of 1939, Charleston voters showed their appreciation. Running against Democrat P.H. Murphy, Dawson doubled his 1935 victory margin compiling 17,986 votes to 14,209 for his opponent and carrying forty-nine of Charleston's sixty-two precincts. Republicans also won the Municipal Judge and Treasurer races (terms of other administrative offices had not expired for this election) and swept Council winning twenty-one of twenty-two seats.[41]

But not all was smooth sailing for Dawson. Just a few months into his second term, he was faced with a budget deficit and was criticized by the Chamber of Commerce for a tax increase. The deficit came as a surprise to Dawson. While campaigning for re-election in April, he promised hundreds of supporters at a ward rally on Court Street a continued balanced budget. Maintaining that he inherited a $150,000 deficit in 1935 and had erased it by 1937, he proudly told his supporters that in the past two years, the city had no deficit for the first time in fifteen years.[42] Now four months later cost overruns on the Municipal Auditorium, a shortfall in the amount of fees and fines projected, and a reduction in property assessments had resulted in a deficit of $126,000. Wasting little time, Dawson and the Council passed an ordinance doubling the gross sales tax to one-fifth of one percent on retailers and to one-tenth of one percent on wholesalers. The Chamber complained that it was not consulted on the proposed increase. In a consoling letter to the Chamber, Dawson explained that as to the type of tax the city had no viable options and that the increase would raise over $65,000.[43] However, in September the Council bowed to the Chamber rescinded the doubling of the tax. As another revenue raising measure, the 1939 budget added an expense item for the installation of parking meters, and in December, Council asked for bids on 450 meters.[44]

Although Dawson was to serve twelve years as Mayor, his major accomplishments were either completed or started during his first term. Just a year into his second term, he announced in December 1940 that there were no new public works and that the current projects would be completed in 1941. His goals were now more prosaic—to install more traffic lights and parking meters, to study the sewer system, and to live within the budget, currently again in deficit due largely to low garbage collection fees.[45]

Dawson's popularity caught the eye of state Republican leaders who persuaded him to seek the governorship. Winning the Republican primary in the Spring 1940, Dawson became the party's gubernatorial candidate in November 1940.But outside Kanawha County, the Democrats were in control, and Dawson was handily defeated by Matthew Neely.

In the last half of 1942, Dawson and the Council took up the issue of re-naming some of Charleston's streets. This question provoked some controversy. Although supported by the post office in order eliminate duplication in some street names, a Daily Mail poll found the public evenly divided on the question. In November 1942 Council passed an ordinance that re-named several streets. The new names lasted except for one. In Kanawha City, Council had changed Virginia Avenue to MacArthur Avenue in honor of General MacArthur who already was a war hero to some members of Council. Residents of Virginia Avenue objected, and the following month Council restored the former street name.[46]

In 1942, as we have seen, the city airport at Institute was closed, but efforts began immediately to secure another site. The Civil Aeronautics Board approved a site at Coonskin Ridge about three miles north of the city. However, the airport plans were assumed by the county, and with the support of the Council, the county moved ahead to open Yeager Airport in 1947.[47]

As WPA funds changed Charleston's infrastructure, other federal money by 1939 began to impact the city's housing. Two years earlier, Congress had passed the Wagner Stegell Housing Act setting up the U.S. Housing Authority that administered the construction of low income housing. Municipalities that wished to participate had to establish their own housing authorities. Unlike the WPA funds that were grants, housing money was disbursed as loans covering ninety percent of the local project cost. Repayment terms were lenient, interest being assessed at just one-half of one percent.

In Charleston the need for low income housing was clear. In 1935 the Federal Emergency Recovery Administration (FERA) surveyed the city's housing and found that over 1400 new housing units would be needed to replace existing slums. Housing was especially poor on the east side of the Elk north of Washington Street in the Triangle area. Here many individuals had built shacks from dump material. Such shelter lacked indoor sanitation and modern plumbing. In the same area, families lived on houseboats anchored in the Elk. These also lacked sanitation facilities. In 1938 the Council established the Charleston Housing Authority, which soon had plans for two housing projects, one in the Triangle area and the other at the west end of Washington Street. But the federal government would not fund the projects until the local housing authority resettled the slum dewellers and demolished their dilapidated housing. Fearing they would be left with nothing, the inhabitants at first resisted resettlement. But the city accomplished the task and demolished the shanties. The Gazette applauded the action, writing that the razing removed "a squalid section that was one of Charleston's most repulsive eyesores."[48]

With a $2.5 million loan and $250,000 of city funds, construction on both projects began in Spring 1939. The West Side project, named Littlepage Terrace, opened in June 1940 with 170 family units, all of which were reserved for white families. The name was given because the project was built on the site of the Littlepage homestead. The Littlepage home was saved, and it became the administrative office of the project. The other project, known as Washington Manor, opened a few months later in November 1940. It would house 304 families, 127 of them Negro who were separated from the white families.[49]

To qualify for a rental unit, a family had to have an income between $900 and $1000 per year. But meeting the income range did not mean automatic admission, as all applicants had to go through an interview process. Rent was modest at both projects. A three-bedroom unit was fifteen dollars per month with utilities paid. Supporting the projects the Gazette wrote that "Littlepage Terrace truly represents the American Way of living."[50]

Dawson finished his second term in Spring 1943 and wanted a third. More popular than ever, Dawson increased his margin of victory over that of 1939. Running against Democrat Jackson Savage, Dawson won by over 4100 votes. The voters, as Republican as they were four years earlier, again returned twenty-one of twenty-two Council seats to the party. And in a carbon copy of 1939, the Republicans captured the offices of Municipal Judge and Treasurer. During the campaign, Dawson was able to turn aside Savage's charges of prostitution and gambling in the city. Likewise his charges of excessive city employees and financial concealment found little support. On a positive note, Dawson ran on his past building projects, which still resonated well with the voters. As Dawson began his third term, there were no large building projects. In 1943 the country was well into World War 11, and the New Deal money so essential to Dawson's first term had become a victim of the war effort.

Charleston at Mid-Century

A long time resident of Charleston in 1950 would still see many similarities to the Charleston of the early part of the century. Capitol Street with its concentration of shopping still drew large crowds and continued to be the focal point of the city. During the Easter shopping season of 1950, a city policeman described the traffic approaching the downtown on Saturday, April 1 as the heaviest he had seen. The Gazette reported that it took a bus an hour to get from Kanawha City to downtown and twenty-five minutes to travel from the State Capitol to downtown. On this day, ten extra policemen had been called for duty and a policeman was stationed at every downtown intersection.[1]

The downtown with many more stores than in 1900 was now serving a population of over 73,000, a seven-fold increase over the 1900 population. Many of the stores would still be familiar to an elderly resident. Frankenberger's on Capitol Street was still a pre-eminent men's store. Long standing department stores as O.J. Morrison's, Coyle and Richardson, and A.W. Cox still appeared to be doing well. But now they were supplemented by The Diamond and Montgomery Ward. Woodrum's Home Outfitting Co. on Virginia Street, judging by its heavy advertising in both Charleston newspapers, was still the city's dominant furniture store even though it now had twenty-nine competitors citywide. Charleston women kept twenty- four specialty clothing stores in business and well-healed men shoppers supported nine tailors. [2]

In banking resources and capital, Charleston banks were much larger that than those in the early part of the century, but its six mid-century banks were smaller in number than in 1910. The four leading banks would be familiar to an elderly observer. All located on Capital Street they were the Kanawha Valley Bank, Charleston National Bank, National Bank of Commerce, and the Kanawha Banking and Trust Company. The city's banking capital was financing a bustling construction industry. The building trades had gotten off to a fast start in 1950. For January and February, the value of city issued building permits totaled $5.5 million. For all of 1949 building permits had totaled just nine million dollars. [3] Downtown the Ruffner and Kanawha hotels were in their fifth decade while the twenty-year-old Daniel Boone was still the largest of Charleston's hotels. The Boone advertised rates of $3.00 and up per night; a double at the Ruffner overlooking the river would cost a couple between $3.50 and $7.50 per night[4]

A busy Capitol Street in 1942. Such scenes remained into the Sixties.

Radio was now a thirty-year-old commercial enterprise, and according to the 1950 census over ninety-five percent of Charleston households had a radio, and residents could turn their dial to seven Charleston broadcasting stations. The city's population had by 1950 spawned over twenty radio repair shops providing employment to many technical minded residents. However, the private automobile deluge had provided the city with a more ample source of employment. The 1950 city directory listed over nineteen automobile parts stores, twenty-five new car dealers, and over fifty automobile repair shops. Finding enough downtown parking space had proved impossible. In May 1950, a citizens advisory traffic committee had recommended that the city Council create a parking authority with the power to acquire property for the construction of parking garages. Private capital said the committee was not sufficiently developing parking facilities. [5]

Charleston had over forty pool halls in 1950, but appeared somewhat short of bookstores. No outlet was devoted exclusively to books, but the S. Spencer Moore store and Coyle and Richardson department store sold books. The pool halls were located in various parts of the city, but the largest concentration was on Summers Street and West Washington Street. Books could be purchased only downtown.

Charleston in many respects, most notably housing, was still a segregated city. The city's major hotels—the Boone, Ruffner, and the Kanawha accepted white guests only. The Ferguson Hotel (of which more later), which was black owned felt compelled to advertise in the city directory that it "accommodated colored people." The public library maintained a branch for blacks on Lewis Street. Before the civil rights revolution of the next decade, it was accepted practice for Charleston newspapers to carry want ads that designated race as a qualification. For example, a Gazette ad in January 1950 read "white couple" wanted. Another ad wanted a "colored man." [6] It was also acceptable to specify an age range. A May 1950 Daily Mail ad read "middle age white woman" wanted. [7]

By mid-century Charleston was not in relative terms the wholesale powerhouse it had been earlier in the century. At the beginning of the century, the city's wholesale business in dollar volume had exceeded that of manufacturing. By 1950 Charleston employed under 2000 wholesale workers versus nearly 6000 manufacturing workers. Of all workers in 1950, just six percent were engaged in wholesale trade, and this percentage would continue to decline throughout the decade to 5.4 percent in 1960. [8] According to data in Charleston's 1962 comprehensive plan, the wholesale payroll in 1958 totaled about $18 million while the manufacturing payroll for the same year was nearly $30 million and that of retail was just over $23 million.

As they had in previous decades, the Gazette and Daily Mail were at mid-century continuing to publish daily, and each had its separate Sunday edition.

There were as yet few by-line articles. The news coverage was heavily international and national as opposed to state and local. International and national articles compiled from wire services usually dominated the front page of each paper. After the Korean War began in June 1950, war news dominated the front pages of both the Gazette and Daily Mail. However, a local election or a fire could on occasion capture a headline. Like the front pages, the subject of each paper's editorials was usually an international or national event. Sports coverage had improved significantly since the early part of the century. Both papers covered major league baseball with box scores, game highlights, and league standings. Professional football and basketball were likewise well covered. Readers could also use either paper to satisfy interest in local and state collage athletic events. Readers, however, had to look elsewhere for national financial news. Neither the Gazette nor Daily Mail had a business section. Stock quotations of only a selective number of companies from the New York Stock Exchange were carrried. Rarely in 1950 did business news exceed half a page. Milestones in the leadership of each paper occurred in the Fifties. First the Daily Mail owner since 1914, Walter E. Clark, died of a heart attack on February 4, 1950.[9] Already a Republican paper when Clark purchased it, he developed it into an independent Republican publication advocating good government. Clark's front-page editorial, "At This Hour," had become, according to the opposition Gazette, one the most widely read columns in the state. Clark's duties as publisher were initially assumed by Fred M. Staunton and in 1956 by Lydell B. Clay, Clark's stepson.

For the Gazette W.E. Chilton Jr., who had been president of the newspaper company and managing editor since the early Twenties, died in September 1950, and Robert L. Smith was elevated from business manager to publisher. Smith remained at the helm until his death in October 1961 and was succeeded by Chilton Jr.'s son W.E. Chilton III.[10]

During the Fifties, the Gazette was located in the second block of Hale Street where it had been since 1918. The Daily Mail in 1950 could celebrate its twenty-third year at 1001 Virginia Street East where it remains today. In September 1960, the Gazette moved into an addition of the Daily Mail building. However, the physical proximity did not bring the newspapers any closer together in political viewpoint; each continued with an independent political stance.

City Government

The Charleston city budget for fiscal year 1950-51 was the largest in its history, over $1.9 million; yet it fell short of the city's needs. Part of the revenue the city administration was counting on was dealt a $180,000 blow by two recent unfavorable court decisions. In 1949 the Supreme Court of Appeals upheld the State Auditor's ruling that municipalities could not share in liquor profits, which the previous year had contributed about $100,000 to Charleston's revenue. [11] Then in April 1950, the Council repealed the city's two-cent amusement tax that moviegoers paid. Earlier West Virginia's high court had declared Huntington's similar amusement tax unconstitutional, a ruling that caused Charleston's City Solicitor to advise that Charleston's tax could not stand a legal challenge. The city had reaped about $80,000 from this tax. [12]

What the city's unmet budgetary needs were depended largely upon one's point of view. In a June 1950 speech to the Rotary Club, Mayor Carl Andrews, who had been elected in 1947 succeeding Boone Dawson and was the city's first Democratic mayor since 1919, stated that the city's greatest need was a professional engineering staff. At present said Andrews the city's one-man engineering department could not keep up. Andrews claimed to the Rotarians that a good engineering department would cost thousands but save millions. [13] In the same month, the Daily Mail took note of the coming budget and saw it as inadequate. The Mail editorialized: "Instead of building new streets, it [the city] will have a hard time keeping the old ones in repair. Instead of building parks and swimming pools, it[the city] will have to scrape to keep the present recreation program in operation."[14] The Mail further wanted to increase the number of policemen and purchase new equipment for the fire department, but concluded that this probably would not be possible. For their part, city employees wanted a salary increase. In 1950 city clerical employees were earning about $160.00 per month, about sixty-five percent of equivalent work in the private sector. Salaries of police and firemen ranged from $197.00 to $262.00 per month[15] Council was sympathetic to employee demands for salary increases, and in August 1950 it increased the gross sales tax by fifty percent to cover salary increases of $15 per month.

The Council adopted the 1950-51 budget at the end of August. Police and firefighting functions consumed the largest relative share of the total with the police receiving $332,000 up $50,000 from 1949 and the fire department receiving $306,000, an increase of $40,000. The next largest expense was payment on the bonded debt that totaled $234,000. Other expenses in round figures included:

Health	$49,000
Engineering	$25,000
Street cleaning	$159,800
Street maintenance	$177,000
Parks & recreation	$66,300
Planning commission	$8,500

The city's revenue sources were principally the property tax that gave the coffers over $603,000 and the gross sales tax that raised about $451,000, a jump of $295,000 over the previous year due to the Council's fifty percent increase. Other revenue sources included:

Incinerator fees $158,000
Police fines $100,000
Building permits $25,000
Parking meters $62,000
Watt Powell Park 29,000
Cemetery revenues .... 18,000[16]

After passage of the budget, the Daily Mail in the spirit of Walter Clark wrote editorially that the budget not only skimped on necessities but had little left over for the "amenities of municipal life." The Mail concluded by opining that someday the public will see that there is little excuse for government poverty and that there is "no underlying reason why every need for long range improvements should be meant with the cry of no funds."[17]

The expenditures that the Council authorized, as the Mail put it, had contributed little to the "amenities of municipal life." In December 1949, Mayor Andrews released a ten-point improvement program for Charleston. Like the budget this was a nuts and bolts program, and showed that Andrews was interested in the same type of capital projects that intrigued Mayor Dawson. Andrews's proposals included a boulevard on the south side of the Kanawha from the South Side Bridge to South Charleston, a bridge across the Kanawha east of the Kanawha City Bridge, street extensions downtown, grade separations at railroad tracks, and a parking garage.[18] Such expenditures should they become a reality constituted what the Mail would call the necessities of municipal life.

Even though the monetary size of the budget was nearly forty times larger than at the beginning of the century, the government in terms of its functions had hardly grown at all. It was still a caretaker government, reacting to events and playing catch-up to the city's needs. The "amenities of municipal life"had clearly eluded the responsible authorities. The city Council of 1950 was no more imaginative and forward looking than its 1900 counterpart. Its principal interest lay in street maintenance, policing, and fire fighting—all necessary functions but in themselves not sufficient to create a city of quality. The single expenditure that can give a city a vision of the future is planning. Adequate plans can define the needs of a city and how resources can be raised and directed to meet them. Although Council had created a planning commission in 1939, it was still an unpaid, volunteer group without permanent staff. At mid-century Charleston was still a decade and a half from employing a professional planner. In the meantime, Charleston would devote a mere $8,500 for planning.

Part of Mayor Andrews ten- point program included a doubling of the city's recreation facilities, but it did happen during his administration. The Parks and Recreation Commission was in 1950 eleven years old and was still without professional staff. As shown above, the Council appropriated just over $66,000 for fiscal year 1950-51, an increase of $1500 over the previous year. As the recreation amenity was starved for public funds, music and art were bereft. The city had opened Municipal Auditorium in 1939, making a home for the symphony, but two decades would pass before the city would build a theatre for live performances.

Music and the Arts

At any time in the first half of the century, it would have been easy to make a case that too little money, either public or private, had been funneled to the arts and music in Charleston. In spite of the monetary deficiency, Charleston thespians and musicians at mid-century were supplying enough interest and perseverance to give the city a respectful standing in the arts. The Kanawha Players, now approaching thirty years of age, had been with local unpaid talent performing year after year. We previously saw that in 1936 the Players lost their rehearsal and stage facility when the former Methodist church burnt and the property taken by the post office. For the two years preceding 1950, the Players had been unable to secure rehearsal facilities and were unable to perform from a stage. Instead the Players read radio scripts until January 1950 when the troupe was ready with a stage production of "Three Blind Mice." After giving four performances at the Thomas Jefferson Jr. High School, the Players went into rehearsal for its next production, "O Mistress Mine."

After weathering a financial crisis in 1949 that was solved in part when many local businesses agreed to purchase symphony tickets for their employees, the Charleston Symphony Orchestra entered its eighth year under conductor Antonio Modarelli.[19] For the last half of its 1949-50 season, the symphony gave three performances at Municipal Auditorium. First on January 31 and again on March 31 when it performed "The Saga of Peer Gynt." The orchestra ended its season on May 4 with among other works a performance of Beethoven's Fifth Symphony. For the 1950-51 season, the symphony had scheduled six concerts. Modarelli would continue yet another season, and beginning in 1953 the orchestra was led by Geoffrey Hobday, a native of England, who would remain nine years.

The symphony's financial problems would continue through the decade and into the Sixties. In a sharply worded article in July 1967, Gazette music and stage writer, Baynard Ennis took the Charleston business community to task for its lack of support. He wrote: "Business and industry by its stand-offish attitude are not helping to raise the standard of orchestra performance here or to enlarge the size of the audience, and it is ridiculous to expect either will alter significantly as long as the attitude is maintained."[20] In the same article, Ennis pointed to John D. Rockefeller IV's recent speech at West Virginia State College in which he criticized wealthy West Virginians for not sufficiently supporting the arts. In this context, it is interesting to note that when such a civic-minded person as Walter Clark died, he left nothing to the arts or to any public institution. His will distributed all assets to family and friends.[21]

Even though the Players and the symphony struggled financially, individuals with a performing interest were not deterred, as the mid-century saw the creation of two new groups. Both would succeed and enter the 21st Century still performing. The first, organized in 1948, was the Charleston Light Opera Guild. In Spring 1950, the Guild gave its fourth performance, staging the opera "Sweethearts" and in the Fall at Charleston High School, it performed the Gilbert and Sullivan operetta, "Mikado."[22] The Guild continued with operettas throughout the Fifties and beginning in 1960 changed its focus to Broadway musicals, showing its talent with such productions as Brigadoon, Sound of Music, My Fair Lady, and Cabaret among the many. Like the Kanawha Players, the Guild began without a permanent home and for rehearsals utilized schools, churches, and fire stations until early in 1967 when it purchased a building on Jefferson Street, which served as its rehearsal center until 1996. In that year, the Guild acquired the much larger Weekly United Methodist Church on the West Side.[23] Its performances, however, have been staged at the Civic Center since 1959 when its theatre opened.

Following the Guild, talented singers found an outlet when Harold Ewing organized in 1952 the Charleston Civic Chorus. Under the Ewing, who would remain as Director until 1967, the civic chorus became a fixture on the Charleston music scene. Over the years the chorus has shown its versatility by performing compositions from Bach and Beethoven to such contemporary composers as Dave Brubeck and Benjamin Britten. Like the opera guild members, the civic chorus singers are unpaid. The singers pay dues and buy their own music in order to perform and enhance the arts in Charleston.

In addition to the performing organizations, Charleston residents in 1950 supported eight dancing studios, one of which taught ballet, and twenty-six music teachers, most of whom taught piano. In all there were in 1950 six music stores, four of them located downtown.

A typical Charleston traffic jam in the 1950's; this one on Lee Street as seen from the front of the public library.

Continuing Problems

The environment as a political and social issue was not at mid-century a part of the public consciousness, but Charleston nevertheless had its share of pollution, and it was the city's contamination of the Kanawha and Elk rivers that began to concern the state authorities. The State Water Commission in 1950 began to order Charleston and other cities to clean up its rivers and streams. It was not common in the Fifties for cities to have sewage treatment plants that filtered pollutants before discharge into rivers. In a report in Spring 1950, the water commission cited Charleston for "grossly polluting streams in the area and threatening the health, comfort, and well-being of a vast segment of the population."[24] The report went on to state that "the continued growth of the community is threatened by the destruction of its streams." Further the report recommended that the city finance the construction of a sewage treatment plant with revenue bonds, for they would not affect the city's debt limit. Then in July 1950 the state issued thirty-day "cease and desist" orders to Charleston and other cities mandating a halt to river pollution. Although Mayor Andrews in his 1949 program had recommended a sewage treatment plant for the city, many on the Council did not react in a cooperative manner, and showed more concern with the state's exercise of authority over the city than the fact of river pollution. In the same vein, Charleston's solicitor questioned the authority of the water commission, and in a July 1950 meeting called the state's action a form of taxation without representation.[25]

The Council dawdled for two more years and into the next administration before it came around to the state's position on river clean up. At a July 1952 meeting, a state sanitary engineer asserted that Charleston's open sewers affected drinking water in communities as far away as Cincinnati. He said: "This condition points a serious finger at West Virginia's capitol city."[26] During the first administration of Mayor John Copenhaver, the Council in June 1952 created a three member sanitary board to set in motion the construction of a sanitary sewer system. The system would be funded by revenue bonds, which unlike general obligation bonds, did not require voter approval. Charleston's water consumers, however, would finance the bonds through a water rate increase. The site of the treatment plant was a manner of some controversy, but in the end the city paid $191,000 for a nine acres site in North Charleston at the mouth of Two Mile Creek. Work got started on the $13 million project before the end of 1952 and would take over six years to complete.

It was not until the Sixties that Charleston's housing problems reached a flashpoint, but the problems had been building for decades. We have seen that the city with federal help opened two public housing projects in 1939 and 1940, but substandard housing persisted in the city. When the federal government passed its second public housing act in 1949, the Gazette urged that the city take advantage of federal funds, eradicate the city's slums, and establish decent housing.[27] In April 1950, the Gazette pointed out that ten cities had already selected sites for low cost public housing and urged Council to move on the issue. While ten years earlier the Gazette praised the apartment like Littlepage public housing in North Charleston as the "American Way of Living," it now advocated that public housing funds be used for single, detached houses.[28] Irrespective of the type of dwellings, the city needed improved housing. Statistics compiled by the 1950 federal census presented a dismal picture of Charleston's housing. Of the city's some 22,700 dwelling units, ten percent or 2217 were rated dilapidated by the census. By comparison, Huntington with about 4000 more housing units than Charleston had just 1600 dilapidated units. Many residents did not have a private bathroom, as about 2400 shared a flush toilet and bathing facilities. According to the census, 534 residents did not have a flush toilet and made do with a privy. Nearly 1000 residents did not have not water in their dwelling.[29]

Although Charleston's population had grown considerably in the first half of the century, the rate of growth in the Forties was the slowest decennial period to date. By 1950 the city had added just under 5600 people to the 1940 population of 67,914. Nearly 3700 of the increase was accounted for by the 1948 annexation of North Charleston. Within the city a clear population trend was in motion. The East End was losing population, the West Side was holding steady, and the area south of the Kanawha was growing. During the Forties, the wards to the south of the river increased in population from 7,418 to 10,420 in 1950.[30] This trend south of the Kanawha would continue in the following decades. The Daily Mail blamed the small population growth during the Forties to the city's "meager and uncertain revenues" and the consequent inability of the city to meet the needs of the people.[31]

In the following chapters, we will take a look at the Mail's pessimistic assessment and see how the city attempted to meet or ignore such problems as traffic, housing, zoning, parks, and encompassing all of these, planning.

Expansion and Planning

At the beginning of the Twentieth Century, Charleston's boundaries north of the Kanawha River encompassed much of today's city on the same side of the river. The eastern side of the city extended from the Elk across the flat area of land to about Michigan Avenue or about a block east of the present day Capitol. West of the Elk, the city limit was approximately present day Park Avenue or about eight blocks west of the river. Northward from the Kanawha, the city laid claim to the area between the river and mountain range. This gave Charleston an incorporated area of bottomland about three miles in length along the Kanawha and about three-fourths mile wide.[1] This municipal land area had expanded from George Clendenin's original plat of forty, one-acre lots extending from the east side of the Elk to present day Capitol Street. The front row of lots faced the northern shore of the Kanawha and looked across Front Street (later Kanawha Street). A second row was placed directly behind the first with the two rows separated by Main Street (later Virginia Street). Perpendicular to Front and Main streets, Clendenin's surveyor drew six numbered streets extending to just the end of the rear lots. This plat was an orderly start to Charleston's physical development, but by the time the city began to grow in the 20th Century, order and design would not be a distinguishing characteristic of the Capitol City.

The shape of Clendenin's plat is known to city planners as a grid, a system of streets intersecting at right angles with building lots between the streets also divided by parallel and perpendicular lines. One of the advantages of the grid is that it can be infinitely extended, giving an entire land mass an orderly design. Since Charleston first developed over a flat area where the grid is especially easy to layout, one would think that a subsequent city government would have extended Clendenin's plat over the entire city. It is after is all an inherent and historic function of government to design and plan cities. Such a grant of power was recognized by the Legislature as accruing to Charleston at least as far back as 1875. In the charter of that year, the Legislature had written that "The Council shall have the power to re-survey said town … to open new streets, and extend, straighten, widen, and repair old streets and alleys; to curb and pave streets, sidewalks, and gutters for public use, and to alter, improve, and light the same…to regulate and determine the width of all streets, sidewalks, and public alleys…."[2] This grant of power was in all subsequent charters. In 1915, for example, the language read that the Council be "granted power to have said city surveyed, to lay out, open, vacate, straighten, broaden, change grade of … widen, narrow, pave and re-pave streets, alleys, roads, squares…."[3] Yet Council after

Council ignored this grant of authority and in the resulting design vacuum, developers largely had their way.

Although this photograph was taken in the 1960,'s, it is placed here to show Charleston original bottomland and illustrate the course of the city's growth. The original city was platted from the Elk River (far left) to about the bridge in center of the p picture. Part of the West Side (left of the Elk River) was annexed in 1895. By 1867, Charleston's boundaries extended a few blocks east of the downtown or the bridge in the center of the photo, and by 1897, an annexation extended the boundaries a block past the Capitol (far left). The area south of the Kanawha in the foreground did not begin serious growth until the 1920's. As late as 1960, it can be seen that the Fort Hill area still has ample room for expansion.

Although most of Charleston' early developers lacked a civic vision, J Brisben Walker was not one of them, and had it not been for a nationwide depression, Charleston's West Side would have grown differently that it did. Originally from Pennsylvania, Walker was a graduate of the United States Military Academy and after West Point spent some time in China. Leaving the Far East, he settled in Charleston in 1870 and soon amassed a large fortune in iron manufacturing. A year after arriving in Charleston, Walker acquired acreage from the west side of the Elk to about present day Park Avenue and from the Kanawha north to Charleston Street (later Washington Street).[4] Over this area, which was not part of Charleston, Walker platted a grid of streets and building lots. The streets were to be sixty feet wide and the lots, selling for $250 to $300, were forty by 120 feet, Unlike future generations of developers, Walker had an interest in urban parks, and approximately in the center of the plat he set aside a large area two blocks in length and one block wide for parkland. In order to connect the plat with Charleston and no doubt to encourage lot sales, Walker constructed a bridge across the Elk where the later Virginia Street Bridge was built. The attractiveness of Walker's plan reached Cincinnati. In February 1872, the Cincinnati Commercial editorialized:" A year ago the territory on the lower side of the Elk river was simply a corn field, but with the advantages of a high level surface. The bottom land having been united in a single tract was laid off for city purposes in the most modern and approved style. Broad avenues, convenient lots, a public square; in a word, care seems to have been taken to profit by the latest improvements in city building. The work of building up the West End has begun in earnest and at present there are over three hundred people located there."[5]

But Walker's ambitious plan never materialized. In the economic Panic of 1873, he suffered financial reverses and lost all of his west side holdings. Walker went west and became wealthy in Colorado. Still interested in city parks, Walker left several acres of his western land holdings to the city of Denver for parkland. Charleston, however, was not so fortunate. Future developers changed Walker's plat, eliminating the park and narrowing the streets. Before the West Side had become part of the city, Walker's former plat west of Delaware Avenue had been altered by the 1891 Glenwood Addition.[6] This Addition established the well known Five Corners intersection where present day Virginia Street, and Central and Delaware avenues meet. East of Delaware Avenue, Walker's plat largely remained. His additional influence on the West Side is still seen in some of the street names. By 1884 the Glen Elk Company began purchasing land along the west bank of the Elk and selling building lots. This endeavor grew to become Glen Elk, and in 1891 the legislature incorporated it as Elk City. Then in 1895, the Legislature repealed its 1891 act, and amended Charleston's charter to add Elk City to Charleston. It needs to be noted here that as with a city's form of government, the Legislature had full authority to increase or otherwise change a municipal boundary. This authority was, however, stripped from the Legislature by the 1936 Home Rule Amendment to the Constitution. With the incorporation of Elk City, Charleston's western boundary now extended to about Park Avenue and its northern limit on the West Side was the Kanawha and Michigan railroad tracks. By 1907 the city's area on the West Side more than doubled when the new charter of that year extended the boundary to Patrick Street.[7]

Edgewood

Charleston's streetcar suburb, Edgewood, dates from the early 20th Century. Although geographically part of the West Side, the developers of Edgewood made no attempt to make their subdivision part of the area's street pattern. It could not be since it was located on a hillside to the north of the city's bottomland. In 1906, the Edgewood Land Company platted several acres on a hilly area about a mile from the Elk and north of today's Washington Street. Overlooking the central city, Edgewood was conceived as a residential neighborhood for the wealthy who wanted an escape from the more crowded conditions of the older city. The lots varied in size and were irregular in shape, devoid for the most part of the grid pattern used by developers of Charleston's bottomland. The design is organic with streets and lots laid out in harmony with the hilly topography. There were deed restrictions in the initial lots sold. These related to minimum setbacks for houses and the value of the house to be built. For example, the 1908 deed for a \$4000 lot required that the house have a minimum cost of \$10,000 and construction to begin within one year from the date of the deed. The deed of another 1908 lot sale mandated a minimum house cost of \$3500 and be set back at least thirty feet from Edgewood Drive. A 1910 sale of a Maple Street lot required that the buyer build his house at least thirty feet from the street at a minimum cost of \$2000.[8] Although deed restrictions were common, the land company made no attempt to influence the design of a house. Accordingly, a wide variety of architectural styles are found. The first houses noted for their stylish exterior were located on Edgewood Drive, the principal street and entrance to the development off Charleston Street. The styles included Colonial, Bungaloid, Greek Revival, and Victorian. Many were designed by prominent architects, including Charleston's H Rus Warne, who designed City Hall and as we have seen the renovations and expansion of the Masonic Building. Befitting the affluent nature of Edgewood, the first homes were designed with electricity and natural gas.

When Edgewood was first platted in 1906, the private automobile had not yet made its mark. The developers in order to insure the success of the subdivision had to persuade the traction company to establish a streetcar route from downtown. A West Side streetcar subsequently ran west on Virginia Street to where it intersected with Washington Street, then up Edgewood Drive to the top of the hill. A quaint streetcar stop was established where a cave opened on the west side of Edgewood Drive.

Attracting many of Charleston's most prominent citizens from government and the professions, Edgewood thrived. In a promotion brochure of 1922, the Charleston Chamber of Commerce called Edgewood "one of the most beautiful, refreshing, and healthful home spots in the state." The development continued its attractiveness over the decades, and in 1989 part of the subdivision that included Edgewood and Highland drives and the streets of Chester, Lower Chester, Beech, Maple, Poplar, and Swarthmore was placed on the National Register of Historic Places. Shortly after Edgewood was platted it became part of the city. Charleston's 1907 Charter incorporated the first 600 feet of the area north of Charleston Street, thereby bringing in the houses along Edgewood Drive. A 1914 city map shows almost all of Edgewood within the city limits.[9]

East of the Elk

It was east of the Elk in the original Charleston where development was particularly random and undirected. We can pick up the story in 1862 when the Charleston Extension Company purchased Cox's Farm and all the land from the Elk east to Bradford Street. Cox's Farm roughly encompassed the area from downtown Virginia St northeast to the mountain range. William Cox first bought this land in 1828 and later built his house north of where Capitol Street ended. In the early years after Cox's purchase what later became Capitol Street was known as Cox's Lane.[10] Following the sale, Charleston's 1867 Charter extended the city boundary to Bradford Street, thus incorporating the extension company purchase into the city. The land company in the absence of any controlling legislation subdivided its purchase and began selling building lots. According to John Hale, when he wrote in 1886, much of the land as of that date is built upon.

The extension company, lacking the civic vision of Brisban Walker, did not layout a network of streets and lots that would guide later development. The land company, moreover, sold much of its holdings to other smaller developers who were free to make their own subdivisions. And so an array of "additions" began to spread over the eastern side of the city. City engineering department maps show them as the Smith Addition in the area of Smith Street and the Smith and Ruffner Addition also in the same area. There was a Lewis Street Addition and others established by the Charleston Construction Company, Quarrier and Miller, and Reed and Hansford. Prominent families as the Noyers and Clendenins set up additions in their names. Sanborn insurance maps in the early 20th Century show disjointed and dead-end streets east of the Elk. This is especially true between the Elk River and Capitol Street. Many of the dead-end streets in this area were due to the private purchase of land for family homesteads prior to any street layout[11]

East of Bradford Street development was somewhat more orderly than in the central area, but it was far from ideal. This area, later known as the East End, was until nearly the 20th Century largely under the control of the Joseph Ruffner's heirs; appropriately it was known as the "Town of Upper Ruffner." In 1897, Charleston expanded considerably when the Legislature incorporated the Ruffner lands from Bradford east to about a block past the site of the later Capitol building. Shortly after the annexation the Ruffner lands began to be dispersed. The First Ruffner Addition had been laid out in 1895 followed in 1902 by the Ruffner Brothers Addition. Farther east between and Michigan and Chesapeake streets, the deGruyter Addition was established in 1904, and in 1914 the Comstock and Kanawha additions east of California Avenue were laid out.

Many of these additions were in themselves an orderly plat of grid design, but they were small and had little effect on subsequent, contiguous plats of another developer. Such was the case of the First Ruffner Addition. The approximate center of the plat was Ruffner Street extending north from the Kanawha River to the K&M Railroad tracks. The east-west streets consisting of Virginia, Quarrier, Lee, Washington and over to Wilson on the north edge of the plat intersected with Ruffner Street. The Addition extended south and laid out Beauregard Street, but this parallel street with Ruffner extended only from Quarrier to Wilson. Why it did not extend south past Quarrier Street is not stated. But we may conjecture that since the developer's primary interest is lot sales, a shortened Beauregard Street was subordinated to the larger lot sizes the company wanted to sell south of Quarrier. Another oddity from the standpoint of street thoroughfare was that the plat brought Lee Street to an end at Beauregard Street while the other east-west streets continued west through Beauregard. As the East End was platted east of Ruffner, there was not another north-south street south of Washington Street until Elizabeth Street, about one half-mile away. This made for very a long city block. The explanation given by one observer was simply that the Ruffner family did not want cross streets through their lands. This small incident is in itself a commentary on the ineffectiveness of the Council. It may have been in the interest of the city to have another street between Ruffner and Elizabeth, but the Council seemingly took no interest and allowed the views of the Ruffners to preview even after their property was absorbed into the city.

Unregulated additions continued throughout the Twenties and into the Thirties. In 1925 the Kanawha Valley Improvement Company purchased land along Piedmont Road between Morris and Chilton streets, carved out fifteen lots, and called it the Logan Addition. The plat was first seen by the City Engineer, who had no objections, and then passed by Council without change. On the West Side, the Higgenbotham-Hill Realty Company in 1928 acquired a tract of land north of Charleston Street (Washington Street) just west of Edgewood. This became the Glenwood Heights Addition, and one gets to it by turning north off Washington Street onto either West or Park streets. In August 1928 Council rubber-stamped this addition, and subsequently the company sold over 100 building lots. Although next to upscale Edgewood subdivision that was established over twenty years earlier, the developer made no attempt to blend the addition with the earlier one. The Glenwood Heights Addition was characterized by narrow streets, small lots, and no driveways. The developer's purpose was clearly to cram the maximum number of lots into the area and make as many lots sales as possible. [12]

Without too much exaggeration, it can be said that Charleston was coming together in the manner of a quitting bee in which the separate patterns stitched took no consideration of the pattern next to it. Consequently lots were lopsided to each other; streets having the same function were of unequal width; the same street might be wider at one section that at another, even when the traffic carried was identical; and the same street might have different names as it ran through the city.

It is better for a city to design a plat early rather than later. But as New York City showed, a plat can still work even if done after streets have been in place for a considerable period. In 1806, not liking what the Dutch and the British had done, the city requested that the New York Legislature appoint commissioners to design a plat for Manhattan Island. Five years later the commissioners unveiled a rectilinear grid for almost all the Island. Broadway survived but little else of the former street pattern was recognizable. After about a decade, however, the plan was realized. The purpose behind the New York City grid was economic. It was thought at the time that the simplicity of the grid encourages economic development. [13]

Compared with later years, developers sailed on smooth seas in the early part of the century. It was an age before planners, before development commissions, before subdivision regulations, and before environmental statues. Once land was purchased and the plat drawn by the land company, the blueprints were presented to the city engineer's office and then to the city Council. The patience of the developer was rarely tried. He got want he wanted. One could appreciate the efficiency, but the process ignored the bigger picture, and thus the Council, bearing final responsibility, ignored the future of the city. Developers of course have little interest in the larger picture. Their investors and creditors want a payoff, and the developers' future horizon extends only as far as the lot sales and the collection of profits. Ideally the city has an interest quite different from this. In short the city's purpose is to achieve a just and orderly urban environment. But to this end, Charleston's city Council never acted by guiding private development with a street design. By the time the private automobile began to deluge the city, Council's neglect was clear.

Sometimes the city got lucky. This occurred when private landowners, recognizing the need for an improved thoroughfare, took the initiative for the development of a street that proved to be of future benefit to the city. This was the case with Quarrier Street east of Capitol Street. At the opening of the 20th Century, Quarrier Street showed on a map extending as far east as Bradford, but lines on a map did not mean it was much of a street. As the Gazette phrased it, Quarrier Street from Hale to Broad was "sort of a street." Early in the century, there were a few businesses in the first block of Quarrier, but east of that stately homes were beginning to be built. One of the landowners east of Hale was William Quarrier who wanted the road fronting his property to be developed into a street that would bear traffic. He and another property owner, the Synder family, donated land to the city so that it could be done. After the work was completed, the street that some residents knew as Third Street became commonly known as "Quarrier Street." [14]

Planning

Although the city government had the authority to lay out a street plan, it did not prior to 1931 have the power to zone and make subdivision regulations. Thus when Council received building plats, it stood on legislative quicksand. It had little foundation from which to criticize. However, Council had never taken the initiative to petition the Legislature for a grant of zoning authority. The Charleston Board of Realtors took this initiative in 1927. Perhaps for reasons in addition to the realtors' petition, the Legislature responded in 1931with an act granting municipalities the authority to establish zoning boards for the purpose of regulating all aspects of business and residential areas. The new authority was, however, conditional upon a favorable local vote. Charleston voters followed up and granted this authority to the Council the following year. A separate Legislative act also in 1931 granted municipalities the power to create planning commissions made up of five to thirteen members; here no enabling vote within the city was necessary. The Charleston City Council, however, waited about five years before creating a Municipal Planning Commission in May 1937 that was composed of thirteen members appointed by the Mayor and confirmed by the Council. [15] (The state law permitted a planning commission to assume the duties of a zoning board, which initially occurred in Charleston). Although it appears that the Council dawdled in creating a commission, Charleston in fact has the longest continuous planning commission in West Virginia. The new commission members, even though they were untrained laymen, took their duties seriously. Within a year, the Commission adopted an interim zoning ordinance, and several months later presented a permanent zoning plan to Council, which passed it in July 1939.[16] In the meantime, the Commission had contracted for a city comprehensive plan that would provide detailed studies of Charleston's demographics, economy, and thoroughfare problems. Adopted by Council in 1938, this plan was an important document in Charleston's history. Not only was it the city's first comprehensive plan, it along with the zoning ordinance gave the

Council a statistical and intellectual basis from which to govern. Moreover, these documents became guides that would tend to provide more legislative continuity between succeeding Councils.

The city's new zoning ordinance was an example of single use zoning, a method that designates certain sectors of a city for specific business and residential use. Charleston's ordinance identified eight uses, four of which were residential. One residential area, for example, was restricted to single family houses while another area was allowed apartments along with single family homes. The ordinance designated other areas of the city for industrial, commercial, and limited manufacturing uses. As it was approved, Charleston's 1939 zoning map did little more than codify existing uses throughout the city. For example, South Hills, Fort Hill, and Louden Heights had earlier developed as single family residential areas, and the zoning ordinance simply gave legal cover to this practice. The West Side in 1939 was a mix of residential and business, which the ordinance codified. Since Charleston's industrial areas were located on the west side of the Elk and along Smith and Piedmont streets, these areas were zoned for industrial use. But lack of creativity is no reason to demean the ordinance. It was overdue and needed. Now as residents looked to the future they could feel assured, for example, that industrial uses would not spread to other parts of the city without laborious proceedings during which time all views could be heard. Residents of single family areas need no longer worry that commercialism would penetrate their neighborhood. Decades later when urban sprawl would become a national problem, critics would flay single use zoning ordinances, but for now it would serve Charleston well enough.

Prior to the ordinance, the Council took a hands-off attitude with respect to residential and business uses within the city. During the Thirties, the Daily Mail was especially critical of the city's laissez faire position concerning problems associated with rapid growth. One incident, occurring three years prior to the zoning ordinance, exemplifies the Council's attitude. On the West Side, an automobile parts store was turning a lot into a junkyard. Many nearby residents were upset and protested to an unresponsive Council. The Daily Mail attacked the lack of response: "Will it (Council) defend readily the rights of the many? Or will it stand up for the rights of one? Will it declare this to be a forward city? Or will it permit it to be a backward one? ... There is all sorts of physical expansion, both private and public. Without direction and restraint it is perfectly possible for such expansion to do more harm than good."[17] After the zoning ordinance, the doctrine of non-conforming uses was in force, and Council would be unable to ignore junkyards in residential areas.

Similarly the comprehensive plan also had the effect of forcing Council's hand, especially regarding street improvements. As the plan stated, its purpose was to guide development and re-development of the city. The use of the term "re-development" is instructive, for it implied that there was much to do over.

Because the first decades of the century were characterized by unguided growth, Charleston was left with a legacy of grade level railroad crossings, a chaotic street pattern, a lack of urban amenities as parks and playgrounds, concert halls, museums, and a quality library. However, the plan principally addressed the traffic problem. The planning document saw Charleston's future as a trade city and encouraged the growth of the service sector and the professions. Thus, an efficient transportation network of streets, roads, and railways was imperative. This network should especially include the warehouse district that needed modern transfer facilities and truck thoroughfares. However, unorthodox streets and traffic problems presented the planning commission with an intractable task, for the private automobile had not waited for the Council to catch up. We saw that in 1930, Kanawha County had over 24,000 vehicle registrations. Although the rate of increase slowed in the Thirties, due to the Depression, the number of vehicles continued to grow, and by 1940, the county registered over 33,000 motor vehicles. Just prior to the Boulevard project, the city conducted a traffic survey at the Washington and Virginia street bridges. [18] In a twelve-hour period, over 11,000 vehicles in either direction crossed each bridge. As the comprehensive plan was being prepared, the authors conducted a survey of eighteen of the city's railroad grade crossings. In a twenty-four hour period in 1938, the survey found that over 80,000 vehicles passed over the crossings. These drivers waited while over 450 railroad cars passed in front of them. In order to put a price tag on the vehicle delay, the study computed that the waiting time was 160 vehicle hours per day. Such items as lost gasoline, wear and tear, and other factors were conservatively estimated to cost two dollars per hour or \$320 per day; thereby putting the yearly loss at over \$100,000. This figure did not count accident losses at the crossing, which amounted to over \$400,000 per year. [19] Those residents who experienced the traffic could have an opinion without citing surveys. In December 1936, the Daily Mail editorialized: "Traffic congestion in Charleston has to be seen and endured to be believed. No mere words can paint the picture or describe the torture, the danger and cussiness of it ... Only people who have experienced the traffic in Charleston and survived know what it is, and they cannot speak of it coherently." [20]

In a mild jab at previous city governments, the plan stated: "While some of the gaps of fifty years ago have been corrected, either by accident of design, there is no evidence that a consistent effort to guide the opening of new streets and extensions along comprehensive lines was ever instituted." This was of course true, although there had been ad hoc efforts. We have seen that Mayor Wertz devoted his two terms attempting to alleviate the traffic problems, yet when he wanted bond issues passed to pay for widening, straightening, and paving streets, his efforts were rejected either by Council or the voters. On occasion, Wertz was successful in spite of voter opposition. In March 1929, Council passed a resolution introduced by the Mayor directing the city engineer to write specifications for widening Washington Street between Capitol Street and the Elk River. The Mayor asked property owners to set back their properties, but if they refused Wertz vowed to take up the sidewalks. In advocating this action, Wertz pointed to increased traffic and to Washington Street as a link in the Midland Trail. He stated: "Some persons may call this drastic and highhanded, but I consider it necessary." This action would not cost the city a cent, explained Wertz, adding that the city is permitted to seize sidewalks and that property owners must pay for new paving.[21]

Because the Council had never laid out a street plan, many property owners over the years had established family homesteads in areas that blocked the continuous development of streets. This was the case between downtown and the Elk River. The Brown family homestead located between Virginia and State (Lee) streets north of Summers Street blocked Brown Street from continuing east to downtown and Laidley Street from continuing south. When Mayor Wertz proposed in 1923 to purchase the Brown property for $350,000, the Brown family opposed and was supported by Council.[22] As the authors of the comprehensive plan wrote in general of this problem: "... it seems apparent that the owners of large holdings consider their subdivisions as isolated communities rather than a part of a larger, orderly-developed whole." The Brown estate remained entrenched for another thirty years. In 1954 the family donated land to the city so that Brown (Quarrier) and Laidley streets could be continued. Later in the Fifties, the estate grounds came to an end when the federal government condemned the land for a federal Building, which is still in use at Virginia and Laidley streets.

Prior to the comprehensive plan, many observers began to see the city's streetcar system as part of the traffic problem. The tracks were thought to hinder automobile movement, and in the Thirties there was a call to replace the streetcars with buses. In December 1936, the West Side Businessmen's Association wrote to Council urging that it not renew the Charleston Transit Company's franchise unless the company reverted to buses.[23] Aside from the traffic problems, the transit company had internal financial reasons for wanting to convert to buses, and previous to the business association's support of buses, the company had applied to Council in November 1936 to use buses on the city streets.[24] Gradually streetcar routes were closed in favor of forty new passenger buses. The streetcar made its final outer loop run from the downtown to the East End on October 19, 1937.[25] For Kanawha City, the Council authorized the new diesel buses beginning May 1, 1937. The authors of the comprehensive plan took note of the streetcar phaseout and supported the move. On June 29, 1939, the transit company converted its entire operation to buses.

In the thoroughfare section of the comprehensive plan, the authors attempted to systematize the problems and outline what needed to be done. Aside from poor street connections throughout the city, past errors to overcome included inadequate street width, the directing of state highway travel through the business center aggravating conditions, railroad grade crossings, and poor bridge placement. The Spring Street Bridge, for example, had no direct contributing streets. At the time of the plan, Washington Street was the only continuous east-west street that was linked to a state highway at each end of the city. It was therefore clear to the plan authors that this street should be widened to sixty feet, which would provide for two driving lanes in each direction. The plan advocated that Kanawha Street be widened to fifty feet, somewhat narrower than what it became with the riverfront project. Other recommendations in the plan included the widening of Virginia Street and its connection to Kanawha Street and the widening of Broad Street. In the area between downtown and the Elk River, the plan echoed Mayor Wertz by recommending the extension of Quarrier and Laidley streets. Lee Street had not yet reached the Elk, and its extension was favored. Ten years later in a 1948 biennial report, the Municipal Planning Commission reviewed the status of these recommendations. Washington Street never became sixty feet wide and Virginia Street was never connected with Kanawha Boulevard. Laidley and Quarrier streets had not been extended (due to the Brown property), but Lee had reached the Elk and part of Broad Street had been partially widened. [26]

Notwithstanding the presence of the planning commission, the Gazette was not satisfied with the progress of the city. In December 1958, the paper editorialized: "We've pretty much taken our city for granted in the past and allowed it to grow without any definite plan or pattern. The presence of slums, our recreational deficiencies, the day-by-day traffic congestion, even the lack of sidewalks in the suburbs and poor street lighting everywhere except in the mid-town area compound into a poor dossier on civic pride." [27]

Interstates

In spite of the improvements made after the advent of the planning commission, Charleston's traffic problems were not alleviated. The much touted Kanawha Boulevard project may have gotten motorists to the East End more rapidly, but vehicles continued to be backed up at railroad crossings, in the downtown, and at Patrick Street. In an attempt to lessen traffic congestion elsewhere in the city, the Council in September 1967 began to allow light trucks on Kanawha Boulevard. Still keeping a close watch on traffic, the Daily Mail in 1960 said essentially the same thing about the problem as it had twenty-five years earlier. In March 1960, the Mail wrote: "But no one who drives in Charleston needs statistical demonstration. The snarl at Patrick Street, the snail's pace at Washington, the constriction along Piedmont, the wail at every railroad crossing—all this is a matter of common experience." [28] It must have looked to many that Charleston was condemned to traffic strangulation, but when the federal interstate highways began to enter West Virginia, many hoped that these four and six lane behemoths would bail out the city for its decades old neglect of planning and street design. However, it was initially not certain that the interstates would go through Charleston. As the 1956 federal act was written, all the nation's interstates would be built around cities not through them. But large city mayors who were experiencing traffic bottlenecks lobbied for amendments to permit urban routes. The mayors saw that the new freeways would alleviate city traffic while the federal government absorbed ninety percent of the cost and their respective states the remaining ten percent. The amendments came through, but in Charleston the in-city route was still not certain. If the 1960 city Council had its way, the interstates would have been built around the city.

In June 1959, the West Virginia State Road Commission released its consulting engineering study that proposed building the interstates through Charleston. Criticism was leveled at this study because it failed to adequately consider a by-pass route. The Gazette was one of the study's critics, both of its omission and conclusion. In March 1960, the paper editorialized in favor of a separate study: "We are convinced such an analysis will indicate the superiority of such a route over the in-town routing."[29] Other critics of the in-city route said that the interstate would be like a "Chinese Wall" blocking many of the city's streets, thereby making traffic worse. The Gazette reported that aerial maps it had seen showed that in-city freeways would dead-end more than twenty-five streets. A few days later, the Gazette issued one its strongest statements against the in-city route: "Charleston has never enjoyed proper planning. Much of the little land we do possess is blighted. Property obsolescence is evident in almost every neighborhood. The lack of recreational areas is a disgrace... Can Charleston, squeezed as it is in a valley between hill ranges, afford the luxury of surrendering hundreds of acres of valuable level land to a road?"[30]

However, the city's engineering department and the Municipal Planning Commission supported the state's engineers in their advocacy of the in-city route. The city Council and Mayor, as of March 1960, had not gone on record with a position, but both sides were urging Council to adopt its respective viewpoint. Municipal Planning Commission Chairman, Robert Spilman, appeared before Council in March to argue for the in-city route, maintaining that the interstate would solve Charleston's traffic problems.

He stated that "Charleston now has the opportunity to cure headaches which had plagued it for years in one fell swoop. It would give the city six grade separations from the New York Central including Patrick, Broad, Brooks, and Dryden."[31] The Daily Mail also looked to the interstates to solve the city traffic congestion. The Mail editorialized: "For the first time in its history, there is a chance for Charleston to catch up with its traffic problem, erase and correct some of the mistakes which have plagued it for years and plan wisely for the future. To oppose it and perhaps discredit it [the in-city route] would be a tragic mistake...

Sending the interstates around the city will do nothing for Charleston."[32] But on March 28, 1960 the Council voted sixteen to five to oppose the in-city route and advocated a separate study on a by-pass route. In a front page editorial the next day, the Daily Mail appeared bitter: "This is the same old mossback Charleston of the 19th Century—the same Charleston which never had the foresight to plan a municipal park, never planned a street system, never believed the automobile was here to stay, never looked ahead, or asked itself what would become of it."[33]

After another four years of debate and lawsuits, the Daily Mail came out on the winning side. Final authority for the interstate routes rested with the U.S. Bureau of Public Roads, and in August 1964, the agency approved the in-city route for Charleston. Some twelve years later, the elevated highways through the city were opened. If the freeways were successful, it came at a human cost. Over 200 pieces of property were condemned for the right-of-way and over 1900 families were displaced by both the interstates and the urban renewal program that was taking place at the same time. The Daily Mail, however, continued to believe that interstates served Charleston well. In July 1992, the paper in its series "Things That Work" looked back and wrote: "... Despite heated debate and numerous court suits ... most people have forgotten the furor and admit that it works after all." William Ritchie, state highway commissioner, when the freeways were built supported the Mail's conclusion: "Seven new bridges came with the interstates. It used to take me an hour to drive from the Capitol to W.Va 21, but now of course it takes three or four minutes." Ritchie was able to speedily drive from the east to the West Side because the interstates had bailed out the city from the plight of its grade level railroad crossings that, as we have seen, had stalled traffic throughout the city from the early 1920's. With a degree of foresight, the highway engineers had elevated Charleston's freeways, thereby leapfrogging traffic over city streets and railroad crossings. The elevated freeways had moreover made moot the Gazette's worry that dead-end city streets would be created if the interstate went through the city. Former city manager, Hugh Bosely, agreed the interstates were good for the city: "I am just convinced that the city as we now know it would not be in existence had we not routed the interstate through the city." Bosely went on to trump the economic benefits that accrued to Charleston following the interstates, maintaining that the Town Center, the Marriott, and the Civic Center expansion were made possible by the interstates.[34] Clearly the interstates along with the Boulevard project of the 1930's and the urban renewal programs (discussed in next chapter) had changed the city's history. These three projects, the largest in the city's history, were all federal programs over which the municipal planning commission played no significant policy role. Instead the commission along with the city Council and administration acted as cheerleaders from the sidelines. But then the city government had never been an active, forward-looking representative of the people. With respect to these projects, the Council was no doubt satisfied with its menial role.

South of the Kanawha

On the south side of the Kanawha River, the newer developing areas of the city did not experience the same problems as older Charleston. South Hills directly across the river from downtown was annexed to Charleston by the 1907 Charter. This charter in terms of Charleston's physical expansion was significant in Charleston's history. As we have seen, it brought a large part of the West Side and part of Edgewood into the city. And south of the Kanawha this charter took the boundary to Ferry Branch on the western edge and Porters Branch on the east.[35] Ferry Branch emptied into the Kanawha roughly across from where the Elk discharged into the Kanawha while Porters Branch entered the Kanawha almost directly across from Ruffner Street. These boundaries would put the later developing Louden Heights in the city but not Fort Hill, which would lie west of Ferry Branch. South Hills was first platted by the South Charleston Improvement Company in 1891. The same year the first South Side Bridge was completed from downtown at Dickinson Street across the Kanawha, providing the sinew for future development. As was the case with Edgewood, this hilly area was not amenable to a grid design, and hence the plat and street layout were drawn in deference to the topography. The lots were irregular and of varied sizes. Unlike Edgewood where the first deeds for lot sales restricted buyers to a minimum house price and set back requirements, deed restrictions in South Hills were usually non-existent. An examination of lot deeds in 1906 and 1907 found only one restriction; a lot that sold for $4400 in December 1906 restricted the buyer only to the prohibition of a stable. In the Thirties, the South Hills Realty Company was developing the Abney Park subdivision and again the restrictions were light to non-existent. Only one restriction was found. On a lot sold in May 1936, the realty company required that the house to be built cost at least $5000.[36]

In terms of planning, Kanawha City was everything that Charleston east of the Elk was not. In 1890, two civil engineers, J.D. and William G. Moher, platted 3200 acres of bottomland in a grid of 6000 lots. Located on the south side of the Kanawha and a little east of Charleston, the 3200 acres stretched from approximately the present day 35th Street Bridge east to 57th Street and from the river bank to the C&O railroad tracks. Since the Mohers envisioned their plat becoming an incorporated city, one of the lots on Central Avenue (later MacCorkle Avenue) at 46th Street was set aside for a city hall. Befitting a city of this period, the Mohers also reserved a lot for an opera house and another for a hotel. The east-west Central Avenue was to be eighty feet wide. Main Street (later 50th Street), extending north and south and intersecting with Central, was laid out 100 feet wide. Other streets were designed with a forty feet width. Most residential lots were fifty by 120 feet and business lots were twenty-five by 120 feet. Except for a city park of one lot, the Mohers reserved nearly all the riverfront for manufacturing.[14]

Had this plat been incorporated, Kanawha City would have been an entirely planned city. However, early growth and development were slow. In the early part of the century, the equally flat East End of Charleston was still filling up; thus there was little pressure to move across the river. Moreover, until July 1915 there was no eastern bridge across the Kanawha to connect the plat with Charleston. But even after the completion of the bridge and the opening of the glass plants in 1916 and 1917 just outside the eastern end of Kanawha City, growth still did not take off. In 1914, the Mohers began to sell off their holdings to investors who formed the Kanawha Land Company. One of the principal stockholders was former Governor William MacCorkle. Initially the land company had no better luck than had the Mohers in selling building lots. By the late Twenties, it was clear that Kanawha City was not going to be incorporated, and in 1929 the Legislature annexed the old Moher plat to Charleston. This annexation also extended west to Porters Branch; thereby connecting the city with the 1907 annexation. Thus the 1929 expansion brought South Ruffner into the city. However, annexation to Charleston was not a spur to development, as Kanawha City's growth continued to be slow. A 1932 photograph shows Kanawha City still largely undeveloped.[38]

Succeeding developers of original plats tend to make changes. We saw this was the case on the West Side when Brisban Walker's plat passed into other hands. When the Kanawha Land Company assumed control of the Moher plat, Main Street never became 100 feet wide and MacCorkle Avenue never became eighty feet wide, a shortsighted decision in the case of MacCorkle, since in the Thirties it had to be widened. Manufacturing never developed on the riverfront and that area was set aside for upscale private homes. As the land company sold lots, it placed deed restrictions on the buyers, especially on lots between the river and MacCorkle Avenue. These related to a minimum cost of the house to be built and its distance from the street. In July 1924, a future home builder purchased for $15,000 a double lot on the riverbank. The deed required the buyer to build a house costing at least $10,000, which had to face Kanawha Avenue, not the river. Since this was a double lot the buyer was permitted to build a second house on the property. For property away from the river, the financial demands were less stringent. In June 1935, a Noyes Avenue lot sold for $1100. For this lot the minimum price of the future house was $3000 with a set back requirement of forty feet. The same month, the land company sold a Staunton Avenue lot (price not in deed). The buyer was required to spend at least $5000 for the house, and also set it back forty feet from the street.[39]

In contrast to Kanawha City, South Ruffner played the orphan. No developer plated the entire area or desired to incorporate it. But like Kanawha City, the area was slow to develop, especially between the river and the railroad tracks, which attracted little interest until Morris Harvey College appeared. The college, since its move to Charleston in 1935, had never intended its cramped quarters on the third floor of the old Capitol annex to be permanent. The administration was forced to hold assemblies in St Marks Methodist Church on Washington Street and to rent office space in the Hubbard Mansion. But while located in the downtown, two significant events occurred that affected the future of the college. It became independent of the Methodist Church, and it absorbed Kanawha Junior College. By 1940, the college's financial position was secure enough to enable the Trustees to make a $47,500 purchase of eleven acres of riverfront property across the Kanawha from the Capitol. However, it was not until September 1947 that the college made its celebrated boat transfer to its new campus. A naval vessel escorted by over twenty smaller boats carried college officials and records from the Capitol Street landing upriver to the State Capitol landing where Governor Clarence Meadows and other dignitaries boarded the vessel for the trip to the South Ruffner landing. Although its first buildings were temporary, the college had its best facilities ever with twenty-six classrooms, four laboratories, music studios, a library, and publications office. Morris Harvey's first permanent building was the gymnasium, completed in 1948. Riggleman Hall, the college's flagship building, followed in 1951. It was named in honor of the college's President, Leonard Riggleman, who headed the institution from 1931 to 1964. In 1957, the Board of Trustees voted to absorb Charleston's Mason College of Music and Fine Arts. By the 1970's, the Trustees wanted to give the college a closer identity with the Charleston community, and in December 1978, the Board changed the college's name to the University of Charleston.[40]

Unlike neighboring Kanawha City, South Ruffner's riverfront never became primarily residential. After Morris Harvey College was established, nearly all the riverfront to the west of the college was purchased for business use. In 1952 National Biscuit Company built a warehouse followed in 1954 by a Coca Cola Bottling Company. Where there had been a tennis club, the United Fuel Gas Company in 1957 completed a $7.0 million building, which later became Columbia Gas. In 1957 the Chesapeake and Potomac Telephone Company opened in a new $4.0 million plus building immediately to the west of the gas company. The riverfront to the east of the college and all the way to the bridge became residential property. However, the first major construction following the college was completed by the board of the Charleston Memorial Hospital. Not on the riverfront, but located behind riverfront private housing at the eastern end of South Ruffner, the $4.0 million hospital opened in August 1951 after a two year building period. This was followed in 1959 by a $436,000 new hospital wing.[41]

Further expansion

After the Kanawha City and South Ruffner annexation, Charleston's boundaries remained the same until February 1947 when a small West Side area known as Chandler's Branch was added to the city. This new addition began at Route 21 and Washington Street and extended northeast. This annexation was concluded by a provision of the state law known as a "minor boundary adjustment." Since Charleston would later expand several times using this procedure, it is necessary to briefly define it. West Virginia law allows a municipally to bypass an election and annex territory by applying to the county commission. A map and population statistics are required as part of the application. After the application is advertised in a local newspaper and posted in five public places, the commission schedules a hearing, and if the minor boundary adjustment is "not substantially opposed," the commission may order the boundary change. The commission's order is subject to review by the circuit court. The law does not specify any physical size that a minor boundary adjustment must meet. [42]

Aside from this minor boundary adjustment, Charleston's first annexation after the 1936 Home Rule Amendment, which gave annexation authority to the people of the affected areas, occurred in June 1948 when North Charleston became part of the city. The initiative could be taken either by the city or by the area wishing to be absorbed. In this case, a tragedy spurred the annexation drive. In February 1947, a North Charleston fire left two dead and nine families homeless. Inadequate fire protection was blamed for the extent of the loss. Moreover, the area lacked police protection. Consequently, North Charleston residents began a petition drive that would result in annexation. In support of the petition drive, the attorney for the residents pointed out to Charleston officials that North Charleston had a population of about 5000, a property valuation of about 2.6 million dollars, which would return about $30,000 to the city.

North Charleston included the old Kelly Axe Handle plant (now American Fork and Hoe) located just west of Patrick Street and bordering the Kanawha River. Older residents remembered that in 1908 when Kelly located to the Charleston area, the city had given a pledge that the plant would never be incorporated. However, the attorney for the North Charleston residents favoring annexation pointed out that the city had been released from its pledge in 1921when the President of the plant, W.C. Kelly, gave the Council a letter stating that the company would not oppose annexation after 1921. Meanwhile the city's Municipal Planning Commission, which had been studying city expansion, concluded that annexation would benefit the city by allowing for more industrial sites and commercial development. [43]

The Council scheduled an election for June 28. High interest was shown in North Charleston, as two-thirds of registered voters cast ballots, approving annexation by a margin of 583 to 472. According to the Daily Mail, Charleston voters were largely apathetic. Only about 2400 turned out, but they approved annexation by a three to two margin. Concurrent with the annexation vote, Charleston voters were also asked to approve a city charter change creating Ward Eighteen that would encompass North Charleston, if it entered the city. This also passed. Geographically, it would make more sense to call the new area of the city "West Charleston," for it was in reality an extension of the West Side, but the term "North Charleston" has always prevailed. Beginning at Patrick Street, the newly annexed territory encompassed all the area south of Washington Street to the Kanawha and extending along the river to about 37th Street. The new boundaries also included area to the north of Washington Street and to the north of Seventh Avenue.[44]

Following the North Charleston annexation, the city concluded three more minor boundary adjustments prior to the major annexation of 1958. First was the Dudley Road area of Louden Heights in 1951. The next year Summit Drive area of Edgewood Hills was annexed, and in 1958, the circuit court approved Highland Hills for annexation.

Charleston's largest annexation to date occurred in December 1958 when the city expanded to include the entire Charleston Magisterial District, north and south of the Kanawha. The effort for this expansion began during the first term of Republican Mayor John Copenhaver, who was first elected in 1951. Copenhaver, an avid and energetic civic booster, was often called "Jumping John." He was re-elected in 1955 and again in 1959, but served only a few months of his third term before he died in August 1959. Eager to expand the city, Copenhaver appointed an Annexation Committee with a Morris Harvey College Professor of Geography as a consultant to study the land supply of the area and make a cost-benefit analysis of contiguous unincorporated land. By the Mayor's second term, the committee recommended that 12.5 square miles with a population of about 11,000 be annexed. Later this area was increased to nineteen square miles. The committee met with neighborhood groups and representatives of industry in the affected areas to present the advantages of annexation. The meetings were largely successful. Especially significant was the agreement of the officials of the two large glass plants just east of Kanawha City to become part of Charleston. (These plants had not been part of the 1929 Kanawha City annexation).[45]

However, there was opposition from Vandelia and Brownemont, two communities just to the south side of the Patrick Street Bridge. Five plants in these areas announced that they preferred to be annexed by South Charleston, a preference that was not surprisingly supported by the South Charleston Mayor. Charleston officials were somewhat puzzled by the companies' position, for Charleston's manufacturing tax was just sixteen cents per one-hundred dollars valuation, while the same tax in South Charleston was nineteen cents. Yet this opposition was not significant, and the petition for an election was secured, which took place December 13. Both the Gazette and Daily Mail supported annexation. Just before the election, the Gazette editorialized: "... the compelling reason which overrides all others is simply this: no community can prosper and progress without growth ... and the only avenue open to Charleston for growth is through expansion of its corporate boundaries." [46]

When the ballots were counted, observers were surprised at the closeness of the vote north of the Kanawha. Here annexation was favored by a margin of just 704 to 639. On the south side where opposition openly developed, annexation passed 1520 to 1269. North side opponents demanded a recount, which was completed the following week. Annexation still carried, but the margin now was just forty votes. Charleston voters had little hesitation about expanding,as annexation proponents crushed the opposition 10,178 to 587. The day following the election, both Charleston newspapers carried front page headlines touting the fact that Charleston had surpassed Huntington in population and was now the state's largest city. In round numbers, the Gazette and Daily Mail reported that Charleston had grown by about 20,000 giving it a population of about 95,000. (When the 1960 census appeared some two years later, Charleston had a population of 85,796 compared to 83,627 for Huntington). [47]

But in terms of numbers, the physical expansion was more impressive. The nineteen square miles of additional territory tripled the size of Charleston. The city had now expanded well outside the narrow valley to encompass the mountain ranges on both the north and south side. On the West Side, North Charleston became about three times bigger, expanding not only to the north but west along Seventh Avenue to the edge of Dunbar. This expanded area would still be Ward Eighteen. At the other end of the West Side beginning at the Elk River, Ward Six, which ran along the city's upstream section of the Elk, was expanded north but mostly to the west so that it reached up and over the West Side to connect with Ward Eighteen. These two wards now formed a large arch over the entire West Side. The other West Side wards—one through five—were unchanged. East of the Elk, wards seven, thirteen, and fourteen were extended north over the mountain range so that these three wards collectively formed the city's northern boundary from the Elk to the Kanawha City Bridge. South of the Kanawha, Kanawha City's Ward Seventeen, South Ruffner's Ward Sixteen, and South Hills's Ward Fifteen were all expanded south farther into the mountain range. West of South Hills from a point across from the Elk to the Patrick Street Bridge was all new city territory. For this area, a new city ward, the Nineteenth, was created.

This ward system would remain fixed for just eight years, for in 1962 the United States Supreme Court mandated that legislative districts had to conform to the principle of "one-person, one vote," meaning that a legislator within a legislative body must represent approximately an equal number of citizens. Charleston's wards following the 1958 election showed ward populations ranging from about 1500 to 8000. In 1966 the city re-drew the ward boundaries in a way to set each ward's population at approximately 5000. In the process, the number of wards was reduced from nineteen to eighteen. The West Side would still have seven wards; the East Side from the Elk River to the far East End would have just five wards, down from eight; the city's fastest growing area south of the Kanawha would be given two additional wards, so that it would have six wards. Since the ward change meant a charter amendment, the proposal had to go before the voters. At the November 1966 election, the ward amendments easily passed 12,215 to 6160 with the most favorable margin coming from the South Side, the area now gaining more relative power in the Council. The amendments also increased the number of at-large council members from five to six in order to keep the Council size at twenty-four.

Population continued to grow on the South Side, resulting in additional annexations. After the 1958 expansion, there were fourteen minor boundary adjustments from 1960 to 1983. Most of these were on the South Side with access to Corridor G. All these adjustments were small; the total land area of the fourteen was less than one square mile. But however small, these annexations meant ward adjustments. In the April 1975 election, an additional council member was chosen from the new Nineteenth Ward. By the April 1983 election, residents of a new Twentieth Ward, stretching along Corridor G to the Southridge retail area, for the first time chose a council member.

Map Notes

The following eight maps illustrate significant patterns of development in Charleston's history. The first two maps, Charleston's downtown in 1884 and 1912, show that the street pattern had changed little even though building had been significant in the intervening twenty-eight years. A point to note, in terms of later motor vehicle traffic, are the many disjointed and discontinued streets. Quarrier Street was not continued west of Capitol Street and would not do so until 1958. Also note that Washington Street was blocked by the Governor's residence. "The West End Extension" map is Brisben Walker's plat with a city park in the center. When Walker lost his properties in 1873, other developers stepped in. The principal development that changed Walker's plat was the Glenwood Addition in 1891. This addition created the well-known Five Corners intersection where Delaware, Central, and Virginia streets meet; however on this plat Delaware Street was then known as Sycamore Street. Note the reservation along the river. This area later became the private amusement park, Luna Park. The 1892 plat of the First Ruffner Addition in the East End is shown next. Note that Lee Street was not continued west and that alleys between the streets were originally planned. Next is shown Charleston's first zoning map of 1939 that followed the city's first comprehensive plan.

Kanawha City was originally planned to be an incorporated city by its designers, the Mohers. Their grid pattern envisioned a 100 feet wide Main Street and an eighty feet wide Central Avenue (now 50th Street and Central Avenue). Unlike Charleston's founders, the Mohers designated a lot for a city hall (shown as lot 114 along Central Avenue). The riverfront was reserved for manufacturing with the exception of one lot for a city park. The page crease mars the park, but it is next to lot 87. The last map taken from the city's 1962 comprehensive plan shows Charleston's voting wards and more significantly its greatly expanded boundaries as a result of the 1958 annexation, the largest in the city's history.

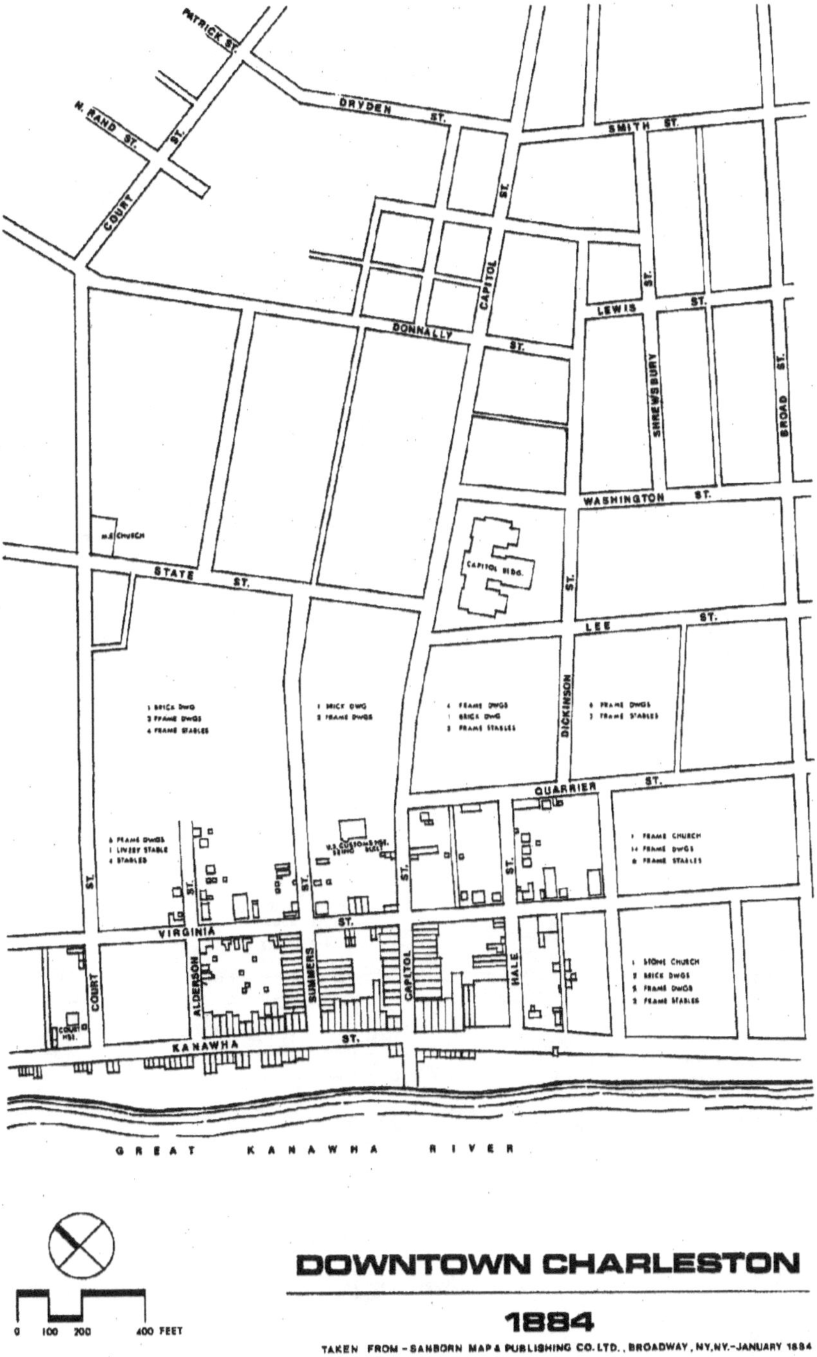

PATRICK ST.
N. RAND ST.
COURT ST.
DRYDEN ST.
SMITH ST.
CAPITOL ST.
LEWIS ST.
SHREWSBURY ST.
BROAD ST.
DONNALLY ST.
WASHINGTON ST.
M.E. CHURCH
STATE ST.
CAPITOL BLDG.
LEE ST.
DICKINSON ST.
QUARRIER ST.
ST.
VIRGINIA ST.
ALDERSON ST.
SUMMERS ST.
HALE ST.
KANAWHA ST.
GREAT KANAWHA RIVER

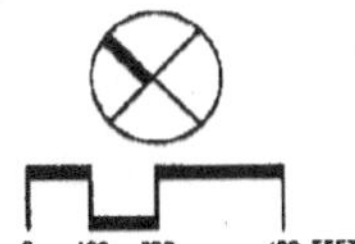

DOWNTOWN CHARLESTON

1884

TAKEN FROM - SANBORN MAP & PUBLISHING CO. LTD., BROADWAY, NY, NY.-JANUARY 1884

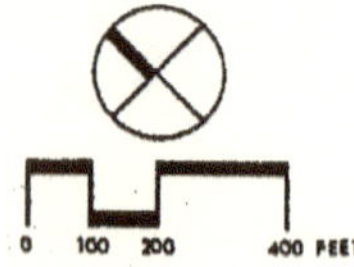

These maps are based on Sandborn maps, but show other information gathered from research and city directories. COURTESY PAUL MARSHALL & ASSOCIATES

DOWNTOWN CHARLESTON

1912

TAKEN FROM - SANBORN MAP & PUBLISHING CO. LTD., BROADWAY, NY.NY. - JANUARY 1912

THE WEST END EXTENSION

PERFECTLY LEVEL, WELL DRAINED, BROAD SIXTY-FEET STREETS.

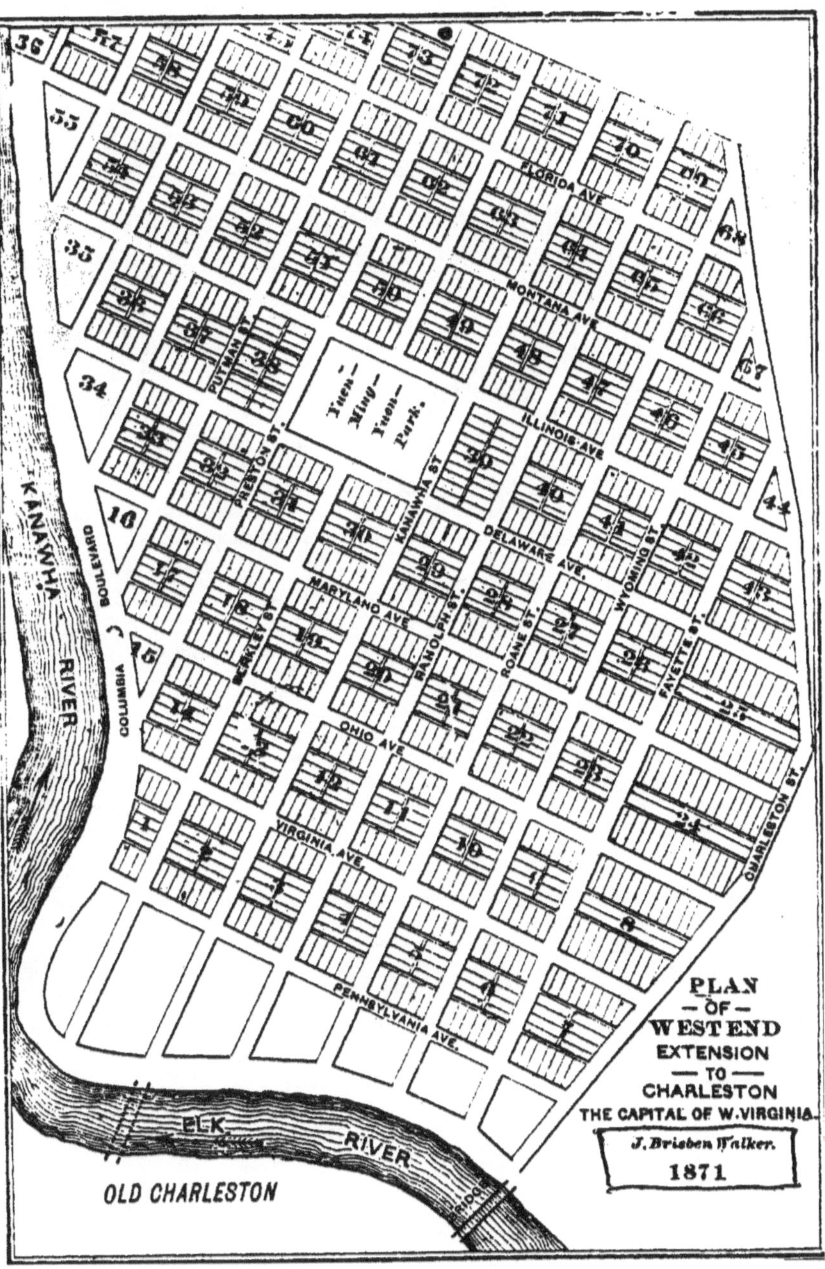

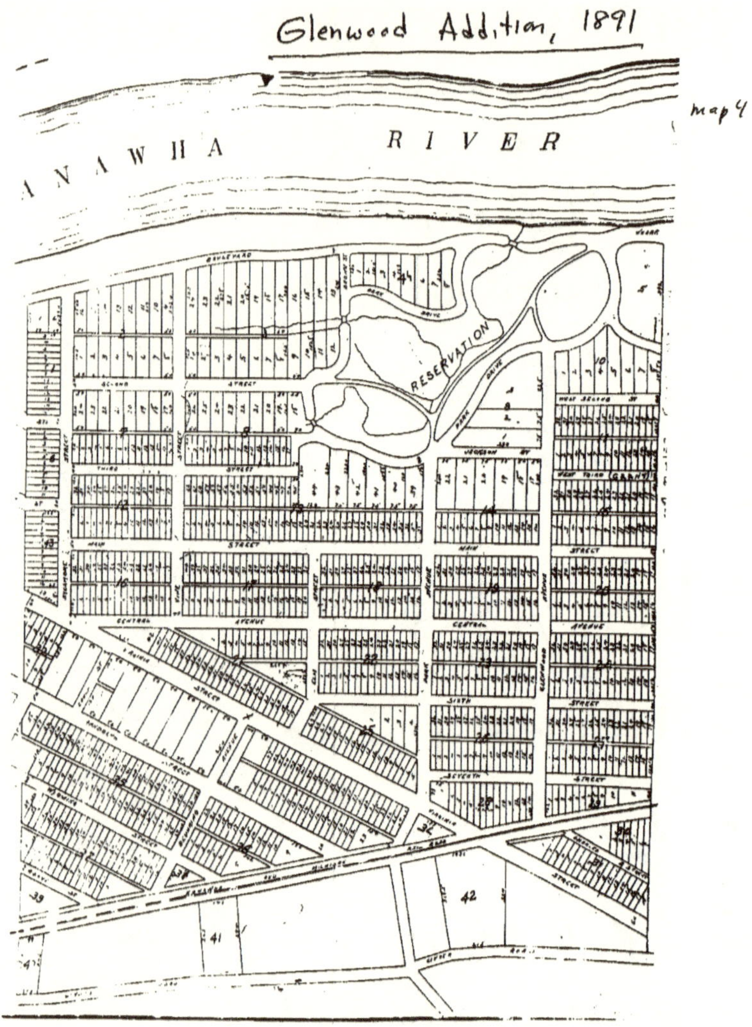
Glenwood Addition, 1891
map 4
A N A W H A
R I V E R
RESERVATION
STREET
MAIN
CENTRAL
AVENUE

LEWIS ST
JACKSON ST
WASHINGTON ST
LEE ST
QUARRIER ST
VIRGINIA ST
KANAWHA ST
BEAUREGARD ST
RUFFNER ST
FIRST RUFFNER ADD
STREETS 50 WIDE
ALLEYS 15 WIDE
MRS. COMSTOCK
A. RUFFNER
SCOTT & WALKER

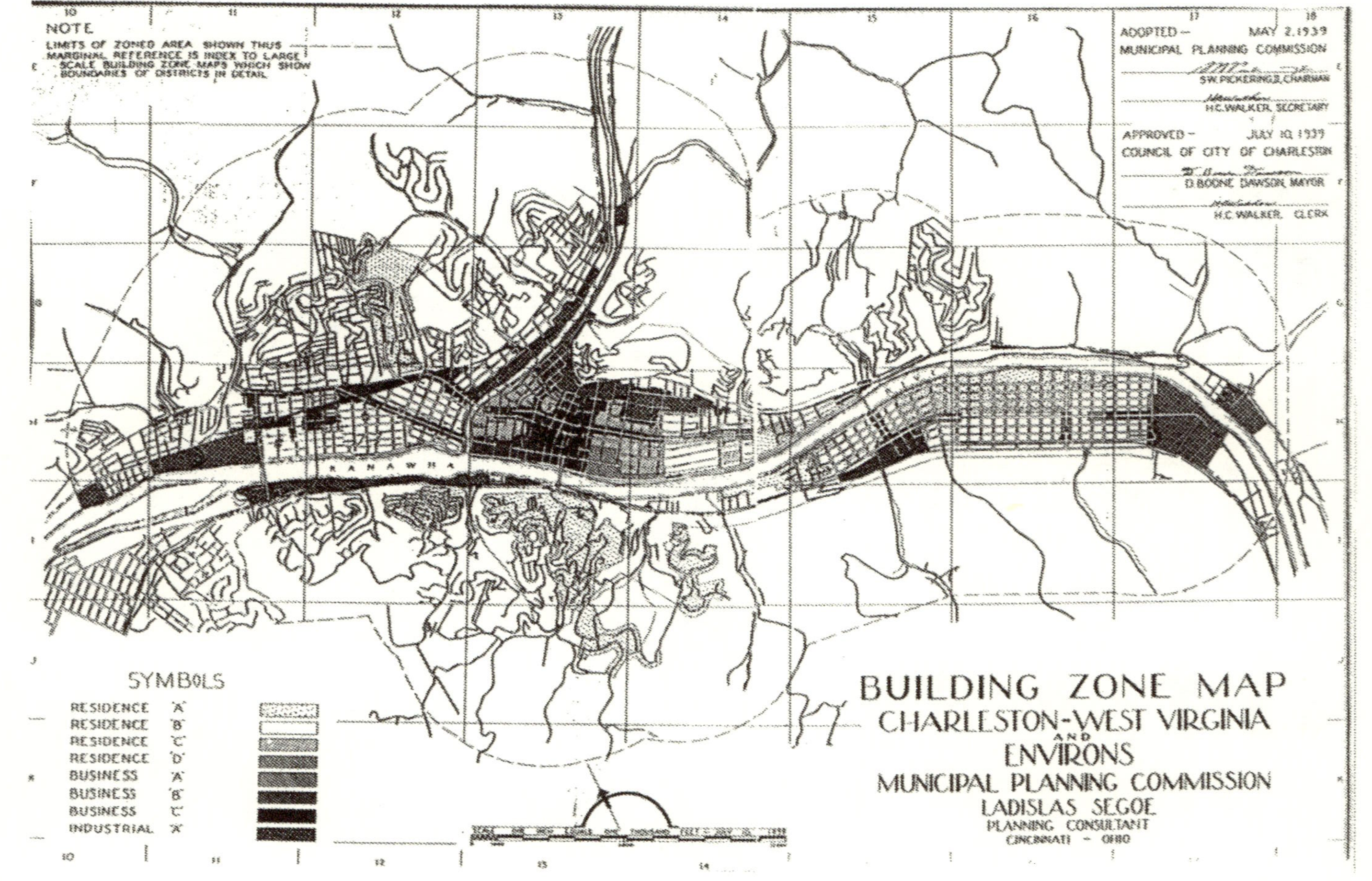
NOTE
LIMITS OF ZONED AREA SHOWN THUS
MARGINAL REFERENCE IS INDEX TO LARGE SCALE BUILDING ZONE MAPS WHICH SHOW BOUNDARIES OF DISTRICTS IN DETAIL
ADOPTED — MAY 2, 1939
MUNICIPAL PLANNING COMMISSION
S.W. PICKERING JR., CHAIRMAN
H.C. WALKER, SECRETARY
APPROVED — JULY 10, 1939
COUNCIL OF CITY OF CHARLESTON
D. BOONE DAWSON, MAYOR
H.C. WALKER, CLERK
KANAWHA
SYMBOLS
RESIDENCE 'A'
RESIDENCE 'B'
RESIDENCE 'C'
RESIDENCE 'D'
BUSINESS 'A'
BUSINESS 'B'
BUSINESS 'C'
INDUSTRIAL 'A'
BUILDING ZONE MAP
CHARLESTON-WEST VIRGINIA
AND
ENVIRONS
MUNICIPAL PLANNING COMMISSION
LADISLAS SEGOE
PLANNING CONSULTANT
CINCINNATI - OHIO

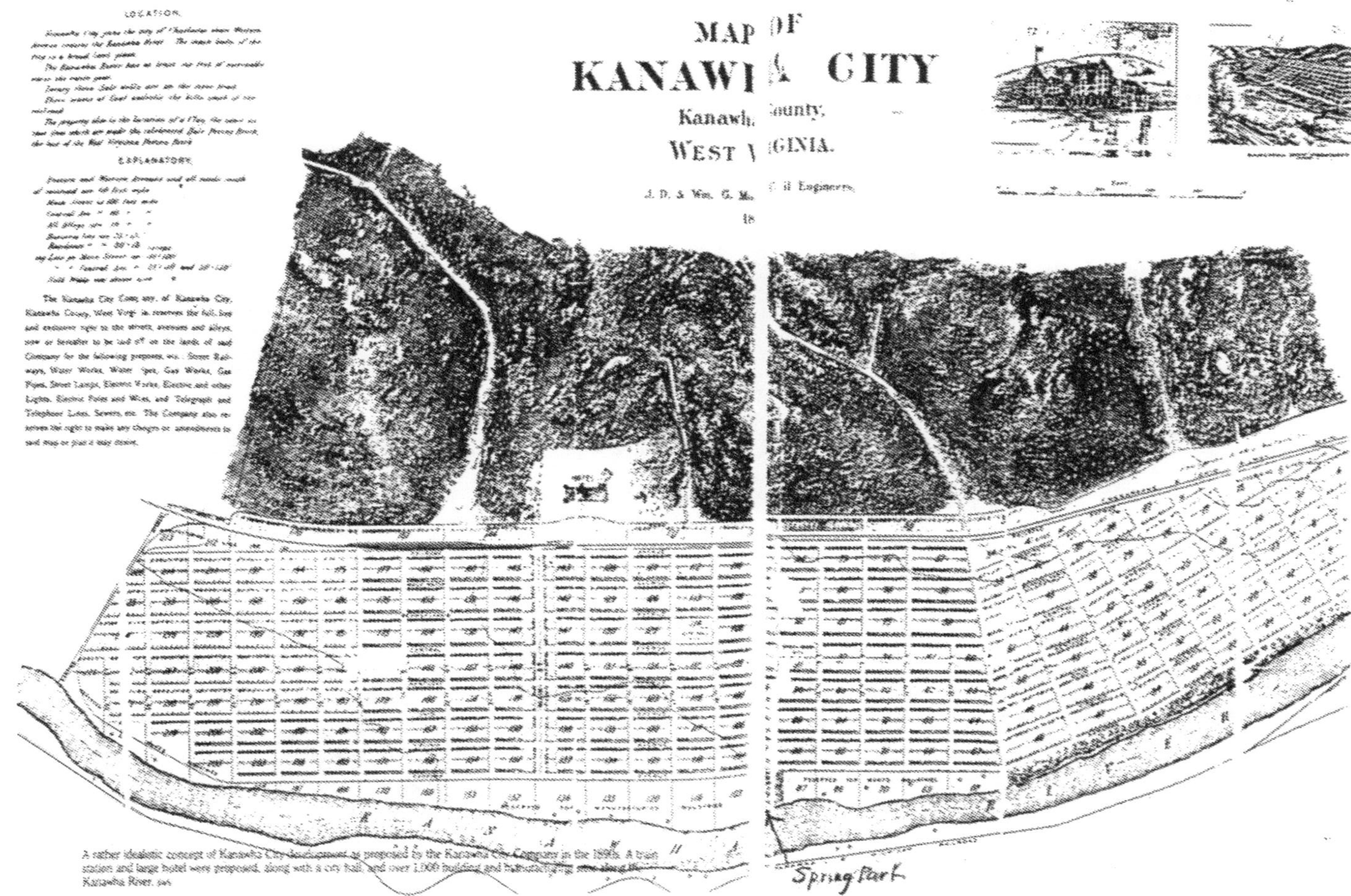

A rather idealistic concept of Kanawha City development as proposed by the Kanawha City Company in the 1890s. A train station and large hotel were proposed, along with a city hall, and over 1,000 building and manufacturing sites along the Kanawha River. (46)

POPULATION CHANGES

BY 1950 WARDS 1950 - 1960

SOURCE: U.S. CENSUS OF POPULATION

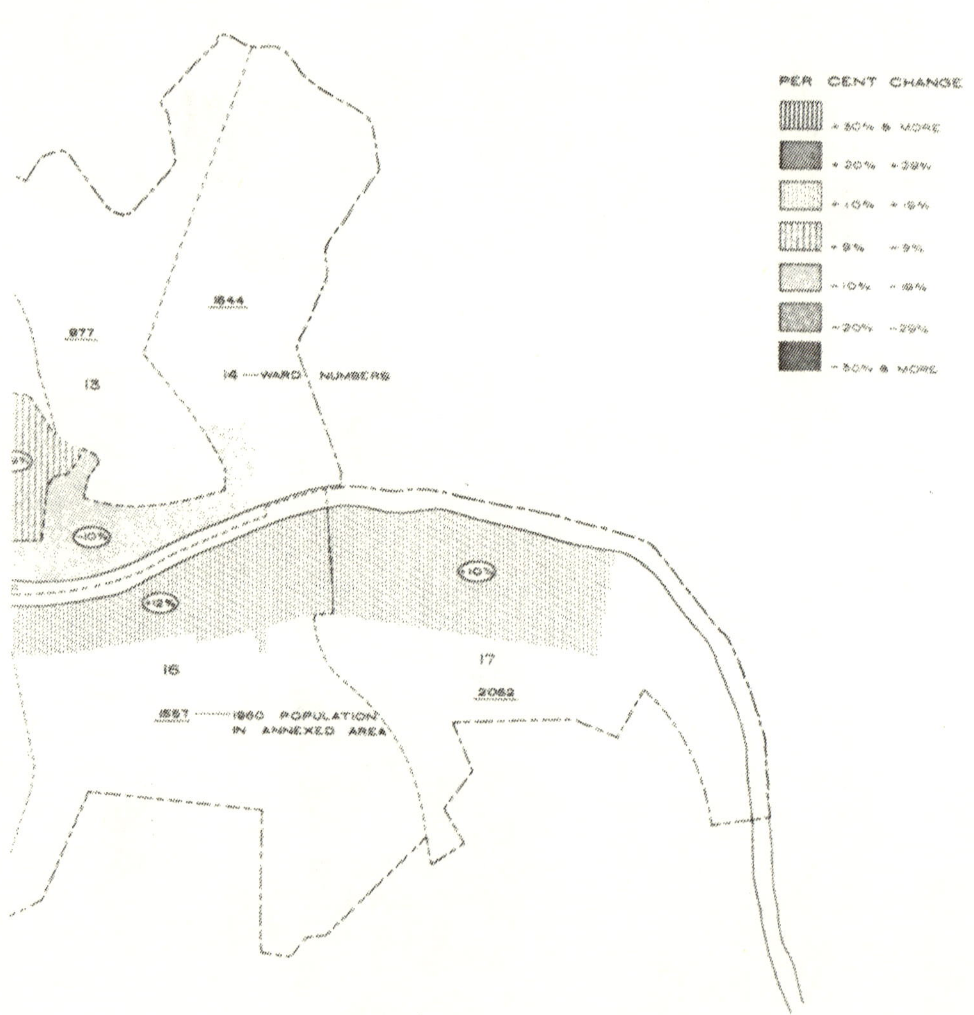

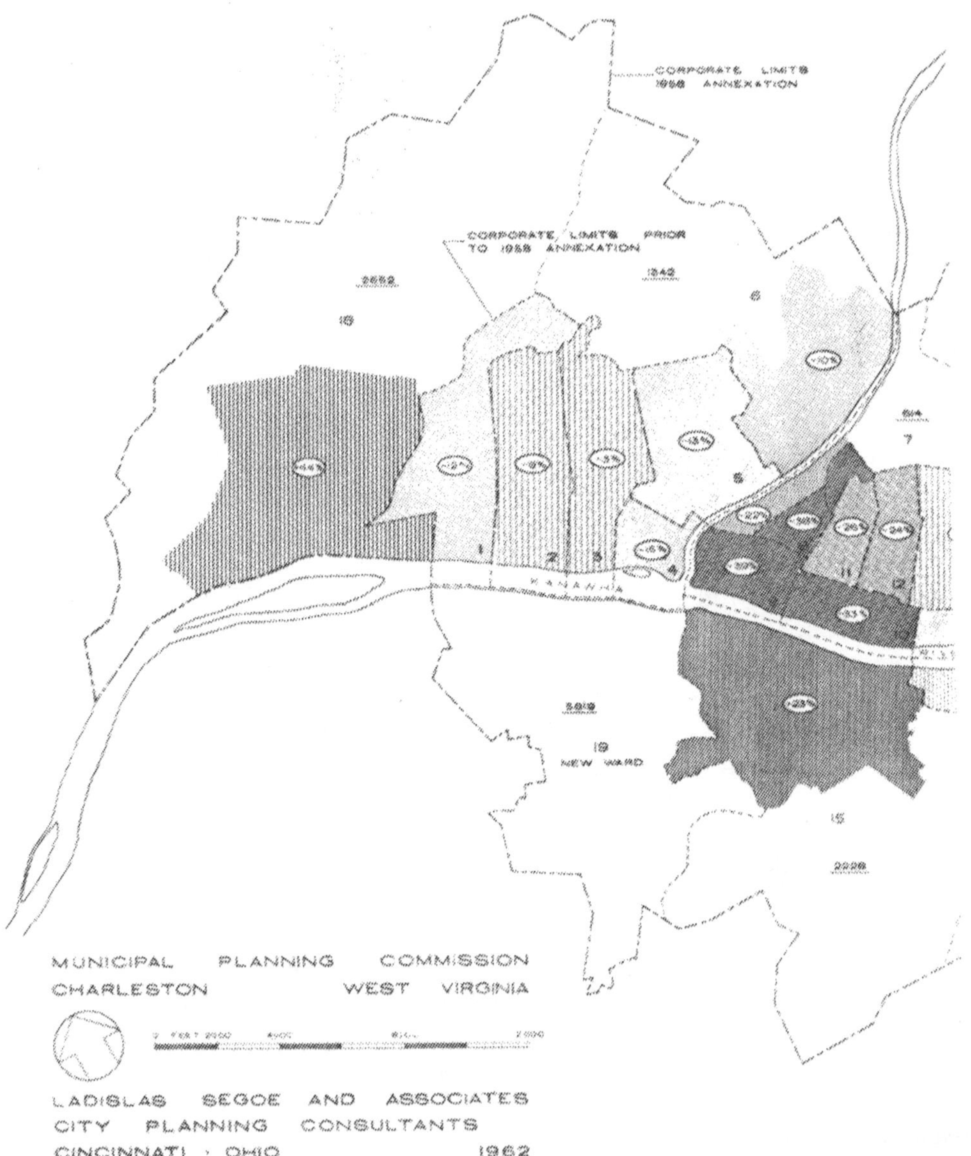
CORPORATE LIMITS
1958 ANNEXATION
CORPORATE LIMITS PRIOR
TO 1958 ANNEXATION
KANAWHA
19
NEW WARD
MUNICIPAL PLANNING COMMISSION
CHARLESTON WEST VIRGINIA
LADISLAS SEGOE AND ASSOCIATES
CITY PLANNING CONSULTANTS
CINCINNATI · OHIO 1962

Two Neighborhoods

In the first half of the Twentieth Century, many aspects of Charleston's social and economic life were racially segregated. Not able to live in certain neighborhoods, eat in certain restaurants, and work at certain jobs left Charleston's black citizens with the unmistakable impression that they were second class. Custom as opposed to local or state law governed nearly all the city's segregation. The most widespread case of legal segregation was the West Virginia Constitution mandate that local school boards maintain separate schools for white and colored students. [1] This constitutional edict was controlling until the 1954 United States Supreme Court decision that voided state segregated school laws. Of Charleston's black schools, the second Garnet High School became the best known. While the city school board (until 1933, it was a city school system, not county-wide) had been criticized for allowing sub-standard conditions to exist at the first Garnet High, which opened in 1909 on Jacob Street, the second Garnet High, opening in 1929 on Shrewsbury Street, was a modern facility with a comprehensive curriculum. [2] Designed by noted Charleston architect, H. Rus Warne, whose work on the courthouse and city hall had been highly praised, the new Garnet housed laboratories for physics, chemistry, and biology and included an auditorium, gymnasium, library, and cafeteria. In the 1940's a south side addition was added, which was designed by West Virginia's first licensed Black architect, John C. Norman, whose office was just two blocks from Garnet High. Students from Boyd, Cabell, and Woodson junior highs went on to Garnet.

But while the school board may be given credit for providing a quality black high school, its policy toward student transportation took on a more unequal cast. The Board had just one bus fleet to serve both white and black students. In the morning the buses would first pick up the black students, getting them to school about two hours early so that the drivers could pick up the white students in order to get them to school as classes were beginning. At the end of the school day, the bus drivers picked up the white students just as classes were over and delivered them to their homes. Then the drivers went to the black schools and picked up the waiting students. [3]

Other than discriminatory public school policy, Charleston blacks experienced other racial insults. The city's prominent hotels—the Ruffner, Kanawha, Fleetwood, Holly, and the Daniel Boone—all refused rooms to blacks. A particularly irritating practice to blacks was the policy of both the Gazette and the Daily Mail to single out blacks by ethnic designation when reporting a crime while ignoring their ethnicity when reporting black achievements. [4] Throughout the1920's and 1930's, blacks read such headlines as "Negro arrested in Brook Tipple Fire," "Negro Held on Charge of Forgery," and "Negroes Held for

Forging Checks on U.S." The alleged crime did not have to occur in Charleston. The newspapers went out of city and even out of state to feature black "crimes." A December 1930 Gazette headline read: "Negro Held in Slaying of Huntington Man." Another read: "Detroit Priest Slain by Negro, Police Believe."[5] It will be noted that none of the above examples involved convictions of a crime. An accusation would do. Blacks of course took note that when crimes involved other ethnic peoples, the Gazette and Daily Mail did not report the ethnicity of the accused.

Housing was not legally segregated by city ordinance, but deed restrictions were just as effective as legislation in maintaining racial purity of a neighborhood. As new housing developments were established, the land and realty companies that marketed the lots commonly would not sell to blacks. Moreover, when the lots were sold, deed restrictions prohibited the buyers from re-selling the property to blacks. Such restrictions were common in the developments south of the Kanawha River in Charleston's suburbs that began during the Twenties. For example, the Louden Heights Company in an August 1926 deed prohibited the buyer from selling to "any person of negro blood of descent." The company used this same phrase in all its deeds and added that the restriction would last for fifty years. Each land company had its own particular phraseology. The deeds of the Fort Hill Realty Company, also marketing land on the south side, prohibited buyers from selling to a member of the "negro race" for twenty years. Charleston's first suburb, Edgewood, was also characterized by deed restrictions designed to keep the area all white. The deeds of the Edgewood Land Company used broader language than their south side counterparts. In the 1940's the deeds prohibited Edgewood lots from being sold to "any person of African or Mongolian blood ... or to any firm or corporation composed of persons of such blood."[6]

In addition to deed restrictions, the policies of mortgage institutions kept blacks from obtaining loans for housing in many parts of the city. The state agency, Bureau of Negro Welfare and Statistics (BNWS), in a 1947 survey of Charleston blacks concluded: "Even though there is no residential segregation in Charleston, it is difficult for Negroes to obtain loans to purchase property outside of areas acceptable to banks and mortgage institutions."[7] In its 1951 publication, the BNWS listed as practicing in Charleston six black lawyers, six dentists, and four physicians. In that year all lived in areas that had a historically black population. Some lived in the East End along Washington and Lewis streets, some lived in or near the Triangle area, and some on the West Side on Second and Fourth avenues. Three lived outside of Charleston in the Institute area.[8]

White owned restaurants were notorious as places of discrimination. It was not until the mid-Fifties that blacks began to be served with any regularity. At a CORE (Congress for Racial Equality, a black civil rights organization) meeting in December 1958 at the Simpson Methodist Church, the co- chairman reported that many restaurants had began to serve blacks, but The Diamond, Charleston's premier downtown department store, still refused service to blacks at its first floor lunch counter and upper floor restaurant.[9] This led in March 1960 to lunch counter sit-ins by West Virginia State College Students. Blacks could shop for clothes and other items at The Diamond, but because of its restaurant policy, blacks had been boycotting the store for about two years. However, by May 1960 the city's Commission on Human Relations, established the previous year by Mayor Copenhaver, persuaded The Diamond management to serve food to blacks.[10]

The popular West Side, privately owned, amusement park, known as Luna Park (discussed later in another context) prohibited blacks from entering the grounds to enjoy the midway rides, picnic areas, and other features. In existence from 1913 to 1923, the advertisements noted that the park was for "the Caucasian race only."[11]

Discrimination extended even to public facilities that black citizens through their taxes helped support. From its opening in 1939, blacks were turned away from the Municipal Auditorium. After an incident in the Fall of 1940, the Charleston Business and Professional Men's Club (a black organization) ran a paid editorial in the West Virginia Beacon Digest urging the city not to rent or lease the building to any organization that discriminated against any person on the basis of race or color. The Council refused to take a stand, maintaining that race was not a factor in determining who would be able to rent the building, but for the period of the lease, the leasee had the right to determine whom it would admit.[12] The Municipal Auditorium was the concert hall of the Charleston Symphony, which in its earlier years prohibited blacks from its performances. It was not until 1946 that the symphony board adopted a non-discrimination policy.[13]

When the public library was raising money in preparation for its 1926 move to the Capitol Annex, many blacks contributed to the library. Not willing to show its appreciation by allowing blacks to use the library, the city school board, which at this time was the governing board of the library, instead established a branch black library on Shewsbury Street. Many blacks were not bought off by the tokenism, and in 1928 the Charleston NAACP sued for the right of blacks to use the main library on Lee Street. In defending against the NAACP suit, the board's lawyers argued that "the usefulness of the library will be severely impaired" if both races use the same building. Moreover, the board argued that since the library was governed by the school board, it was part of the state mandated segregated school system. The lower court supported the school board, but on appeal, the West Virginia Supreme Court of Appeals held that the public library was not part of the segregated school system. However, the victory was only partial, for the court ruled that the school board may establish separate sections for white and black library patrons. The black branch continued, later moving from a house on Shrewsbury Street to a room at Garnet High. [14]

Although blacks were admitted to the city's hospitals, they were given a separate section away from the white patients and for the most part were cared for by black physicians. Black nurses could not gain employment in Charleston hospitals until the Fifties. The nursing color barrier was broken by St Francis Hospital in the Spring of 1950 when the administration hired the first black woman to work as a nurse in any of the city's larger hospitals. Later in the year, the hospital hired two additional black nurses. After the first black nurse was hired, twenty white nurses demanded that she be dismissed and threatened to quit if the hospital administration refused. The protesting nurses said they were acting to protect their professional standing in the community. The walkout occurred, but the administration of St Francis remained resolute and kept the black nurses. The gap in patient care was met when the administration brought in staff and student nurses from Catholic hospitals in Parkersburg, Clarksburg, Wheeling, and Pittsburgh. Racial lines, however, continued to be drawn at other Charleston hospitals. [15]

Even in death segregation prevailed in Charleston. According to the 1921 city code of ordinances, a separate section in the city owned Spring Hill Cemetery was set aside for the colored. [16]

A poor photograph of the "Block" at Washington and Shrewsbury streets; the center of life in the area from 1920 to 1960.

Another center of life in the Washington- Shrewsbury area was the Ferguson Hotel. It housed a nightclub, theatre, and several businesses on ground floor. This photo is from the 1930's.

A recent view of liveless Shrewsbury Street looking north from Washington Street. To the front right was the sight of the "Block" from which several businesses faced Shrewsbury Street. Large Building in background on left side of street is the former Garnet High School.

A 1930's identical view of the accompanying contemporary view of Shrewsbury Street. The lively street was a well integrated area of residences, retail, and restaurants from the 1920's to the 1960's.

Parking lot of Motel 8 is former sight of A.H. Brown's building, the "Block."

Broad Street from Washington Street looking toward the interstate ramp. In 1970 before the interstate ramp, there were thirty businesses in this two block area. By 1975 after the interstates took the area, the number of business had dropped to eight.

Community life

Faced with discriminatory practices in both the public and private sectors, Charleston blacks developed a community life of their own. Beginning about 1920, the hub of black economic, social, and cultural life was concentrated in two areas: the Washington and Shrewsbury streets area located just northeast of the downtown and the Triangle area abutting the northern edge of downtown and continuing to the Elk River. For about a half century ending around 1970, Charleston's black community spawned many business entrepreneurs. Though not confined to the Washington—Shrewsbury and Triangle areas, these locations held the heaviest concentration of black owned businesses. These businesses ran the gamut from restaurants, grocery stores, pharmacies, real estate, law, dry cleaning, barber shops, billiard halls, medicine, dentistry, printing shops, and nightclubs. [17]

As a tandem, perhaps the best known of the many black entrepreneurs were Anderson H. Brown and Gurnett E. "Cap" Ferguson, both of whom in the 1920's constructed buildings on the north side of Washington Street between Broad and Shrewsbury streets. A Charleston native, Ferguson returned to the city after serving as naval officer commanding troop ships during the First World War. After the war, a prosperous Charleston got many black visitors, many from the entertainment field, but they had few places to lodge. Ferguson then built a brick, three-story, seventy-two room hotel midway in the Washington Street block. Opening in March 1922, the hotel at street level was designed for a café, barber shop, theatre, and smoke shop. In a short time, a thriving nightclub, known as the Alhambra Club, became part of Ferguson's building. [18]

Ferguson's colleague in black development, Anderson H. Brown, was born in 1880 in Dunbar, grew up in Charleston, and in his early twenties began to travel widely with a band as a trombone player. Settling in Boston in 1907, Brown began to study real estate while playing in an orchestra. In 1914 he returned to Charleston and for the rest of his long life, he enjoyed a successful real estate career. Shortly after Ferguson completed his hotel, Brown added to the vitality of the Washington—Shrewsbury area by constructing the two-story, brick Brown Building next to the hotel. It extended west to Shrewsbury Street, rounded the corner, and was large enough to house several businesses on the Shrewsbury side. This bustling corner at Washington and Shrewsbury became known as the "Block." With the Brown and Ferguson establishments as the focal point, community life sparkled in this area. The Brown Building housed many long-lasting black businesses. [19]

Many of these were not only profit making establishments; they were also gathering places. At the corner with a Washington Street address was the M & S Pharmacy. Known for its hot dogs and camaraderie, the pharmacy lasted for about forty years until the mid-Sixties. Around the corner facing Shrewsbury, the

West Virginia Restaurant under different owners served meals and offered a place to hangout for about thirty years. A.H. Brown took a second floor office in his building and managed his real estate business for over forty years. From the Thirties to the Sixties, Brown's son, Willard Brown, practiced law from his Father's office. Other businesses in the "Block" included a barbershop, a beauty salon, a printing shop, an electrical business, and a tailor. In 1956, A.H. Brown's daughter returned to Charleston and opened an art gallery in the Brown Building. These long lasting black businesses did not survive because they served a captive black clientele. Like any successful business, quality service was essential. Writing of black owned businesses in southern West Virginia, the historian Joe W. Trotter stressed the modern service and courteous treatment offered by black businesspeople. This appeared to be the case in Charleston. The Bureau of Negro Welfare and Statistics, wrote that the Hotel Ferguson takes rank as one of "the foremost modern and elaborately furnished and equipped hotels catering exclusively to Negro patronage in the country."[20]

From Washington Street, Shrewsbury extended for three blocks to the railroad tracks at Smith Street. All of the three blocks on both sides of the street were lined with a harmonious mixture of homes and black owned businesses. In addition Garnet High School was located on the street, one block from Washington. Another block north of Garnet stood the Simpson Memorial M.E. Church. During the Thirties, businesses in the first block of Shrewsbury Street included a restaurant, an advertising agency, a printer, a barber shop, and the Charleston Colored Day Nursery. By the Fifties, the block was still humming with two restaurants, a taxi company, a barbershop, a sweet shop, and the Knights of Pythias Lodge. As in the Thirties, several individuals made their homes in the block. Another prominent black owned building, but lasting for just the decade of the Thirties was the Susan Anthony Building. Built in 1929 and owned by Mary Brown Clark, a teacher in the county schools, and her brother, Andrew Brown, a dentist, it was located across Washington Street from the "Block" and to the west side of the Baptist Church. The Ruth Lowe Drug Store and Hill's Sandwich Shop occupied the first floor and on the second floor at various times a physician, a dentist, and two lawyers maintained their offices.[21] In the late Thirties, this building was acquired by the federal government, which needed the space for Charleston's new post office. About twenty years later, the post office needed more land and in the late Fifties purchased the First Baptist Church property. The church rebuilt one block away on Shrewsbury Street across from Garnet High.

Funeral homes have enjoyed high prestige in black communities. The current Preston Funeral Home had its start on Shrewsbury Street. In the early 1940, the day nursery sustained minor fire damage and moved to a house next door. After repairing the house, the owner offered the building to Merrill Preston and Roy Lawson who had recently completed their mortuary training in Philadelphia and

Cleveland respectively. Opening in September 1940, the Preston-Merrill Funeral Home struggled in its early years, but by 1945 the partners were able to purchase a house about one block away at Dickinson and Donnelly streets. A short time later, the partnership dissolved and Merrill moved on. In 1948 the business was incorporated as the Preston Funeral Home. Over the decades the business prospered, and the house was expanded and the car fleet enlarged. In 1983 Preston died and the business continued under his widow, daughter, and son in law.[22]

Just two blocks north of the Preston Funeral Home the Harden and Harden Funeral Home had been in operation since 1946 from its Broad Street location. Silas Harden had begun the business in 1922 on Alterson Street near the downtown. In 1928 he married Elizabeth Mason, who in 1940 became the first licensed black female funeral director in West Virginia. The business then became known as Harden and Harden. After Silas died in 1946, Mrs. Harden purchased a stately, four-column house at 514 Broad Street and continued the business from the new location. She later married Virgil Gilmore, who was also a funeral director, and the two practiced together under the original name. Beginning in the Fifties, Mrs. Gilmore was active in the civil rights movement in Charleston. Gaining prominence, she was named in the Seventies to the West Virginia Board of Regents. She carried on the business into the Eighties when her health began to fail. She died in 1986. Prior to her death, the business became the Scott Funeral Home.[23]

According to the Bureau of Negro Welfare and Statistics, "the Negro Church represents the most important agency of Negro group experience in Charleston. It is the center of most of the Negroes' social life."[24] The church was in most cases the largest building in the community and its facilities were used for lectures, meetings, concerts, and community programs. As if presiding over the Washington—Shrewsbury area, the First Baptist Church stood on Washington Street across from the Brown Building looking down Shrewsbury. First founded in 1868, the Washington Street church was completed in 1889 and served the community at that location until 1959 when the congregation moved to a new building at Shrewsbury and Lewis streets. From the Twenties, the church developed a number of social welfare programs and printed a weekly news bulletin that was supported by many business advertisers.[25]

The Knights of Pythias Hall was another focal point of the community. The K of P was a national black fraternal organization, and according to BNWS these organizations have played a large role in Negro life. In a1923 study, the BNWS reported that one-third of West Virginia Negroes belong to one or more fraternities, the largest of which was the K of P. The BNWS study stated that in general "The local bodies [of fraternities] spend thousands of dollars annually in sick benefits, contributions to dependents at the death of members, assistance to the aged, widows, and orphans, contributions to churches ...."[26] In the early part of the century, Charleston's Samuel Starks played a prominent part at both the organization's local and state levels. Starks, like Elizabeth Gilmore, became known outside the black community. In 1901 he was appointed State Librarian by the Governor, a position he held until 1908 when he died at age forty-two. Under Starks leadership, the local K of P chapter floated a bond issue among its members in order to raise the capital for the purchase of a lot and the construction of a building. In 1906 the building was completed at the northwest corner of Washington and Dickinson streets, just a block west of the Brown Building. Three stories tall, the Hall housed black owned businesses on the first floor. In the early years, the Gem Pharmacy and the Peoples Grocery did business at the street level. In later decades, a pinball vending company and the Mutual Savings and Loan, a black owned bank rented space. The second floor housed offices for black professional people, while the third floor was reserved for lodge meetings and social functions. One of the more prominent professional men occupying the Hall was John C. Norman, who as we have seen designed the Garnet High addition. Norman designed many other structures in Charleston and Kanawha County including the faculty circle homes at West Virginia State College, the Ferguson Hotel, and many private homes in Charleston. Norman maintained his offices at the K of P Hall for forty-five years.[27]

The cohesiveness of the black community in this area is typified by the Mattie V. Lee Home, which in 1920 had relocated to 810 Donnelly Street next door to the Preston Funeral Home. In the second decade of the century, many young black women were coming to Charleston in search of employment, and the need for safe living quarters for the women became apparent to many established blacks. Helped with funds from a number of wealthy white women, a house was secured in 1915 at 1007 Quarrier Street, which could house twelve women. More than bed and roof, the home became a social center where community and civic meetings were held. A governing board was responsible for securing funds. After five years on Quarrier Street, the board launched a $35,000 fund drive for the purchase of a new building, and in January 1920 the home on Donnelly Street opened. Named for West Virginia's first woman black physician, the board secured a state charter of incorporation to promote the spiritual, intellectual, social, and industrial development of black women.[28] Until 1958, the Home was financed by membership dues and contributions, and after 1958 it began to receive United Way Funding. Because of the historic role the Home has played in the black community, it was placed on the National Register of Historic Places 1992.[29]

Although the Washington—Shrewsbury corner was the hub of the area's business and social life, black owned businesses extended east of the "Block" to Bradford Street. In the segregated years, the area west of Bradford along Washington Street and north to the railroad tracks was generally considered to be the black area. Many businessmen located to the east of the Brown Building enjoyed long and successful careers. One of these was R.C. Barnes, who owned the Q Ball Inn on the north side of Washington about a half block west of Bradford Street. Barnes started his billiard business in the Thirties on Summers Street. After a few years there, he relocated to an existing building on Washington Street. In the Forties, Barnes built a new Q Ball Inn at the same Washington Street site. A restaurant that was already beside his building was acquired and attached to it. It was known as Bob's Café. According to Black Past, the new "Q Ball Inn was a show place of billiard halls—spacious, clean, orderly." By the Fifties, the café had become a favorite place for visiting parents of West Virginia State College Students to dine. Barnes kept the business going into the Seventies when failing health brought it to an end.

Morris Street north of Washington was the site of the successful Northside Pharmacy. Aubrey Harris, a pharmacist, opened his drugstore in 1937 at 914 Morris Street. Morris, his wife, and children lived in the same building over the store. Popular with all ages from children buying candy to adults filling prescriptions, Harris kept both his business and residence at Morris Street for about forty years. In 1966-67, Harris served a term on the Charleston City Council.

Another durable enterprise was Earl's Barbershop. Earl Green got his start in barbering in 1930 at a white owned shop at Capitol and Quarrier streets. In 1933 Green opened his own shop with two chairs on Jacob Street, two blocks east of Shrewsbury Street. Green's gregariousness and skill attracted customers from the start. A place to enjoy the company of others as well as to get a haircut and shave, Green's business prospered on Jacob Street for half a century A favored pastime for those who gathered at Earl's shop was to listen to a baseball game while they shot pool and socialized. In 1985 after more than fifty years in the business, Green retired.[30]

This neighborhood covering several blocks in the area of Washington and Shrewsbury streets grew organically over the years unimpeded by Charleston's later single use zoning ordinance that sometimes artificially separated work and housing and even different types of housing. However, in this area work, housing, and social life all existed in harmony and literally side by side. On Shrewsbury, Dickinson, Lewis, Broad, Jacob, and Washington streets private homes were located beside and across the street from shops, businesses, and places of entertainment. Some business owners lived over their shops. Ferguson lived in his hotel, Merrill Preston and the Gilmores lived in separate quarters in their funeral homes, and Aubrey Harris lived over his pharmacy. Because of the variety of the area, one could walk for most items and services needed. Physicians, dentists, and lawyers were nearby as were grocery and drugstores, restaurants, barber and beauty shops, hardware stores, and churches. Socializing took place in the retail stores and shops and on the sidewalks, but for more planned events, one walked to the church or K of P Hall.

End of the community

By the mid—Sixties, unplanned events and uncontrollable outside forces had begun to take a toll on the Washington—Shrewsbury area. On March 26, 1966 a fire began in the attic of the Ferguson Hotel. Although the fire was confined to the attic and third floor, smoke and water damage caused all residents to leave. In the Sixties business had begun to wane, and Ferguson had turned the hotel into a rooming house for poor blacks as well as whites. A few months before the fire, Ferguson had agreed to sell his hotel to the Heart O' Town Motel Group. The fire did not affect the sale because the motel group was interested only in the real estate, and in May 1966 the sale was concluded. [31] In January 1967 the new owners demolished the forty-four year old building in order to use the property as a parking lot for their new motel at the corner of Washington and Broad streets. Anderson Brown sold his Brown Building in 1970, thus bringing to an end the focal point of black life that had lasted for about a half century in this area of Charleston. By 1970 many of the Shrewsbury businesses were gone. Shaffner's Grocery and Pal's Beauty Shop, both located in the first block off Washington, had ceased business. In the late Sixties, the Palace Barbecue, next to the Brown Building, had given way to a youth oriented police community center. In the early Seventies, the Red Star Cab Company, a fixture for over twenty-five years in the first block, closed doors. During the same period, the Trio Beauty Shop, across the street from the cab company, also closed. [32] After Brown sold his building, he moved down Shrewsbury about a block and constructed a second Brown Building in 1971 next to the First Baptist Church. Garnet High School building was still standing and would remain so, but integration had closed it. The school's last graduating class was May 1956.

Charleston's interstate highways also took their toll on the area. The highway designers wanted an exit ramp at Broad Street, forcing residents and businesses from the street during the construction period of the mid—Seventies. Since the aesthetics of an interstate ramp are rarely appreciated, these businesses and residents did not return. The ramp split Broad Street, and the street became characterized by automobiles and trucks racing down the ramp to Washington Street. As late as 1970, five years before work on the ramp had begun, there were twelve businesses on Broad Street in the first block off Washington. (By now many of the businesses were white owned). These included Appalachian Tire, White Enterprises, Pepsi Cola Bottlers, a car wash, and an ambulance service. By 1975 when the interstates had claimed the area, there were just four businesses left. In the second block beginning at Lewis Street and extending to the railroad station at Smith Street, there were eighteen businesses in 1970. Two restaurants were in the block, a drugstore, a barbershop, a loan company, and a rug company. Safeco Insurance Company was located at Lewis Street next to

Rollyson Motors, and a few doors away was Coyle and Richardson's wholesale outlet. The Harden and Harden Funeral Home and Parkison Motors were closer to Smith Street. Near the center of the block there was an apartment building with eleven tenants. By 1975 the fate of this block had duplicated that of the first. Only four businesses remained in the wake of the ramp that had pierced the block. In 1975 the apartment building still remained, but was empty of tenants. [33] This area of Broad Street was now a shadow of its former self. Yet this was not the extent of physical dislocation of the neighborhood wrought by the Broad Street ramp. This ramp had an ancillary ramp that turned sharply to the right or west, thereby completing a U—turn from the eastbound interstate. Spanning the block from Broad to Shrewsbury streets, the ramp connected with Christopher Street, thereby providing the link with the downtown. Since ramp traffic did not have to stop at Shrewsbury, the ramp had the effect of splitting the street. Yet by 1976 when the ramp was under construction, the vitality of Shrewsbury Street was already gone.

Behind the physical changes of the area were profound sociological changes that by the Sixties had affected the larger society. Charleston was, of course, not immune to these changes. Traditional families were breaking down, single parenthood was increasing, blue-collar work was declining, and welfare roles were expanding. All this changed Charleston's black community. Moreover, the back of segregation had been broken, and Charleston's blacks did not have to live in exclusively black areas. Professional blacks who formerly lived in and served the black communities could now move out and establish a practice in the larger society. Consequently black institutions began to decline. In a 1993 newspaper interview, the black sociologist Andrew Billingsley said: "Sad to say many black institutions fell victim to integration and social change and upward mobility and increased opportunity. Even progressive changes have their downside, and the downside of racial progress that started thirty or forty years ago was the closing of black schools, the scattering of black professionals, and the abandonment of black institutions as we integrated with white ones." [34] Billingsley's remarks were given in the context of the country as a whole, but the same theme had earlier been made by Ben Starks, publisher of the Charleston based black owned newspaper, the West Virginia Beacon Digest. In a 1980 Gazette interview, Starks said that with integration and urban renewal "the number of black owned businesses in the city has virtually vanished as have black neighborhoods." (Words of Gazette). Starks further stated in his own words that "The old segregated neighborhoods were imbued with ownership. They gave residents a chance to control their own destiny." [35] Aside from the changing family relationships and the ramifications of integration, declining population would play a role in community breakup. From 1960 to 1970, Charleston's population in round figures had fallen from 86000 to 71000. The black population reflected this general decline. In 1960, Charleston's blacks numbered 8264; by 1970 the figure had fallen to 7389.

Triangle

The Triangle area differed markedly from the Washington—Shrewsbury area. Less traditionally middle class, the Triangle was poorer than its neighboring black area a few blocks to the east. The clearest distinction between the two areas concerned the ownership of real estate. Whereas the Washington—Shrewsbury blacks largely owned their business real estate, Triangle blacks largely did not. The Triangle became a recognizable community during the Twenties. However, as a physical space, it originated in 1909 when the Legislature created a triangular shaped ward against the Elk River extending east to Court Street and bounded on the north by Slack Street and on the south by Washington Street. Early on the Triangle gained a reputation for notoriety. The area was known by such epithets as Isle of Vice, Little Chicago, and the back end of town. The usual vices could be found there—prostitution, gambling, and liquor during prohibition. Fry's Alley, a narrow east-west street running through the area, stood out as the vice center.[36] But the street was also known as the place for good music and good ribs. Many whites frequented Fry's Alley for the women, liquor, and a good time. Although in many areas the vices are associated with violent crime, this was not the case in the Triangle. The area had very little crime against people or property. Former Police Chief John Bailes, who as a patrolman worked the Triangle in the Fifties, once stated that although there was crime in the area, it was victimless crime.[37] In its later years, about 5000 people lived in the Triangle. Not all were black. A few poor whites were scattered through the area, and when the Washington Manor public housing project was completed in 1941, the area got more whites.

Many of the Triangle residents were poor and lived in substandard housing, but there were also many owner occupied middle class, single family homes. Many of these were on Margaret, Joseph, and Donnelly streets. There were many small businesses in the area, and many blacks earned their livelihood from them. Donnelly Street in the Thirties was home to an ice cream manufacturer, a printing company, a battery store, a barber and beauty shop, and a restaurant. Two blocks north on Dryden Street were the Checker Tire Service, National Lunch, Blue Haven Inn, Tri-State Brewing Company, an oil well supply company, and a railway garage. On Bullitt and Young streets one found grocery stores, a tire and wrecking service, a rooming house, and a Baptist Church.[38] Throughout the Triangle, there was no segregation of housing and business. Like the Washington—Shrewsbury area, the Triangle developed before single use zoning, and the mix of houses, work sites, and entertainment places worked in harmony. Fry's Alley for all its notoriety was principally a residential street.

By the Fifties, small businesses were still common in the Triangle. The Checker Tire Service was still on Donnelly Street. Other businesses on the street were a radio store, a meat shop, a restaurant, a garage, and a towel supply business. Fry's Alley had been renamed Christopher Street, and it was still primarily a residential street, but it had legitimate businesses also, such as a Firestone retread shop. Bullitt Street in the fifties was home to two restaurants, a used furniture store, a grocery store, and a lumber company. [39]

Yet in spite of the area's viability, sub-standard housing and vice continued to plague the Triangle, and these conditions gave the city government through the urban renewal program the rationale to seek the eradication of the Triangle. But before getting to urban renewal, two blows from other forces need to be mentioned. These were not vindictive attacks on the Triangle; rather the double assaults involved two agencies carrying out their special interests and the Triangle was unfortunate enough to be in the way. The West Virginia Water Company delivered the first blow in 1966 when it purchased acreage in the eastern part of the Triangle near Court and Smith streets in order to construct a new water treatment plant. This meant the eviction of 215 tenants and the razing of their housing. The removal and relocation went relatively smooth. An organization of housing groups called Action for Housing helped with the effort and by August 1966 all residents were out. [40] Following the Water Company's action, the Triangle next endured the efforts of the interstate highway officials chipping away at the size of the area. The previous chapter discussed the traffic aspects of the interstates. Here only the route is relevant.

For Charleston, the state Road Commission proposed route for I-64 and I-77 had been approved by federal officials in 1964. At that time, the Road Commission announced that up to 1000 families would be displaced. As planned by highway authorities, I-77 as it entered Charleston from the north would curve to the east to extend along the northern hillside of the city. The curve would slice through the northwest corner of the Triangle in a way that would eliminate Dryden, Rand, and most of Bullitt and Young streets as viable areas. In addition to housing, businesses would also be lost. By August 1968, many residents had received notices demanding that they move. In frustration, demonstrations began to occur. Legal Aid attorneys filed a motion in federal court asking that demolition funds be denied. In April 1969, the U.S. District Court denied the motion. Because of the protests, federal Secretary of Transportation, John Volpe, issued an order in July 1970 halting all interstate related demolition so that the I—77 route could be reviewed. The city Council supported Volpe's order, and an organization in the Triangle collected over 300 signatures thanking the Council for its support. In addition to Triangle residents, prominent non-residents also signed the petition including West Virginia Secretary of State John D. Rockefeller, Rabbi Samuel Cooper, Delegate Si Galperin, and Rev. John Wilkes, head of the city's Human Rights Commission. But Gov. Arch Moore, who supported the interstate route criticized Volpe's desist order. Volpe's action, however, was merely a delay in the highway march. In November 1970, the Department of Transportation approved the route as originally drawn.[41]

Yet even with parts of the Triangle excised by the water treatment plant and the interstates, most of it still would remain. Then came urban renewal. A critic of the national experience with interstates in urban areas wrote that the removal process amounted to treating black neighborhoods as a "land reserve for downtown expansion."[42] Coupled with Charleston's urban renewal, this conclusion was also the experience of the Triangle.

City neglect

Unlike the plans of the water company and the highway officials whose programs within their own framework had a positive aspect, the plan of Charleston's Urban Renewal Authority was harshly negative. With the blessing of the city government, the local urban renewal officials planned, plotted and delivered the deathblows to the Triangle. The Achilles heal of the Triangle was that the historic low percentage of owner occupied real estate had changed little since the Twenties. The Bureau of Negro Welfare and Statistics reported that in 1921 only thirty-two of 310 Negro living units were owner occupied or just over ten percent. This contrasted with other East Side areas in which over one-third of Negroes owned their homes.[43] In 1965, the Gazette reported that about eighty-five percent of Triangle businesses and residents did not own their real estate.[44] It was largely a rental area owned by absentee landlords who cared little for their property except to collect rent. Maintenance of Triangle property was nearly non-existent. The Gazette estimated that fifty percent of the property was "deteriorating or dilapidated." Herein lay the city's failure. As in the first decades of the century when the Council abdicated its planning authority to private developers, Councils of the Thirties, Forties, and Fifties had turned their backs on the city's housing plight. Although Charleston had had a building code since 1915, administered by an inspector of buildings, the Council and administration refused to enforce housing and health regulations. The code did not relate to design or physical placement of structures; its purpose was to protect the health and safety of residents. Provisions of the code included mandating that exterior walls and roofs are of non-combustible material, defining the thickness of walls relative to height, and setting height requirements relative to material used. Bathroom plumbing requirements were given in some detail. For example, the floors had to be of waterproof material, fittings were specified in order to prevent leaks, and certain taps were required for waste material piping. With respect to electricity, the code included the provisions of the national electrical code.[45] In August 1965, the Gazette published a series of articles on Charleston's housing problem called the "High Cost of Indifference.' On a tour through the Triangle, the Gazette writer found that it does not take a trained building inspector to recognize many unsafe housing conditions. He found lack of fire escapes, overused electrical fixtures, poor plumbing and drainage, and poorly supported porch roofs. The Gazette study concluded "For more that a decade the city has steadfastly shrugged it off whenever a slum problem knocked on its door."[46]

An attempt to deal with Triangle housing fizzled in 1953. In that year the Council on the recommendation of the Municipal Planning Commission created the Slum Clearance and Redevelopment Commission for the purpose of improving Triangle housing. On the strength of a $15,000 grant from the federal housing officials, the local authority conducted a study, and about $450,000 under the 1949 Federal Housing Act had been approved for slum clearance. But before anything was done, Council for reasons not entirely clear disbanded the agency. John Copenhaver, whose eight years as mayor encompassed most of the Fifties said at the time that "vested interests" which were profiting from renting sub-standard housing were able to force the program's abolishment. This explanation does not appear plausible, for slum landlords traditionally have been happy to sell their slum property when the opportunity to make a capital gain presents itself. There may have been many reasons for Council's action; not the least may have been the Gazette's explanation that some members denounced the program as a "socialistic scheme."[47] In 1957, another Council reactivated the Commission, announcing that it would make a citywide review of housing and make recommendations, but there would not be a slum-clearing program. During the Fifties, in spite of the 1955 public housing project known as Orchard Manor, the Copenhaver administration showed little interest in upgrading Charleston's housing stock. Mayor Copenhaver's interest lay in the Civic Center, completed in 1959, paving streets, extending Quarrier Street west from the downtown, and presiding over the large 1958 annexation. Copenhaver gave his administration a moralistic tone by attempting to censor the novel Peyton Place from private bookstores and on occasion challenging the public library over some of its book selections. His interest in the Triangle had nothing to do with housing and everything to do with vice. In his first term, Copenhaver created a vice squad, whose favored place to raid appeared to be the Triangle. The Loveless Hotel on Dryden Street, thought to harbor prostitutes and bootleggers, was repeatedly singled out by Copenhaver's raiders.[48]

Although federal funds for urban housing blight had been available since 1949, Charleston was about to close out the Fifties holding an empty bag. The Gazette editorialized on this theme in December 1958: "Urban blight has been allowed to feed so long upon itself or neighborhood areas that it has grown into a local scandal. While other cities, particularly in the Northeast and Midwest, have moved ahead with urban renewal projects, Charleston has done next to nothing to rid itself of slums, regardless of the millions in federal funds available for the purpose."[49] In 1958, the Kanawha Welfare Council issued a report that detailed the high number of substandard homes in the city. Showing some interest, Council in 1960 formally set up the Charleston Urban Renewal Authority (CURA). However, the city's blighted housing was not an urgent matter with this body. Somewhat surprisingly CURA's priority was a commercial project in the three-block area along the Kanawha Boulevard from Capitol to Court streets and extending to Virginia Street. Mayor John Shanklin in 1961 defended the priority in these terms: "We have got to do everything we can for downtown Charleston because that is where the business people are ... We've got to do it so they can make money; so they can pay taxes and the budget can be composed to take care of the rest of the facilities of Charleston." [50] Recognizing Charleston's serious housing problem with no action being taken, the Charleston Board of Realtors in 1961 asked the advisory team of the National Association of Real Estate Boards to make a survey of the city's housing. In a fifty-one page report, this organization concluded that the Triangle area was the heart of the housing problem and urged CURA to concentrate first on housing in the central city. Mayor Shanklin turned the report over to the city's Municipal Planning Commission, which amounted to burying it. [51]

While the city government and the Urban Renewal Authority continued to do nothing about Charleston's blighted housing, the Triangle Improvement Association (TIC) was formed in 1964 as part of the federal war on poverty program. Its purpose was to improve housing in the Triangle, and in early 1964 TIC members began a door to door survey of houses in the area. The organization sent letters to landlords urging them to correct slum conditions. During the same time period, TIC members began to appear at Council meetings urging that the city put pressure on the landlords. Still showing little interest, Mayor Shanklin did no more than he did four years earlier when he buried the realtors housing study. He now in 1965 ordered the Charleston Housing Authority (the body that administers low income housing) to make a housing study. The Director said it would take time. During this period interest groups were increasingly speaking out on the housing plight. In August 1965, TIC President, Spencer Burton, issued a statement: "... housing and the job situation for the average Negro is critical and can't wait for another round of more talks and more studies." [52] The same month, Rev. Homer Davis, head of UNION (United Neighborhood Interest Organization Network), a coalition of Negro groups, stated that "the establishment has been criminally negligent in the slums, especially in the Triangle." Davis further charged city hall with "indifference and incompetence." With no help from the city, TIC's effort to force landlords to upgrade Triangle was failing. Burton in December 1965 stated: "We would hate to admit this, but what our effort thus far has produced amounts to nothing—nothing." [53] Meanwhile as if to announce its neglect of housing as well as other duties, the city in 1965 lost its recertification status with the federal Urban Housing Administration. This agency notified the city that it had not updated its housing code, that it was weak on enforcement of its existing code, and that it did not have a current comprehensive plan of city government. This meant that all urban renewal funding was at risk. Funds were not cut off, but it took the Council three years to update its housing code.

In its neglect of Triangle housing, the city was not just allowing a sizeable number of its citizens to live in unsafe and unsanitary conditions, nor was it just allowing the aesthetics of the city to suffer. It was also cutting its financial throat and thereby causing the middle class and all other taxpayers to pay more than necessary to support their government. Slums in themselves are a public expense. First of all, the city loses property tax revenue because blighted housing has a low assessed value, and in an attempt to offset this, other property is assessed higher. Moreover, the cost of police and fire protection is higher in slum areas. The Charleston Police Chief in 1965 said that it costs five times as much to police a slum area as it does other areas of the city. The Fire Chief at the same time reported that his department spends one-third of its time fighting fires in the Triangle area. Furthermore, the Health Director reported that over sixty percent of the department's funds are spent in the Triangle because of the high incidence of disease. [54]

Urban Renewal Authority

Having completed most of what it could do with the first urban renewal project on the Boulevard, the Charleston Urban Renewal Authority (CURA) was by 1966 ready to tackle the problem of Triangle housing. Because of the pivotal role played by CURA over the next several years, it will be helpful to briefly review the federal guidelines under which the local urban renewal authority operated. Congress established the urban renewal program as part of the Federal Housing Act of 1949. The purpose of this program was to eliminate slum areas and to provide a decent home for American families. A major guideline gave local governments responsibility for initiating and implementing a specific project; in doing so maximum reliance had to be placed on private enterprise. Participating city governments were required to create a local urban renewal authority, appoint board members, who then hired staff. Congress through the Department of Housing and Urban Development funded up to seventy-five percent of the program. Much of the cities' share could be in-kind services. Federal law required that the project area be blighted, and gave the local urban renewal authority full power to decide what was blighted. Nationally this power was abused, for if a city wanted to clear out a large area, it would declare all houses blighted when many were not. Such abuse also took place with respect to housing in the Triangle area.

Residents in many of the nation's cities who had been given an eviction notice because their house was scheduled to be demolished challenged the law.

Their challenges failed. The federal act gave local urban renewal authorities the constitutional power of eminent domain. As the challenges reached the United States Supreme Court, the high court put a new twist on the condemnation power. Formally it was thought that eminent domain meant the right of government to acquire (with compensation) private property for public use. The federal act gave local urban renewal authorities the right to take private property; then sell it for private use. The Supreme Court decided in 1954 that this practice was constitutional.

Once a local urban renewal authority picked an area it wanted to renew, the regulations required it to write a plan for approval by the city government and by Washington, after which funds would be released. A key requirement in the process was citizen participation, meaning that the affected community, its neighborhood groups and organizations had to have full opportunity to participate in development of the plan. With respect to the Triangle, its residents felt, as we will see, that the Charleston authority slighted this requirement.

Nationally, the urban renewal program was in almost all cases a land clearing program. It was certainly that in Charleston. Armed with condemnation power and ample funds, local urban renewal authorities purchased real estate, demolished it, and sold the land to private developers, who then erected new buildings and housing units to satisfy the local plan. It became immediately clear to local urban renewal officials that they possessed the power to not only change the physical appearance of a neighborhood, but more significantly to change the neighborhood's character. If it was previously a low income area, local officials could turn it into a middle or high income area, or even turn a predominantly residential area into mainly a business district.

As the urban renewal program developed nationally, it began to acquire racial overtones. Of the individuals forced from their homes, about two-thirds were black or other minorities. Given the extent of housing discrimination coupled with their low incomes, minorities were increasingly finding it difficult to find other housing. One critic of the program wrote that urban renewal rather than eliminating slums merely shifted slums. Many of the blacks forced from their homes began to call urban renewal a "Negro removal program," a criticism later made by Triangle residents. Because of the extent of urban renewal and problem of finding new housing, Congress in the 1955 Housing Act added a provision for housing rehabilitation to the urban renewal law. However, neither nationally nor in Charleston did rehabilitation play a significant role. In practice, urban renewal did not mean rehabilitation, renovation, or preservation. It meant land clearing.[55]

Plan and counter plan

After being prodded for over a decade to deal with Charleston's housing problem and doing nothing about it, the city Council and administration must have been relieved when the Charleston Urban Renewal Authority (CURA) turned its attention to the Triangle. CURA had its own board, its own staff, its own funds, and its own legal powers. Once Council created the local authority, the details of rectifying the city's blighted housing was in the hands of the renewal officials. In February 1966, the Council voted twenty-one to zero to apply for a $248,000 planning grant for a study of Triangle housing. Presiding over the plan study was CURA Chairman, Howard McJunkin, a millionaire industrialist, who had been appointed by the Mayor to head the five member local board. McJunkin would prove to be unsympathetic to the wishes of the Triangle residents. Upon being named as CURA Chairman, he called the Triangle "a blotched up part of our city." The plan took nearly three years to complete, and the area covered was larger than that of the recognized neighborhood. Whereas the southern boundary of the Triangle was Washington Street, the study area extended another block and a half to the south to take in the area between Washington and Lee streets and half of the block between Lee and Quarrier streets. The eastern boundary also extended farther than the traditional neighborhood; in one section nearly to Capitol Street. The plan assumed that the interstate highway officials would be successful in their condemnation and planned razing of the northwest corner of the Triangle, and thus that area of the neighborhood was not part of the plan study area. The three year period during which the study was carried out and approved was characterized from the start by tension between CURA officials and Triangle residents. Citing federal guidelines, the Triangle residents' representative organization, the TIC, maintained that they were illegally shut out of the study process. Four Triangle residents were initially appointed to the study group, but William Preston, TIC President, who succeeded Spencer Burton, later charged that they were dismissed by Chairman McJunkin when they would not support the direction of the plan. Under federal guidelines, TIC members did not have an automatic right to be part of the planning process. Local participation had to be formalized by the creation of Project Area Committee (PAC), which was to be made up of a cross section of the community. A PAC did exist, but Preston charged it was in effect window dressing, because CURA excluded the organization from planning and had to rely instead on information from CURA Director, Eric Hemphill.[56]

By Summer 1968 when the CURA plan was nearing completion, TIC's Preston had no knowledge of its content, and he wrote to McJunkin asking for a copy. He received a July 10, 1968 letter from the Chairman promising a copy. A month later Preston had not received his copy and he arranged an August 21 meeting with McJunkin and CURA Director Hemphill. Other TIC members were present, as was a Gazette reporter. Parts of the meeting degenerated into a shouting match, but in the end McJunkin promised Preston a copy of the plan the same day.[57] Upon reading the plan, Preston and TIC members were stunned. In short, CURA wanted to bulldoze the Triangle and reconstruct a district unrecognizable to the residents. McJunkin and his Board without Triangle participation had written a land clearing plan. Of the eighty-three acres in the project area, the plan called for fifty acres to be razed. This meant that of 483 structures, 471 would be demolished (in some of the reporting, the number of housing units has been stated to be in excess of 1500. This is not inconsistent with 483 structures because a structure could contain several housing units). Spared from CURA's wrecking ball were St Francis Hospital, two churches, and a commercial building owned by a city Councilman. Although the low income housing project, Washington Manor, was within the plan boundaries, it was excluded from CURA's jurisdiction. After the land clearing, CURA envisioned private developers constructing 200 high density units, 200 family living units, and a senior citizen high rise. All of these would be on the north side of Washington Street, and would total about 700 housing units, all high density. Also on the north side of Washington Street, the plan called for a community building, a swimming pool, and an elementary school to replace Fruth School already in the area. The area south of Washington Street was reserved for commercial development. The implementation of this plan meant that the Triangle would not be rehabilitated. It would be transformed into another type of neighborhood.[58]

To fight the plan, the Inter-City Council of Neighborhoods, a coalition group of which TIC was a member hired Peter Abeles, head of a New York planning firm of Abeles and Schwartz to study the Triangle and write an alternative plan. The alternative plan recognized the historic boundaries of the Triangle, and the residents' plan moved the boundary to the north and west to include the areas taken by the water company and the highway officials, but as we have seen CURA had no control over these land condemnations. More fundamental, the TIC plan called for rehabilitation of existing housing with many single family homes to remain. Housing density would be no greater than sixteen units per acre compared to the CURA plan of twenty to thirty units per acre. The thrust of the TIC plan, according to its head, William Preston, was to insure that the current Triangle residents remain residents and that homeowners remain in the area as homeowners.[59]

To understand why the TIC favored housing rehabilitation and was adamantly opposed to demolition of their homes does not require a vivid imagination. It is easily appreciated that if individuals suffer both from racial discrimination and poverty, they will have an overpowering tendency to fight to keep the shelter they have. As the first TIC President, Spencer Burton, put it: "If you are white, you may move out and find a better place, but if you are poor and a Negro, you are trapped here until you die; you have no place to go."[60]

But this position went unappreciated by McJunkin and his CURA Board. Except for a few small details, such as allowing more than two churches, the Board rejected the TIC amendments. McJunkin added that because the city Council had to approve the plan by March 1969 in order to receive funding, there was no time to re-write the plan. It would therefore remain a land clearing program.

It is true that the Triangle had many dilapidated houses. The photographs of the CURA assessors show this.[61] But the TIC had a cogent argument supporting housing renovation. If as the Gazette said that fifty percent of the housing was dilapidated, then fifty percent was not. The assessors' photographs, which show all housing proposed for condemnation also show many solid and substantial looking houses. In addition James Randall, who co-authored Black Past, printed in his book two pages of Triangle houses in a good state of repair.[62] Moreover, credence was given to the view that there was substantial housing in the Triangle when in late 1969 the Washington office of urban renewal reversed a portion of the approved plan and decided that some blocks of housing should be renovated and not demolished. However, at this point we are in early 1969 nearly a year before this reversal, and McJunkin and his Board was single-minded in support of demolishing the Triangle.

Taps for the Triangle

Preston and his organization and supporters now had to make their case before the Charleston City Council. About 400 people showed up at city hall on the evening of February 17,1969 for a public hearing on CURA's plan for the Triangle. Twenty-nine individuals spoke all of whom were against the plan. Preston argued for housing rehabilitation, stating that "this and strong enforcement of the city housing code against landlords would renew the Triangle and increase the housing supply without swallowing up the community." Negro pastor Rev Bushnell asked rhetorically: "Do you cure a man of cancer by taking his life? Do you cure the Triangle by bulldozing it?" The Charleston chapter of the NAACP had formally come out against the CURA plan the previous month. At the hearing, its President, Richard Payne called the plan "Negro removal and extermination of low-income communities." Three attorneys representing Triangle businesses protested the loss of their clients' livelihood. Charleston legal aid lawyers supporting Triangle residents told the Council that they would appeal any adverse decision through the courts.[63] The Council adjourned without a decision and met two days later to appoint a six member committee that would attempt to resolve the issues. Two Councilmen were named members, as were the leaders of the Triangle. Improvement Association and the NAACP.

This committee traveled to the Urban Renewal Administration regional headquarters in Philadelphia and at this meeting, the federal officials agreed to attend a city Council meeting in Charleston. At its regular March 3 meeting, the Council again postponed a decision because foul weather kept Philadelphia officials from arriving in Charleston. [64]

While waiting for a Council decision, both the Gazette and Daily Mail editorialized in favor of the CURA plan to raze the Triangle. The Gazette wrote: "…the urban renewal proposition confronting council is basically one of reviving the inner heart of the city within the next five years or permitting the area to remain as it is—stagnant, ratridden, dilapidated, deprived—for the next twenty years." [65] In supporting the plan, the Daily Mail stated: "It is a chance to undo the neglect of a generation and to restore to usefulness one of the city's worst examples of urban decay." [66] On March 11, federal urban renewal officials met in Charleston with the Mayor's special committee and other Council members. Afterwards it was announced that an agreement with TIC was close, but providing a measure of drama, the members said they would need another week.

The Triangle had at least one on the record Council supporter. This was the black Council-at-Large member Virgil Matthews, who announced that he would vote against the CURA plan unless the Council amended it to reduce housing density by allowing no more than six units of public housing per block, make a provision for housing rehabilitation, allow no structure to be built higher than forty feet, and allow all residents of the Triangle to stay if they choose. But the amendments got no further with the Council than similar amendments did with CURA six months earlier. On March 18, 1969, the Council formally voted twenty to one to approve the CURA plan. Councilman Matthews cast the only vote against it. The plan then went to the Urban Renewal Administration in Philadelphia where it was approved in October 1969. There was one last flickering light for the Triangle residents. In late 1969, the urban renewal regional office in Philadelphia relented to TIC and decided that several blocks of housing should be rehabilitated and not demolished. But by this time the residents felt defeated. The bulldozers were at work in the northwest part of the Triangle where the interstate would be built and residents had begun to receive eviction notices. Seven homeowners held out and rehabilitated, but most decided not to renovate and sold their homes to CURA.The district as they knew it would be gone.

As urban renewal funds were released to the city in March 1970, CURA Director, Eric Hemphill said: "This will allow us to clear out one of Charleston's most blighted areas and allow construction of new housing for these people who need it most." [67] As the residents were helped out of the Triangle with federal relocation grants of $4000 to each tenant and $15000 to each homeowner plus the value of the house, the demolition crews moved in. Toward the end of 1971 when the demolition was complete, a Gazette reporter surveyed the scene and wrote that the Triangle was nearly gone; as "barren as the Utah Salt Flats." Contrary to what the Triangle residents had been promised after the plan was completed and what Hemphill said upon release of federal funds, the residents who were evicted did not get housing in the Triangle. The hope of the urban renewal program was that following the demolition stage, a developer would appear who would rebuild the area. This of course happened in the Triangle, but not for ten to twenty years. By 1979, ten years after evictions started and eight years after the area was leveled, only thirteen housing units had been completed, compared to over 1500 demolished. Of some 1180 families displaced, 615 moved to private rental housing, 509 to public housing, and fifty-seven purchased homes. Some moved to the West Side, some to the East End, and others to the new City Park Village near Spring Hill Cemetery. Many moved out of Charleston.[68]

In an assessment nearly a decade after the razing of the Triangle, the Gazette questioned whether the program was urban renewal or Negro removal. Critics, according to the paper, maintained that city officials saw the destruction of the Triangle "as an end in itself and exaggerated its condition to gain support for the administration's campaign to remove blacks from the downtown area." The city's federal-state program director, Norman Kirkpatrick, said: "It turned out that relocation was often too early, too brutal, and too unnecessary." Mayor John Hutchinson in 1979 said: "Whether or not [Negro removal] was the purpose, it could certainly be contended that that was what happened."[69]

Postscript

If there was little housing for the displaced Triangle residents ten year later, the housing situation had barely improved after yet another ten years. Indeed by 1980, it had become clear that urban renewal in the Triangle meant much more than improved, albeit much less housing. During the 1980's, any observer could see that the entire character of the neighborhood was changing. New housing finally began to arrive. First against the Elk River just north of Washington Street, the high rise, privately owned Charleston Arbors opened in 1979. With 204 living units, it was designed for senior citizens and the handicapped. Luxury townhouses followed the high rise to the area. These units were first proposed in December 1983 and would be located along the north side of Washington Street and across Clendenin Street from the Charleston Arbors. One side of the complex abutted Washington Manor and was separated from the public housing project by a brick wall. Ten units of the fifty-two unit complex were reserved for low to moderate income renters. When it opened in 1984, the all brick complex was known as the Charleston Center Village. The third and final housing development in the old Triangle, known as Clendenin Square, opened in the Summer of 1986 at Court and Donnelly streets. This was a fifty-unit condominium complex with each unit having an initial purchase price of $63,000.[70] With the completion of the condominiums, only about 300 housing units would be built of the 700 units promised in 1969. Of the 300 units, about one-third of them would have been clearly out of the affordable price range of the displaced residents. The remaining 200 units were restricted by age. Yet the possibility of the original residents returning was moot. After more than ten years, they were scattered over the city and county. There is other housing in the Triangle, and due to amendments in the original 1969 plan, more lots, principally on Margaret and McCormick streets, were made available for single family housing. The later amendments also spared a few houses from the wrecking ball and were allowed to be renovated. Between I-64 and Donnelly Street, an athletic field, swimming pool, tennis courts, and a recreation building were developed. This area formerly contained housing that was demolished for the interstate. The notorious but lively Frys Alley, later Christopher Street, had ran though the recreation area and interstate path. A truncated Christopher Street remains, but all of it is east of Summers Street.

The remaining Triangle planning area became the site of large scale commercial and retail establishments, the largest of which was the twenty-six acres, $160 million Town Center Mall opening in November 1983.[71] (To repeat the original Triangle neighborhood extended just to Washington Street on the south, whereas CURA's Triangle planning area extended one and one-half blocks farther south). The front of the mall was at Court Street, and being just three blocks from Capitol Street, the architects designed a pedestrian walkway connecting downtown with the mall. Known as Brawley Walkway and Slack Plaza, which were outside the planning area, these connectors were dedicated on July 4, 1984. Other significant developments in the Triangle planning area were the Marriott Hotel at Lee and Clendenin streets opening in August 1982 and Cagney's Restaurant at Washington and Court streets. The last development of CURA's Triangle was Embassy Suites that opened in December 1997, twenty-eight years after the first approved plan.

Although our focus is on the Triangle urban renewal project, a word is needed on the other two urban renewal projects between the Elk River and Capitol Street, for collectively, these three projects had a significant impact on Charleston's new and enlarged downtown. Reference has been made to the city's first urban renewal plan of the early Sixties. Known formally as the Summers Street—Boulevard Project, this plan called for the razing of all structures along Kanawha Boulevard for three blocks from Capitol to Court streets and one block to the north. Its non-controversial nature and small size—nine square acres compared to the Triangle's eighty-two—enabled this project to move relatively swiftly. Its plan was approved in 1963; and about four years later, the major developments were in place. The Charleston National Bank purchased the first square block beginning at Capitol Street at the end of 1964 and completed its steel and glass tower building in Summer 1967. The Holiday Inn Charleston House, however, opening in September 1966 and occupying the second block to Laidley Street was the first building completed. In the third block behind City Hall would be the city's parking garage. [72]

This new construction was the final blow to the old Kanawha Street as a retail shopping area. As Charleston's first retail area, it was by the Sixties showing considerable wear and was a shadow of what it had been. The late 1930's riverfront project with the help of federal WPA funds had eliminated all retail from the river side of the street, and now some thirty years later, another federal project would eliminate retail from the north side. The design of the bank was especially detrimental to the vitality of Charleston's first street. Taking up the entire block, the bank's entrance was placed at Virginia Street with view from the Boulevard dominated by four garage doors leading to underground parking.

The remaining urban renewal project in the larger downtown was called the Government Square Project. Its first plan of thirty acres was approved in June 1969. Situated somewhat between the other two projects, its boundaries extended from Clendenin to Laidley streets. Part of the Town Center Mall is within the original boundary of Government Square. Like the Triangle, this project developed slowly, taking several years to complete, as the original plan underwent several changes. Briefly, the structures built within this project were the Union Bank in 1985, the Courthouse Annex, in 1988, and the federal building opening in 1998, all either fronting or alongside Virginia Street.

Ignoring the human costs of forced residential removal in these areas, the urban renewal programs from an investment perspective gave the city a major financial boost. Unlike many urban renewal projects across the country in which property assessments decreased following a renewal program, Charleston's three projects from Capitol Street to the Elk River resulted in a sizable increase in real estate assessment. [73] In the smallest of these projects along Capitol Street, real estate assessment in 1962 prior to urban renewal was about \$3.2 million. After completion of the bank, the hotel, and the parking garage, the assessment in the same area five years later was projected to be about \$10.5 million. [74] To evaluate the city's increased assessment, nearly a thirty year period has to be used, for it took that long to complete all new structures. For Charleston as a whole, the increase in property assessment over this period was significant. In 1965, the citywide Class II and IV real estate assessment was \$31,197,350. This figure, as do the following, excludes personal property and public utility property. We now go to 1993, for by then most pieces of the Triangle project were on line. The city's real estate assessment in that year was \$766,004,094, a figure that excludes the assessment for Embassy Suites, since it was not yet completed. [75] These citywide figures do not of course give a precise measure of the increase in property value within the urban renewal areas, but during the time frame in question, construction between and Elk River and Capitol Street dominated building projects in the city and most of the increased assessment can be attributed to the urban renewal development. In order to have a realistic comparison between the 1965 and 1993 figures, the rate of inflation should be considered. When the 1965 figure is assigned the value of the 1993 dollar, the city's assessment for 1965 would have been about $157,000.

In obtaining nearly a five-fold increase in real estate assessment, the city's investment was miniscule. In 1968, the projected cost of the Triangle project was $14.2 million. This would be reduced by land sales to just over $7.0 million. Under the federal-local funding formula, Charleston's share came to less than $2.0 million, but much of the city's share could be paid with non-cash credits such as street and sewer improvements. This would leave the city with a cash obligation of less than $1.0 million. The cost of the Summers Street—Boulevard project was $3.8 million reduced to $1.7 million by land sales. Charleston's share was about $425,000, of which $307,000 was in cash. The city's Government Square cost was about $1.0 million, but there would be continuing revenue from the parking garage. Yet even using $1.0 million for the latter project, Charleston's cash outlay was less than $2.5 million.[76]

Map Notes

There appear to be no extant photographs of the Triangle area prior to urban renewal. The following three maps are presented to illustrate a few points regarding the area. The first two are small details of the area from the Kanawha County Public Library's collection of Sanborn maps. The first one made in 1947 shows a part of the southern section of the Triangle that abuts Washington Street. Note the number of businesses along Washington Street as well as others to the right of Washington. These were all destroyed by the urban renewal program. The second map from 1950 also shows a number of businesses, especially along Dryden and Summers streets. The structures at the upper part of the map between Dryden and Frys alley were largely demolished in the wake of Interstate 77, which was built over these two streets.

The third map from the Charleston Gazette is an overview of the Triangle area excluding the part at the top of the map that was demolished for the interstate. This map from late 1968 shows what the Triangle would look like according to the Urban Renewal Authority plan completed in the fall 1968. The residents who were evicted were led to believe there would be new housing for them after the area was razed. Accordingly, this plan shows public housing along Street No. 1 and No. 2, and along Washington Street. Moreover, there was to be high-rise for the elderly along Summers Street. None of these were ever built.

The high-rise shown against the Elk River was built, as well as one of the two private housing projects shown on Washington Street. In addition, a private housing project on Court Street was completed. All this, however, was far short of the housing promised in the plan. When the housing was finally built ten to fifteen years had elapsed since the area was demolished.

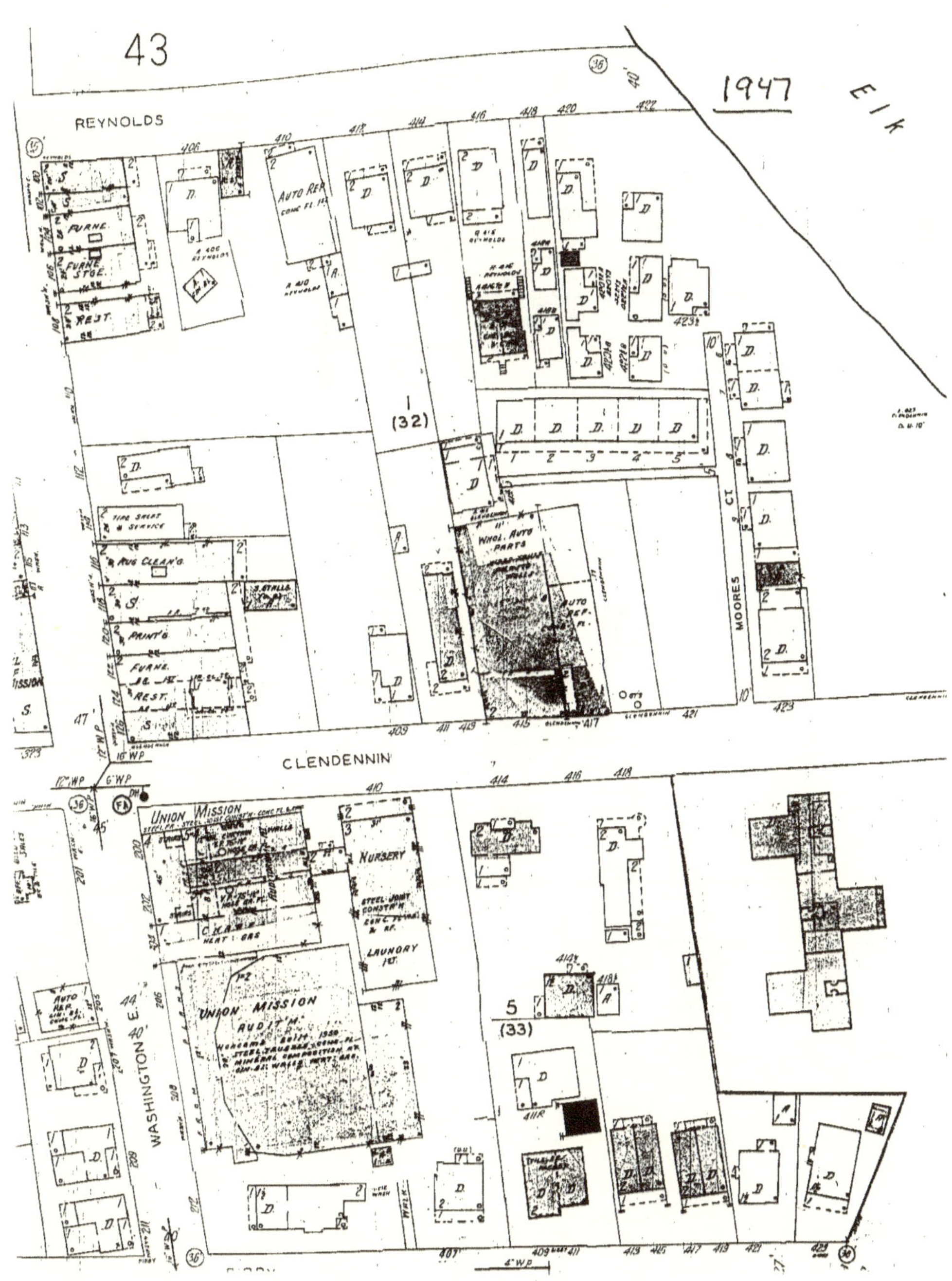
43
1947
ELK
REYNOLDS
CLENDENNIN
WASHINGTON E.
MOORES CT.
UNION MISSION
UNION MISSION AUDIT'M.
NURSERY
LAUNDRY
AUTO REP.
WHOL. AUTO PARTS
RUG CLEAN'G
PRINT'G
FURNE.
REST.

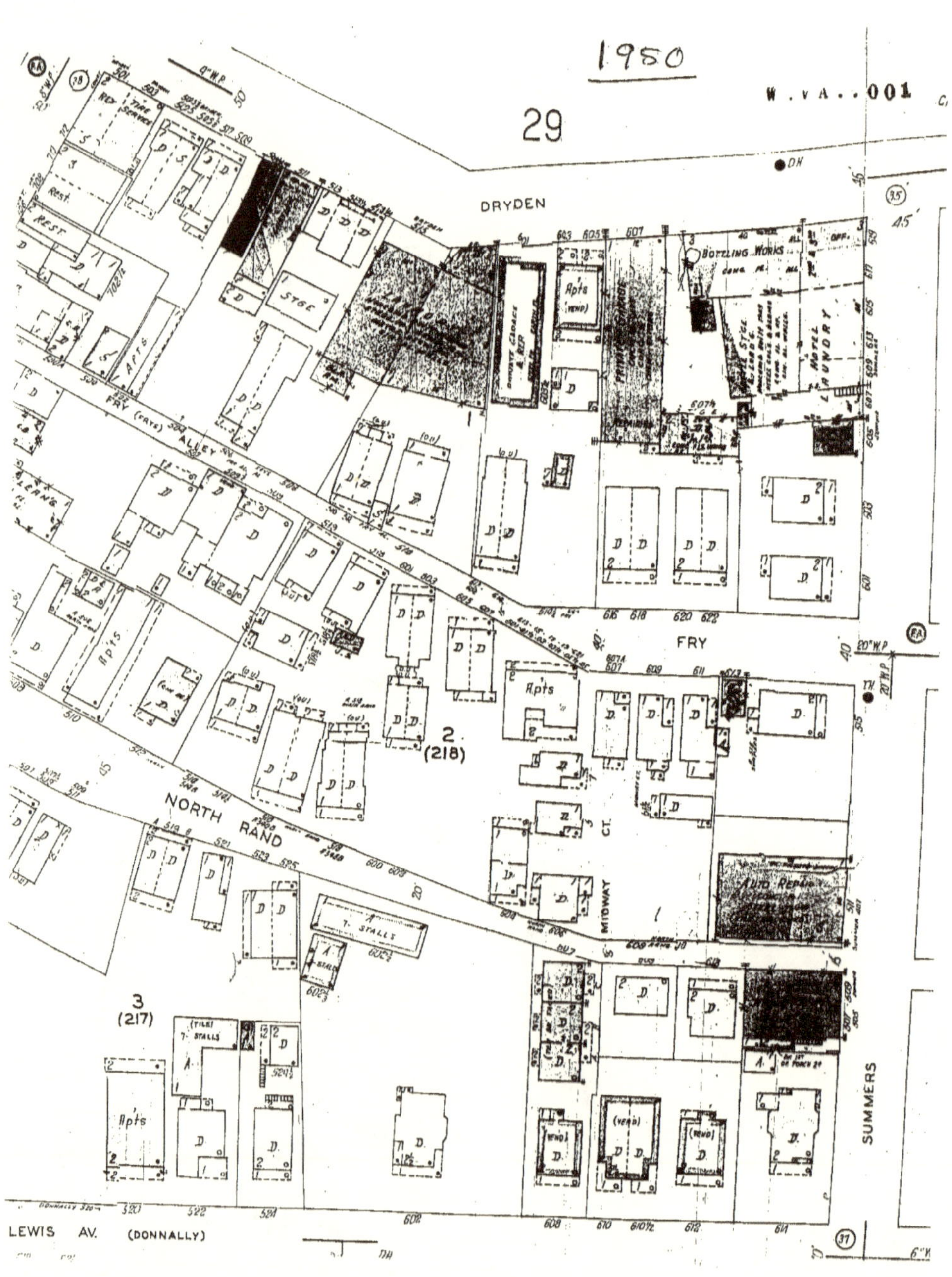
1950
29
W. VA. . 001
DRYDEN
BOTTLING WORKS
HOTEL LAUNDRY
FRY ALLEY
FRY
NORTH RAND
MIDWAY CT.
AUTO REPAIR
SUMMERS
LEWIS AV. (DONNALLY)
2
(218)
3
(217)

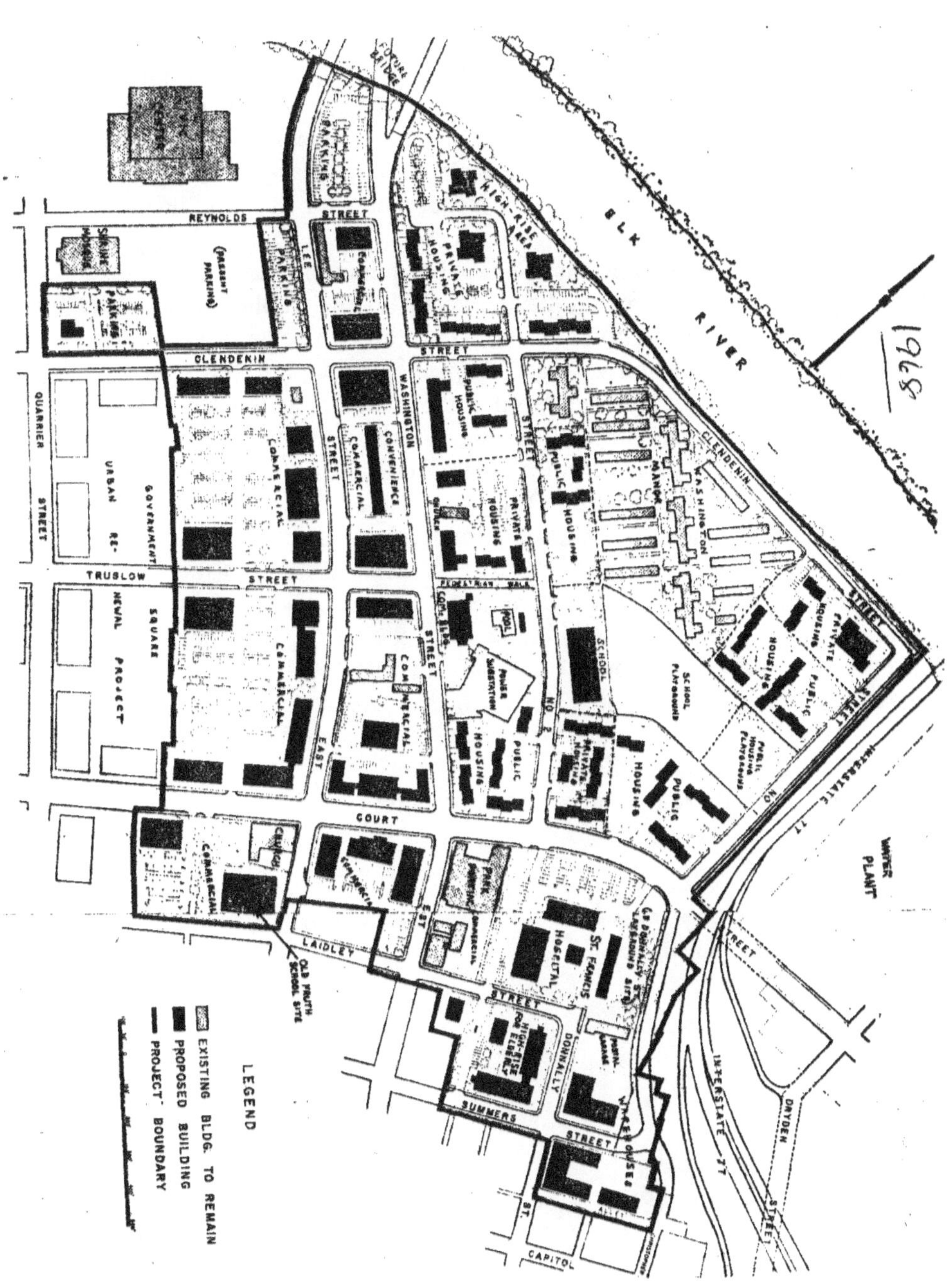
LEGEND
EXISTING BLDG. TO REMAIN
PROPOSED BUILDING
PROJECT BOUNDARY
ELK
RIVER
1968
CIVIC CENTER
REYNOLDS STREET
CLENDENIN STREET
QUARRIER STREET
TRUSLOW STREET
WASHINGTON STREET
EAST STREET
COURT STREET
LAIDLEY STREET
SUMMERS STREET
DONNALLY STREET
CAPITOL ST.
DRYDEN STREET
LEE STREET
HIGH-RISE AREA
PRIVATE HOUSING
PUBLIC HOUSING
COMMERCIAL
CONVENIENCE COMMERCIAL
URBAN RE-NEWAL PROJECT
GOVERNMENT SQUARE
PARKING
(PRESENT PARKING)
SCHOOL
SCHOOL PLAYGROUND
WASHINGTON MANOR
POOL
POWER SUBSTATION
ST. FRANCIS HOSPITAL
CHURCH
OLD FRUTH SCHOOL SITE
HIGH-RISE FOR ELDERLY
WAREHOUSES
INTERSTATE 77
WATER PLANT

The Public Sphere

Charleston has never been known for the vitality of its public sphere. Historically, the city grew dominated by private, profit making interests. Charleston's government, which of course has the responsibility for creating the public sphere in the interest of the people at large, has historically been weak with a caretaker mentality. Without a large vision for the city, the Council has been largely uninvolved, reacting to events rather than making events. An exception to this generalization is the Dawson administration of the late Thirties. Mayor Dawson, while showing little interest in the public sphere, was future oriented and had the drive to start and carry through several large projects that forever affected Charleston's future. However, it should be remembered that these projects would not have occurred without federal New Deal funds. Whether or not one agrees with its projects, the city's urban renewal program represented another case of an active government with a vision for the city. Between the Elk River and Capitol Street, its three projects planned during the late Sixties were designed to turn the area into a large commercial and retail center supplemented by high-density middle to upscale private housing. But as in the Thirties, so in the Sixties. Urban renewal was a federal program and without it Charleston would not have experienced the changes of the Sixties and beyond. Yet these exceptions to the city government's lack of vision barely touched the public sphere. Dawson's projects provided infrastructure needed by the public while urban renewal was a program of private development. Public parks, public buildings, and neighborhoods—what here constitutes the public sphere—were largely ignored by these two large developments.

Kanawha Street as seen from the South Side about 1915. Note how close the street is to the river, making parkland impossible.

The Elk River flowing through Charleston never had a chance for a river front park. Washington Manor housing project is against the river.

Riverfronts

With regard to public funds at its disposal, Charleston's city councils have always had priorities that that did not include parks and other public places. With both banks of two rivers intersecting the city, the potential for at least part of the shore becoming a public treasury in the form of a park would have appeared to be great. But the will was never there. In an atmosphere of an unimpeded private sector, Charleston's riverfronts principally developed as private domains with industry and wealthy individuals for the most part appropriating the shoreline. In this regard, Charleston was like most American cities, such as Pittsburgh, Philadelphia, Cincinnati, and Morgantown that had turned their riverfronts over to private interests. Those cities that went the other direction toward public waterfront parks stand out. Few cities can match Chicago's thirty-mile stretch of parkland along Lake Michigan from the southside through the downtown to the northside. And few would not agree that the lakefront park has added immeasurably to Chicago's quality of life. Charleston's quality of life has never been enriched in this manner.

With the exception of the walkways along the northside of the Kanawha River that date from the late Thirties, Charleston's riverfronts along both the Elk and Kanawha rivers have been and are characterized by private use with little public access. In the early part of the 20th Century, industry had located on both sides of the Elk. On the river's east side, the Charleston Lumber Company was located near Rand Street and the railroad tracks, and at Spring Street the Diamond Ice and Coal Company took up a large riverfront area. From Washington Street to the north, Water Street ran parallel and too close to the river to allow for parkland.[1] In some areas, private housing had been built against the river. In 1939 after slum housing had been cleared from the banks of the Elk, the Washington Manor housing project was built, but it was designed with a street in front of the project close to the river, making a park in that area impossible. It was much the same story on the westbank. Private housing and industry dominated the shoreline. When the Glen Elk Company prior to 1900 began purchasing land from the suspension bridge at Charleston Street up the Elk and began to sell building lots, public access to the shore was denied.

Likewise the south bank of the Kanawha has never seen developed parkland. Early in the 1900's when parts of the bank were in a natural state, nearby residents found places to swim. One popular swimming "hole" was near the point were Lick Branch (across from Elizabeth Street) emptied into the Kanawha. But the city never assumed any control of the riverbank for a permanent park or for recreation use. Part of the problem was the C&O railroad tracks that had been laid in 1873. In the area between the tracks and the river, Route 61 developed. West of the South Side Bridge, the area between the highway and the river was too narrow for a satisfactory park. Yet early in the 20th Century, there was some industrial use in this area. We have seen that the Ward Manufacturing Plant, for example, which lasted until the Thirties, was located just west of the bridge. East of the bridge in the South Ruffner area, the highway and the railroad tracks veered away from the river leaving ample riverfront acreage for parkland, but the city never acted. Beginning in 1947, the South Ruffner riverbank began to fill up with private educational and business concerns.

In Kanawha City, the Mohers original 1905 plat had set aside a riverfront lot for parkland, while other riverfront property was platted for manufacturing use. It all remained undeveloped and in 1929 when Kanawha City was annexed to Charleston, it was still undeveloped and remained so throughout the Thirties. As with South Ruffner, the city showed no interest in riverfront parkland in Kanawha City. As we have seen later developers eliminated the Mohers' riverfront park site, and subsequently the entire Kanawha City riverfront was taken for upscale private homesteads and a private marina.

The north bank of the Kanawha, which included the original Charleston, has never received consideration for parkland. Prior to 1900 private commercial interests developed along the riverbank from the Elk to the downtown area. East of the downtown, except for eight houses between Morris and Bradford streets, Kanawha Street ran close to the river, and houses and other developments never took place on the river side. Likewise, there was never any space against the river for parkland. The riverfront project of the late Thirties resulted in public space along the Kanawha for nearly five miles from the Patrick Street Bridge east to the Kanawha City Bridge. This was and continues to be a pleasant amenity, which previously had been denied to the public, but what was left for pedestrian use was a mere sliver of land. During the riverfront project of the late Thirties, fill and stabilization of the embankment allowed Kanawha Street to be widened to four lanes, but a park was never part of the planning. Instead of parkland the public got a street level sidewalk separated from speeding automobiles by an approximate one-foot concrete barrier. No room was allotted for a row of trees to better separate the thoroughfare from the walkway. A second lower walkway was quieter and safer, but was just as narrow as the upper walk. As with the upper sidewalk, the design of the lower walk did not allow for a row of trees. Ideally, trees could have been placed between the sidewalk and the river in order to protect walkers from the Summer sun. So narrow were both walkways that pedestrians could not be separated from bicycle riders.

Any rational design attempts to connect public recreation space and parkland to nearby neighborhoods. But obviously, the Boulevard with its four and five lands of traffic bordering the walkway serves as a barrier rather than a connector to the neighboring residential areas. This fact only emphasizes that the primary purpose of the entire riverfront project was to move automobiles as fast as possible and only secondarily to provide a pedestrian amenity. However, after completion of the

1930's project, the city developed two areas along the river wider than the walkways, one of which allows for recreation. Having limited recreational use was Magic Island located just west of the Elk River and the interstate bridge. Not even in existence when the Boulevard was constructed, the landmass originated in the Spring of 1948 as an accumulation of silt and debris in the aftermath of heavy flooding. Later dumping and filling resulted in an "island" about one-half mile long and 500 feet wide. When the fill attached it to the shore, it became city property. (As an island, the Corps of Engineers had jurisdiction). The name incidentally resulted from a contest in which residents submitted proposed names. In the first decades of its existence, the city ignored its possibilities, and in the words of the Gazette, it became "a beer strewn swamp." In 1987 with the support of Mayor Mike Roark and West Side councilman, Steve Brown, the city committed funds to clean it up. In June 1990, the Charleston Urban Renewal Authority provided $200,000 to help turn the former island into a park. Opening in April 1992, it is used for volleyball and a play area.[2] The lack of trees give it a barren look, but its real failure is not as park in itself, but in its separation from the West Side neighborhood by the four lane thoroughfare.

The second area on the riverside of the Boulevard that expands beyond the two walkways is Haddad Riverfront Park, extending from Capitol Street three blocks west to Court Street. This site had been constructed as the city levee as part of the late Thirties riverfront project. However, the switchback ramp had turned into a parking area as boat use declined. In June 1984, the Council passed an ordinance that provided for a riverfront park at the levee. Various designs were considered beginning in 1983 with one that would cost $2.3 million and ending in 1991 with a final approval of a Corps of Engineer design for $8.5 million, of which the Corps paid one-half of the cost. Other large contributions toward funding the cost included $1.5 million by the Charleston Urban Renewal Authority, $300,00 by the Clay Foundation, and $500,000 by Charleston businessman Fred Haddad, for whom the park was named.[3]

Opening in June 1995, Haddad Park has been a disappointment. It began with a mark against it because like Magic Island, it was separated from downtown by four lanes of traffic. Moreover, although called a "park," it is principally a 5000 seat, concrete amphitheater. Small, slopping, grassy patches are at each end, and at the east end are two small buildings, one housing restrooms, the other a concession stand. The park is used for just one event per year: the regatta extending a few days on each side of Labor Day. But even for this event, the amphitheater has been slighted. A performer at the 2000 regatta preferred to do his show in the blocked off Kanawha Boulevard rather than the theatre.[4] Since the "park" is not part of a larger greenspace area with recreation facilities and picnic areas, its separation from downtown gives it an isolated look. Its treeless, barren, and concrete surface insure that Charleston residents largely ignore it.

Magic Island as it looks today from under the interstate bridge. Four lanes of traffic divide it from the West Side neighborhoods.

Although a rainy day when this contemporary photograph was taken, Haddad Riverfront Park, downtown, is usually just as devoid of visitors on a clear day.

Lost opportunities

Before moving from the riverfronts to attempts to establish parks elsewhere, we should define the type of park under discussion. By a "park" it is here meant a reasonably large, well maintained greenspace area that the public uses for walking, reading, picnicking, meetings, festivals and the like. A well-maintained park would have floral landscaping, benches, and walkways. A small area of the park would be set aside as a play area for small children. Such a park can be called a greenspace park in order to distinguish it from ball fields where formal athletic events are scheduled. In the following discussion, some Charleston officials have called a greenspace park a "passive" or "quiet" park. The ideal location of such a park would be within existing neighborhoods, making accessibility easy for many residents. Huntington's seventy-five acres Ritter Park represents such ideal urban park. Charleston's downtown Davis Park and the East End's Ruffner Park, although pleasant sitting areas, are far too small for an ideal urban park. Parks of their size are commonly called pocket parks.

Although not greenspace parks, mention should be made of two amusement parks. Beginning about 1900, Edgewood Park was established at the top of the Edgewood subdivision. Owned by the Charleston Traction Company, it was a pleasant, shady place where families took a picnic lunch listened to concerts and spent the day. Its major attractions included a skating rink, penny arcade, and a merry-go-round.[5] About the time Edgewood closed, a larger amusement park, known as Luna Park, opened on the West Side in June 1913. It was larger than Edgewood and more centrally located along Columbia Boulevard (Kanawha Blvd) in the area of present day Park Avenue and Park Drive. Streetcars brought many residents to the park. One line ran east on Central Avenue to Park Avenue, which was the main entrance. The popular park attracted many excursion boat visitors from the Ohio River cities of Point Pleasant and Gallipolis. Features of the park included picnic areas, a roller coaster and other midway rides, a skating rink, and pony rides. Sections of the park were wooded with revines and walking paths. However, residents and visitors enjoyed the park for just a decade.[6] On May 10,1923, a spectacular fire swept through the park. The damage was so great that the owners could not raise funds for rebuilding. The acreage was shortly acquired by the Luna Park Land Company, which divided it into building lots and began to sell them. By 1928, there were still over four acres of the former park that had not been developed and were being used by neighborhood children as a playground. These empty acres provided the city with its best opportunity ever to secure a centrally located, bottomland park. The city all but had it in its hand, but gave it back.

The Peoples Exchange Bank, which held title to the four acres, offered it to the city for $40,000. Mayor Wertz responded favorably and took the offer to the Council meeting on October 1,1928. By a ten to eight majority, the Council authorized the Mayor to purchase the former parkland. However, in the next few days opposition to the proposed purchase developed as a petition on the West Side began to circulate. Wertz felt bound to call a special Council meeting a week later on October 8 in order to reconsider the Luna Park issue. Several Councilmembers had changed their minds regarding the purchase, maintaining that disapproving constituents had contacted them. Wertz spoke at length defending the Council's previous action to authorize purchase. Moreover Wertz maintained that in his campaign the previous year he had promised the West Side a park. In addition, he stated that no one over the past week had contacted him to protest a possible purchase of the park. Instead Wertz could point to the action of the West Side Woman's Club that had went on record supporting the park purchase. At this special meeting, the Mayor came armed with thirteen appraisals, all which stated that $40,000 was a fair price. The Charleston Real Estate Board put the value of the acreage offered to the city at $45,000. All of the other twelve appraisals valued the land between $40,000 and $50,000. The Council was undeterred and voted seventeen to four to rescind their vote of the previous week.[7] Wertz cast one of the four dissenting votes. Later the acreage was developed for building lots, and other than the street design, no trace of the park remains. Some of the streets in this area depart from the grid pattern of the adjoining areas. This is because the developer platted lots along the park's walking paths.

We have seen in chapter six that Brisbane Walker's plat on the West Side included a bottomland park of two square blocks. Of all Charleston's developers and land companies, only Walker and the Mohers in Kanawha City rose above the profit motive to set aside part of their developments for parkland. Well located, Walker's proposed park would have been surrounded by residential neighborhoods. However, Walker's plan, to repeat, never materialized because of his financial reverses in the 1873 Panic.

While Luna Park failed to become a municipal park, the city during the Wertz administration was establishing a municipal park on a hillside just below Spring Hill Cemetery overlooking the East End. When the Charleston General Hospital in 1924 vacated its hillside location below the cemetery, Mayor Wertz proposed that the city owned twenty-eight acre site be turned into a municipal park. There were no funds in the budget for the development of the park, but city officials hoped to secure tangible support from civic organizations such as the Women's Club, the Rose Society, and the Garden Club. The city Council, consumed with streets and traffic during the Twenties, never committed city funds for this park.[8]

It was not until the following DeVan administration (1931-1935) that the city put any effort into developing the park, now referred to as City Park. In May 1933, Mayor DeVan had city workers under the federal WPA program clearing and improving the hillside land. Roadways through the park were built and civic organizations hoped to have shrubbery, floral gardens, and other attractions by Spring 1934.[9] Little of City Park appears in the record, but it continued to exist for about forty years. In its surveys of Charleston published periodically from 1901 to 1940, the Charleston Chamber of Commerce first listed City Park in its 1931 publication. It remained an entity until the early 1970's when the city sold the land for construction of high rise housing following the displacement of Triangle residents. We know from 1966 remarks of a parks commission member that City Park was a" passive park," that is, without recreation facilities. However, the Daily Mail did not appear to give City Park any credence. In remarks over the years, the newspaper refused to even acknowledge it as a "park." As the Kanawha Boulevard was nearing completion, proposals were made to call the thoroughfare a "parkway." In disagreeing with this designation, the Daily Mail in 1940 wrote that there was not a park within ten miles.[10] City Park was in fact about one mile from the eastern end of Kanawha Boulevard. Again in 1960 the Daily Mail still did not acknowledge City Park, for in connection with the interstate controversy, the paper wrote that Charleston "never had the foresight to plan a municipal park." Finally the Mail in a 1966 editorial wrote: "For a number of reasons, none of them credible, Charleston has never had a municipal park."[11] A park to be worthy of the name must be more than a vacant piece of land with a sign at its entrance. Apparently the Daily Mail felt that City Park did not rise above vacant property with a name. In any case, its location at the far northern edge of the city on a hillside made its accessibility inconvenient and not within walking range of many residents. It added nothing to the aesthetics of Charleston's bottomland and little to the enjoyment of the residents.

As the days of City Park were numbered, the possibility of another municipal park arose that would replace City Park. This was the proposed Copenhaver Park. It never materialized, but if it had its disadvantages would have been identical to those of City Park. It was too remote and inconvenient from most city residents to be of much use to them. Located on the West Side in the far hillsides of North Charleston, it was even farther away from the population centers of the city than was City Park. Its remoteness may have played a part in the tepid effort to make the proposed park a reality. The Daily Mail, which had historically criticized the city for its lack of a municipal park, supported the establishment of Copenhaver Park. Unfazed by its remoteness, the Mail in June 1966 editorialized: "The geography, which in some ways is a handicap to the development of the conventional park, has its compensations, notably in the isolation of the area from an otherwise densely settled community."[12] The proposed park site covering eighty acres had originally been purchased by the city as a site to dump residue from a sewage treatment plant. But in the Summer of 1959, the city had an opportunity to secure $50,000 worth of free bulldozing and grading. Just prior to his death in August 1959, Mayor Copenhaver (hence the park name) wanting to make use of the free grading proposed a park for the site. Copenhaver's successor, John Shanklin, in March 1960 agreed to spend $5000 for a feasibility study of the area for a park.[13] While the bureaucracy dragged on, Mayor Shanklin continued to express support for the park and had named a Copenhavor Park committee. In early 1966, this committee presented a plan for the proposed park's development. However, in March 1966, the Parks and Recreation Commission rejected the plan of the park committee. Three reasons were given: the plan was for an all sports complex and the Commission wanted a "quiet" park for family picnics, citing the present use of City Park; secondly, funding priority would go to Legion Field along Seventh Avenue, which was being developed for athletic events; and finally the Commission was concerned about a clear title to the site and that no cost study for maintenance had been done.[14]

As individuals made sporadic attempts to establish a municipal park, they were handicapped by a lack of a strong park constituency in Charleston. Without an active interest group, the Council as it had dawdled with respect to creating governmental machinery for planning, saw no urgency in creating a parks commission that might spearhead parks development. The newly created Municipal Planning Commission recognized this deficiency in 1938. In its first biennial report, the Commission wrote: "The lack of public recreation areas has been found by the Planning Commission to be perhaps the most serious deficiency in Charleston."[15] Upon the recommendation of the planning commission, the Council in September 1939 created the Charleston Parks Commission and in June 1944 renamed it the Parks and Recreation Commission. Council poorly funded the body and for years went without permanent staff. In 1940, Council appropriated $3000 for the Commission, $4000 in 1941, and $7000 in 1942. The name change to include the word "Recreation" has ever since largely defined the thrust of the Commission. In spite of the funding pittance, the Commission set about to maintain a system of children's playgrounds throughout the city. In 1943, the city operated sixteen segregated playgrounds, four of which were for Negro children.[16]

Even with a Parks and Recreation Commission in place, there was no apparent push for a large greenspace park, preferring instead to concentrate on juvenile recreation. This outlook did not change even after the Council in the Spring of 1974 created the Parks and Recreation Department with a full time director. Soon after the department was established, the Commission made up of volunteer citizens began to dissipate. The Daily Mail in November 1981 took note that the Commission had not met with the director or staff in about five years.[17] But whether as a commission or department, Charleston's park officials have within the city's governmental structure been politically weak with the director serving at the pleasure of the Mayor and the department at the mercy of the Council for funding.

For an effective model of park management, Charleston need have looked any farther than Huntington. After the city of Huntington established Ritter Park by land purchase and private land donation, city administrators early in the 1920's were concerned that there was no consistent plan of park development. A city Civic Club led by the Rotary and Kiwanis clubs began a drive for more parkland. The club raised funds, purchased land, and gave it to the city for park development. Significantly, the club went further and provided for a new park management. It petitioned a cooperative state Legislature to create a Board of Park Commissioners, and in 1925, this independent body began to function. Structurally, it was as strong as it could get with six elected members and the power to set a funding levy for park acquisition and maintenance independent of the city Council.[18]

If Charleston lacked a governmental thrust and a citizen constituency for park development, there remained the possibility of contributions, but the city has never had a history of strong, philanthropic giving.[19] Isolated examples of philanthropy can be found, as Humphries$100,000 to the library, but given the large amount of wealth created by the coal, gas, and chemical industries, little of it has found its way to the city by way of wills and trusts. Mayor Dawson, in his campaigns for Mayor advocated the establishment of a municipal park, yet he did not push Council for funds. Instead he made a pitch for public donations of property. In his city outlook for 1938, Dawson said: "While a park is badly needed, I do not see how we can purchase one during the coming year. I had hoped and still hope that some civic minded citizen who owns a suitable site would come forward and donate it outright … to the city."[20]

Within a year of Dawson's plea for a private contribution of parkland, the Union Mission offered the city its 800 acre Abney Park located in Mission Hollow on the South Side, about two miles off MacCorkle Avenue behind the present Watt Powell Park. This offer from the Board of Directors of the Mission was contingent upon the city agreeing to further develop the area for parkland and recreation purposes. In its biennial report of 1939, the city's Municipal Planning Commission favored taking possession of the property, and by the Spring of 1939 the Commission had completed a proposed development plan that included playfields, tennis courts, hiking trails, a lake, and an aquatic garden.[21] Once the Mission's Board approved the plan, it would be ready to deed the land to the city. But when it came to acting on his statements purporting to be in favor of a city park, Dawson backed off. While giving lip service to a park, his interests were in the current riverfront project, street paving, a new bridge, and other large capital projects. Unlike Mayor Wertz, Dawson did not even try to obtain the parkland. In September 1939 the Mayor announced that because of the large investment on public improvements, the city would not have funds for Abney Park and, moreover, the city would not have funds for several years.[22] Although this park would not have been centrally located within existing neighborhoods, much of it was flat, and would have given the city a valuable park and recreation area. The land lay unused for nearly three decades, and during this period, there is no record that the city tried to obtain the property. The city's 1962 comprehensive plan made a reference to the fact that Abney Park never materialized. Later in the 1960's, Union Mission began to make use of the land. The Mission had lost its properties on Court Street and Summers Street to urban renewal and began to move its facilities to Mission Hollow, taking up the bottomland of the property. In the 1960's, the Mission leased a portion of the 800 acres to a private company for a landfill where Charleston's waste was dumped. Later in the Sixties, it sold the landfill area to the leasee. As part of the original 800 acres offered the city, there is still about 250 acres of hilly land in its natural state. In its 1996 comprehensive plan, the Municipal Planning Commission recommended that the city attempt to develop the site for park use.[23] However, this acreage is at the southern end of the property originally offered, and with development of the northern end of the property by the Mission, public accessibility would be poor.

A case can be made that the city's refusal to purchase Luna Park and to accept Union Mission's offer of parkland had negative repercussions beyond these possible parks. When a city already has parkland, as opposed to having none, it becomes easier to organize a private park trust fund in order to raise funds, accept contributions, and establish an endowment from which additional parkland can acquired. Without a base of at least one park, it is difficult to secure investor interest. In July 1928, the same year that the Charleston City Council refused to purchase Luna Park, the city of Wheeling accepted the 1615 acres Waddington Farm from the will of Earl Oglebay. Having the showplace of Oglebay Park, the Wheeling Park Commission (an independent body in the manner of Huntington's park commission) was able to establish in 1945 the Parks System Trust Fund.[24] Over the years, this trust has received many contributions and bequests. Charleston has attempted a trust of this sort. In December 1967, Charleston at-large councilman, John Wells, persuaded the Council to establish a private non-profit corporation for the purpose of acquiring and developing parkland in the city. Called the Capitol Park Authority, Inc, it received a few contributions, including $1000 from councilman Wells, and passed from the scene.[25] Without an existing base of parkland, it appeared to have little legitimacy. A similar private trust was recommended in the 1996 city comprehensive plan for the purpose of acquiring "openlands" and to "develop park spaces," but no action has been taken.

Cato Park

Charleston seemed to have an affinity for remote hillsides as possible park locations. After the failure to establish Copenhaver Park, city officials began a pursuit of the Edgewood Country Club's golf course that overlooked the city from its West Side hilltop. By 1968, the country club was establishing a new golf course at Sissonville and had decided to sell the Edgewood course, adjacent to its clubhouse, which would be kept along with the pool, and tennis courts. Mayor Elmer Dotson wanted to purchase the site, which included some additional land just outside the golf course, but by April 1968 the parties were unable to agree to a price. Fearing the course might be sold to another party, the city sued the Edgewood Building Association in an attempt to force a selling price. Before the end of the year, the city had agreed to purchase the 91 acres site for $450,000 and paid $50,000 down. In May 1969, the Council voted to pay another $175,000. The remaining balance of $225,000 was to be funded by a grant from the federal Bureau of Outdoor Recreation. Although the city took possession of the property in November 1969, it was not until February 1972 that a development plan for the park was ready. Approved by the Council later in the month, the plan retained the golf course and on the additional land added an olympic size swimming pool with a bathhouse, twelve tennis courts, a picnic area, and a children's play area. By August 1975, the $678,000 pool and bathhouse opened; the tennis courts were ready for play by Spring 1976. The total cost for the entire project amounted to about $1.3 million. Another Bureau of Outdoor Recreation grant covered $300,000 of the total and a bequest of $224,000 from the estate of Judge Henry S. Cato reduced the amount obligated by the city to something over $700,000. Hence the name Cato Park and not Edgewood Park.[26]

This 91 acres acquisition, however, did not give the city a greenspace park. The area remained for the most part what it had been when the city purchased it: a nine-hole golf course. The swimming pool and tennis courts gave the city a fourth swimming pool and additional tennis courts. By October 1994, the Gazette reported that the tennis courts had not been maintained, that the surface was cracked with weeds protruding, making the courts unusable. More than three years later, nothing had been done to repair the courts, and in the Spring of 1998, the Parks and Recreation Director announced that the courts would not be repaired and instead he would accept a contribution from a benefactor to turn the space into a soccer field. In June 1997, a six-tenths mile trail, called the Garrison Trail, was completed. Making a circular route through a wooded area above the golf course, the well-designed scenic trial includes a chipped wood walking bed and educational markers describing the flora and fauna of the area.[27]

There are other parks to mention, but these will be better considered within the context of the discussion of public buildings and neighborhoods.

A 'sidewalkless' street in Fort Hill, typical in the south side neighborhood.

Neighborhoods and single use zoning

The public sphere is not limited to municipal owned property as public parks and buildings. It includes neighborhoods with variety enough to encourage residents to use them in a collective manner. For this to happen, the neighborhood must be of mixed use, meaning that among the homes are such conveniences and necessities of daily life as parks, grocery stores, lodges, restaurants, dry cleaners, and the like that for many people can be reached by walking. One urban critic has called these neighborhood centers and shops "third places,"[28] that is, places of socialization outside of home and work. Recent writings by urban planners, academics, and others have made the argument that the nation's widespread use of single use zoning tends to thwart neighborhood vitality while encouraging sprawl. [29]

Charleston's zoning practices, since its first zoning ordinance in 1939, has been hostile to neighborhoods that encourage random and easy socialization. Like most cities in the country, Charleston has striven to separate residential from commercial use, and both from industrial use. On a limited scale, there is an argument for such separation, and as we saw earlier, when first adopted, single use zoning tended to rationalize the city's random growth. But carried too far it can be like monocultural farming: a bland, dull sameness, resulting in a denial of community and, in an increasingly environmental conscious society, overuse of the automobile. Had single use zoning been in practice early in the 20th Century, the vitality of the Washington-Shrewsberry area would never have occurred. The area would have been either all residential or all commercial. Areas of the West Side also developed with a mix of small businesses and housing. Like the Washington-Shewsberry neighborhood, the West Side grew organically with Charleston's early entrepreneurs opening small stores and businesses needed by nearby neighbors. At mid-century, Main Street, while largely residential, had a food market in the second of its six blocks. In the eastern most block of the street, over ten businesses were located. Central Avenue, extending west from the Five Corners area, was a mix of businesses and private housing. Businesses in the seven-block length in the 1950's included restaurants, several grocers, a dry cleaners, a bicycle shop, and a printer. The West Side's principal thoroughfare has been Washington Street (early it was called Charleston Street); it grew primarily as a commercial and shopping area.[30] The streets that intersected with Washington, Main, and Central were generally residential, and residents of the cross streets enjoyed walking access to much of the West Side's retail area. Again like the Washington-Shrewsberry neighborhood, the West Side in the first half of the century was characterized by stable, home owning families. For many of the same societal and economic reasons that adversely affected Washington-Shrewsberry—decline of blue collar jobs and changing family patterns—the

West Side began in the 1960's and 1970's to become more unstable with a higher crime rate.

The south side suburbs of Louden Heights, South Hills, and Fort Hill had a different history than the West Side. They were from the beginning platted as exclusively residential communities. South Hills in the area just across from the South Side Bridge had its first plat in 1906, but most of the South Side began to be platted in the 1920's, nearly two decades prior to Charleston's first zoning. However, developers of the South Side enforced their own brand of "zoning" through deed restrictions that mandated one single-family house per lot at a prescribed minimum cost. Lots in such plats were not set aside for hardware stores, food stores, and dry cleaners. Like the earlier developed Edgewood, the South Side was seen as an escape from the commercialism of the central city. With the growing ownership of the automobile, it was thought that homeowners could drive across the bridge to downtown for shopping purposes. When Charleston's zoning appeared, the ordinance, as we have seen, merely codified the deed restrictions of the South Side developers. A single exception to residential zoning in South Hills is a small commercial area just at the top of Bridge Street hill. This developed well before the zoning ordinance when entrepreneurs carved out a small shopping area. This area persisted, and the city's zoning map from the beginning has put a commercial stamp on this small and, for nearly residents, a convenient area.

Charleston's zoning since 1939 has remained single use, but more gradations within the residential and commercial zones have been made. While the most restrictive use is reserved for single family housing, a less restrictive zone permits four unit apartment buildings to be mixed with single family houses. Still another zone allows for larger apartments and tourist homes. Density of housing here is the guideline between zones. In all residential zones, land uses other than for homes are permitted, but these are generally limited to a park, church, or school. By special permit, the zoning authorities will consider other narrow uses such as a museum, art gallery, or home occupation. It is interesting to note that in spite of the city's historic weak effort to establish parks, the zoning ordinances over the years have permitted parks in all residential zones.[31] Yet while putting a positive value on parks, city zoning law does not require that a developer when designing a new subdivision to set aside acreage for parkland, thereby all but insuring that the development will not have a park. By accident, one park has appeared on the South Side. This is Danner Meadows Park in Fort Hill. The park's evolution began in the early 1980's when an interstate contracting firm got permission to dump stone and dirt at the site. This turned into a seven acres greenspace park set within a pleasant middle class neighborhood. It features benches and an exercise track around the perimeter of a grassy area.[32] Although it is a type of park that would be an asset to any neighborhood, the Council in the

Summer of 2000 took steps to negate its value to the Fort Hill residents by designating it as a soccer field for organized leagues.

When it comes to commercial use, the zoning ordinance draws a hard line between such use and residential areas. The ordinance lists several pages of small business categories, none of which is permitted in residential zones. More experimental developers who may want to design new communities with mixed uses are under the city's zoning law prohibited from doing so. Only a monocultural development is permitted.

As a result of deed restrictions followed by the city's practice of single use zoning, the South Side is largely an area of bedroom communities. Any activity that occurs there largely takes place in the private home or yard. Perhaps what most epitomizes the dearth of public life in the South Side neighborhoods is the lack of sidewalks. A few sections do have sidewalks, such as Bridge Street from the bridge to the top of the hill, but for the most part, South Side communities have no place for walking other than the street. The area's hilly terrain has resulted in streets that are narrow, curved, and slopping, making them hazardous for driving. To walk on them is even more hazardous. Consequently, few people are found outside their property. It of course adds to the developers' cost to install sidewalks, and just as they saw that setting aside parks would reduce profits, so they also ignored sidewalks as a luxury they could not afford. The city's subdivision regulations have been no more enlightened, for even today sidewalks are not mandated. Without nearby public areas or retail outlets, single use zoning tends to force residents to drive out of the neighborhood for nearly everything, putting a premium on the private automobile. Since it is illegal to integrate small retail stores that are necessary to daily life, single use planning typically carves out an area along a feeder road and zones it for commercial use, allowing a developer to construct a plaza along with a large mandated parking lot. The feeder road then develops into a busy, congested thoroughfare leading inevitably to a large road-widening project. All this has happened on Charleston's Corridor G or route 119, which serves as the South Side's feeder road.

As single use zoning puts a premium on the private automobile, so it also can elevate the importance of the private home. Since property values are important to all homeowners and paramount to many, owners can feel secure that in an area zoned exclusively single family residential, the property values will be maintained and most likely appreciate. Since the initial 1939 ordinance zoned the South Side as single family home lots, homeowners could feel that with all neighboring lots having the same characteristics, their own homes could not fall in value. (Of course since the South Side has expanded, later zoning has permitted more density in certain areas). In response to such property friendly zoning restrictions, individuals of means have built many outstanding houses in Louden Heights, South Hills, and Fort Hill. The Grosscup Road area of South

Hills became an early favorite site for the wealthy to build expensive and what proved to be historically significant houses. First known as Grandview because the houses on the northeast side of the road commanded a spectacular view of the Kanawha River and the older Charleston. Between 1906 and 1920 over twenty significant houses, ten of which were designed by H. Rus Warne, were built on property marketed and restricted by the South Charleston Improvement Company and the Grosscup-Meyers Real Estate Company. The original owners of these homes were some of Charleston's major industrial and political leaders. Because of the quality of the houses and the importance of the owners in the city's early 20th Century history, twenty-two houses on Grosscup, Roscommon, and Roller roads were included in 1983 on the National Register of Historic Places. The area is known as the Grosscup Road Historic District.[33]

The development of the East End differed from that of the West Side and South Side. Long before Charleston's affluent residents began moving to Edgewood, the East End had become the city's most fashionable and upscale neighborhood. Prior to the advent of subdivisions and land plats, wealthy Charleston businessmen in the 19th Century began building distinguished homes along Kanawha Street that looked across the river. The oldest house still standing is the Holly House built in 1815 by Daniel Ruffner and now located on the west side of the Governor's Mansion. In the first decade of the 20th century, businessman, O.F. Payne and coal operator John Carver built homes to east of Ruffner Avenue that still remain. East of the present Capitol, families of means occupied several fine homes in the 1920's. By the 1920's, the East End streets of Virginia, Quarrier, and Lee were replete with expensive and stately houses. Unlike the South Side in the Twenties, deed restrictions did not prohibit apartments, and consequently many apartment buildings were erected along Virginia, Quarrier, Bradford, and Ruffner streets. The eight units Virginia Apartments on Bradford Street, completed in 1907, was one of area's first apartment buildings.[34] Another departure from single family houses was the construction of the Woman's Club building on Virginia Street at Elizabeth Street. Dedicated in March 1929, the building was designed by Walter F. Martens, who had been the architect of the Governor's Mansion that was completed on the boulevard in 1926. The appearance of the stately houses and buildings of the East End was enhanced by the wide sidewalks that were constructed as the Ruffner additions of the early century permitted the streets to be continued to the east.

As if to show that Charleston's initial zoning was not a refined process, the 1939 zoning map designated Virginia, Quarrier, and Lee streets to the east of Ruffner as residential B, the second lowest density category. This was the same zoning type given to most of the West Side where it was common for houses and businesses to be located on the same street. However, Virginia, Quarrier, and Lee streets were devoid of retail and commercial outlets. But residents of these and other East End streets had only to go as far as the bordering streets of Washington and Duffy to find food markets, drug stores, restaurants, beauty and barber shops, a hardware store, an appliance store, a jewelry store, and a movie theatre. Businesses of this sort were principally concentrated from the 1920's to the mid 1960's on Washington Street from Elizabeth Street to about one block west of the Capitol. Duffy Street also held a number of businesses, and its intersection with Elizabeth was an especially busy area.[35] However, as the Capitol grounds in the 1960's were readied for expansion, the commercial area of the East End began to suffer. Demolition of housing along Duffy, Washington, and other nearly streets resulted in a business decline and consequently fewer services for neighborhood residents. Coincidentally, as Washington Street several blocks to the west at Shrewsbury Street was commercially declining, so for different reasons, the upper end of Washington Street was suffering the same economic pains.

Aside from the commercial decline of Washington Street, the most pronounced East End change was taking place along Kanawha Boulevard. When the 1939 zoning map was formalized, the upper Boulevard, reflecting current reality, was designated as single family housing. That is to say, according to this map, Kanawha Boulevard had no apartments or commercial activity from Ruffner Street to the Kanawha City Bridge. However, by the Sixties, changing family patterns and the pull of suburbs had caught up with the Boulevard's large houses, and families were moving out. According to the 1955 Charleston Directory, there was just one apartment on the Boulevard north of Ruffner, this being about a sixteen-unit building in the 1500 block. But by 1965, a different street was apparent. The East End Boulevard now housed an art gallery, a home interiors company, and a realtor's office. In addition, the AFL-CIO and the Boy Scouts of America had offices between Ruffner and the Capitol. Yet in spite of the changes, the property values continued to hold, and partly because of the cost, families were not buying them. In the vacuum, law and accounting firms, labor unions, and statewide associations began to secure special zoning permits and buying the old homes. In order to protect the value of the properties, the planning commission could not be rigid. It was clear that the commercial interests wanting the houses had the financial means to maintain them. The commission then began to rezone the Boulevard. Over the years, the zoning went from the lowest to the highest density. The presence of law firms and state associations did not result in a high density of people, but the apartment buildings did, and these dwarfed the older apartments of other East End streets. The largest was Carroll Terrace, a high-rise residence for the elderly located between Ruffner and Elizabeth streets.[36] At thirteen stories and 210 units, this building's non-conformity with the Boulevard's stately houses was blatant.

As the nation's bicentennial approached, East End residents were increasingly concerned about such non-conforming structures as Carroll Terrace. After a two-year period of study by the state Historic Preservation Office, a 110-acre section of the East End was placed on the National Register of Historic Places. The boundaries of the historic area extended from the east side of Bradford Street to the Capitol grounds and included Kanawha Boulevard, Virginia and Quarrier streets as well as Ruffner, Elizabeth, and Greenbrier streets. East of the Capitol, the new historic district included only Kanawha Street from California Avenue to East Avenue. Lee Street had been included in the study area, but it failed to qualify.[37] Although there can be federal income tax breaks for homeowners, a historic designation area is largely symbolic. Increased status may accrue to the area, thereby increasing property values, but the area is not protected from unsightly buildings. In order to guard against unwanted building design, a review board is necessary, something that is not part of the historic designation process. In 1983 with the approval of the East End Association, the city Council passed an ordinance creating an architecture review board that would enforce strict building and renovation standards on property. New standards, for example, included a limit of eighty-four feet or seven stories as maximum height for Kanawha Boulevard structures and a thirty-five feet height limit elsewhere in the historic district.[38] Thus, there would be no more Carroll Terraces.

City Hall in the 1930's, about a decade after its completion. Note lack of public space around the building.

The Kanawha County Courthouse in 1970. Like City Hall it also lacks public space around the building, though there is now a small sitting on the west side of the building.

Public Buildings

From its beginnings, it appears that Charleston's founders and early developers had adopted the common American view that public buildings, while necessary, are not of paramount importance. This generalization is based neither on the architectural style nor the cost of public buildings, but on their usual commonplace and undistinguished location. Since Charleston did not have a founder who laid out a plat for the entire city, public buildings did not have a prominent site or any site on which they would be built. Cities that have grown from a designed plat are more likely to have their public buildings better sited than those cities than grew more randomly. For example, when William Penn platted Philadelphia in 1682, his design included a large, centrally located square for a city hall. It was not built for almost ninety years, but the land remained reserved all the time. Penn's plat, incidentally, was in area just two miles by one mile, making it smaller than Charleston's all bottomland area in 1900. Yet this small plat included four eight-acre public squares, which today remain as fine examples of small urban parks.[39]

Charleston's history was different. Not only did the city lack a citywide plat, but also its early founders and large landholders never set aside any part of their holdings for public use. Neither Thomas Bullitt, who in 1775 acquired 1030 acres east of the Elk River and 1240 acres west of the river, nor his brother, Cuthbert, who held the same land as of 1778 when Thomas died, donated any of their lands for a governmental, educational, or any public purpose. In 1787, George Clendenin acquired the same 1030 acres east of the Elk from Bullitt. Of the forty acres he platted into building lots, which marked the beginning of Charleston, none of the forty lots was reserved for a governmental or public purpose. They all began to be sold as private real estate ventures. Shortly Clendenin grew impatient with Charleston's growth, and in August 1796 he sold the 1030 acres minus the lots already purchased to Joseph Ruffner. Ruffner held the land until his death in 1803 when his will distributed the lands to his sons. The Ruffners, however, showed no more interest than the Bullitt Brothers and Clendenin in assigning any of their land for a civic purpose. What they did not keep, they began to sell.[40]

The property on which the courthouse and the city hall were later built was part of Clendenin's original forty lots. When the county authorities decided to move the county's business from Fort Lee, they entered the real estate market like any other corporation or individual. In 1797, the county court in effect paid $100. for the lot at Front and Third streets (later Kanawha and Court streets). The owner of the lot was George Alterson, who agreed to let the county take title to the lot in satisfaction of $100 he owed the county.[41] After purchasing the lot at Front Street, a log courthouse was built that served the county until 1817 when a more substantial two-story brick building was constructed. In December 1888, it was razed so that construction of the present courthouse could begin. Completed in 1892, it faced the river and was about midway between Kanawha and Virginia streets. This allowed for an attractive, tree-shaded plaza in front of the courthouse overlooking the river. The county spent $153,000 for the Romanesque Revival style building designed by architect Walter Higham.

In 1917, the attractive plaza was sacrificed for a $107,000 extension that took the building to the edge of Kanawha Street. The well known Charleston architect, H. Rus Warne, who we met in connection with his work on Garnet High and the Masonic Building, designed the addition. Just nine year later, the county needed still more space, and Warne's firm was again approached to add a $125,000 extension on the Virginia Street end. This addition turned the courthouse around so that the main entrance was at Virginia Street. With this addition, the courthouse now occupied the entire block between Kanawha and Virginia streets. Charleston architect, Paul Marshall, has praised the compatibility of the three sections: "Each of the three design units is noteworthy, but especially important is the manner in which the architects of the extensions were sympathetic with the previous construction and subjected their detailing to reflect the character of the adjoining work."[42] In 1990, the courthouse was placed on the National Register of Historic Places.[43]

Just across Court Street from the courthouse and facing Virginia Street is the Charleston City Hall. Like the courthouse, it is located on one of Charleston's original lots. Though not the first owner of the lot, Joseph Ruffner owned it in 1799 afterwhich it was sold and re-sold many times. The city first acquired a part of the lot in October 1882 for construction of the first city hall, which lasted until 1921. For a larger city hall, additional property was needed, and city officials opened negotiations to purchase additional sections on the same lot as well as some sections of the adjoining lot. The heirs of the Barlow and Wherle families owed the property in question, and they and the city settled on a price of $84,000.[44]After a two and one-half year construction period, the new city hall, designed by courthouse architect H. Rus Warne, was dedicated on August 31, 1923. In an editorial, the Daily Mail praised the architectural beauty of the building. However, the conservative paper added that the size of the building was suitable for a much larger city, and cautioned that the citizens should be watchful that the city government would not uselessly expand— "a fad of the present day amounting to almost a rage."[45] The new building, financed with a bond issue, set the taxpayers back about $665,000. Like the courthouse, the building itself is impressive. Its style is Renaissance Revival with four massive columns along the second floor front. Broad front steps lead to three arched front doors. Unlike the courthouse, the city hall has not been altered.

Although city and county officials took care to construct distinguished government buildings, designed by prominent architects, the location of the buildings are not prominent. They are lined up in a row with Virginia Street's other buildings, thereby symbolizing that the functions of local government are no more important than the commercial, cultural, and other endeavors of Charleston life. In the location of its public buildings, Charleston reflected the common American practice of siting government buildings so that they do not dominate the city or even an area of the city, thereby adhering to the American ethos that government is not above the people. Exceptions from Charleston's practice is more European than American. [46]

Although not sited prominently, the courthouse and city hall were historically located within easy reach of many residents of the city. In a city with a dearth of public open places, there is no record of any consideration given to placing public buildings in a campus or park like setting. Except for a rejected urban renewal plan in the 1960's, which proposed a small park along Virginia Street, there has been no thought given to creating a public space around either building. Such inattention given to open areas around public buildings contrasts sharply with the state Capitol complex in the East End. When the Capitol was completed in 1932, it stood on a sixteen acres site, hardly large enough to give the Capitol a grand campus setting. The Capitol architect, Cass Gilbert, was well aware of this shortcoming, and in a 1932 letter to Daily Mail publisher, Walter Clark, Gilbert wrote: "It is obvious that the property should be enlarged to prevent the too close intrusion of higher buildings and to provide for more ample grounds for the State Capitol."[47] Gilbert never got to see the expansion of the grounds, for he died in 1934; but some forty years later his suggestions began to be realized.

Planning started in the mid-Sixties on an enlarged Capitol complex. Initially the State Building Commission and the Charleston Planning Commission proposed a Capitol campus of eighty acres or a five-fold expansion of the present acreage. In addition to expanding to the west and north as was done, this plan called also for an expansion to the east acquiring all property from California Avenue that ran alongside the grounds to Michigan Avenue.[48] However, this plan was scaled back, and there would be no eastern expansion. As approved the project was done in two parts. First west of the Capitol, the grounds were expanded one block to present day Greenbrier Street. Until this time, there was a Duffy Street that extended between the Capitol and the Governor's Mansion, and thus Virginia and Quarrier streets extended one block farther east than they now do. The state had to negotiate and use eminent domain authority to acquire all the housing and businesses along Duffy from Washington Street to the Boulevard. On the now vacant land between Duffy and Greenbrier streets, the state began construction of the $10.6 million Cultural Center that would house the State Library, the Department of Archives and History, the museum, and an auditorium when it opened on July 11,1976. With the completion of the Cultural Center, Duffy Street had been turned into a walkway in front of the Center.[49]

As early as 1952, the state began its expansion to the north of the Capital. Across Washington Street at Duffy Street, it opened an eight-story office building. Then in the mid-Sixties, the state began to condemn and demolish private housing on the north side of Washington Street for additional offices. A two-building complex opened for state workers in July 1970. [50] However none of these office buildings initially meant an expansion of the campus, for Washington Street remained a busy city street extending uninterrupted to the rear of the Capitol and in front of the office buildings. It was not for eighteen years that the Capitol grounds would stretch across Washington Street to the office buildings. In July 1988, Washington Street at Greenbrier Street was permanently closed when work began on the War Memorial, which would be partly built on the former Washington Street.[51] For a while the traffic circle in back of the Capitol remained open with access provided from the other end of Washington Street. The War Memorial scheduled for completion within a year dragged on for nearly seven years. But the Capitol grounds were united by 1990 when Washington Street was turned into a pedestrian walkway and the traffic circle was re-designed for pedestrian use.

After the expansion, the state campus had grown to forty-three from sixteen acres. Unlike a municipal park, structures occupy much of the land area, but there still remains significant greenspace that has come to be used for festivals, relaxation, dog walking, reading, and protests—all the functions that characteristically take place in a city park that Charleston never had. The Capitol grounds have in a sense become Charleston's "municipal park."

Map Notes

1. The first map from the Sanborn Company, made in 1933, shows the former Luna Park (bottom) on the city's West Side gradually filling up five years after the city Council rejected an offer to purchase the area for a city park.
2. The second map, Sanborn Company,1933, is the eastern end of South Ruffner, and illustrates the undevelopment of the South bank of the Kanawha. Yet the Council took no action to develop A city park.
3. All the structures shown in the third map, Sanborn Company, 1933, were later demolished for the expansion of the Capitol grounds. Duffy Street no longer exists and the area is now the walkway in front of the Cultural Center, which spans over the former Quarrier Street. The large structure at the right denotes the first wing of the State Capitol.

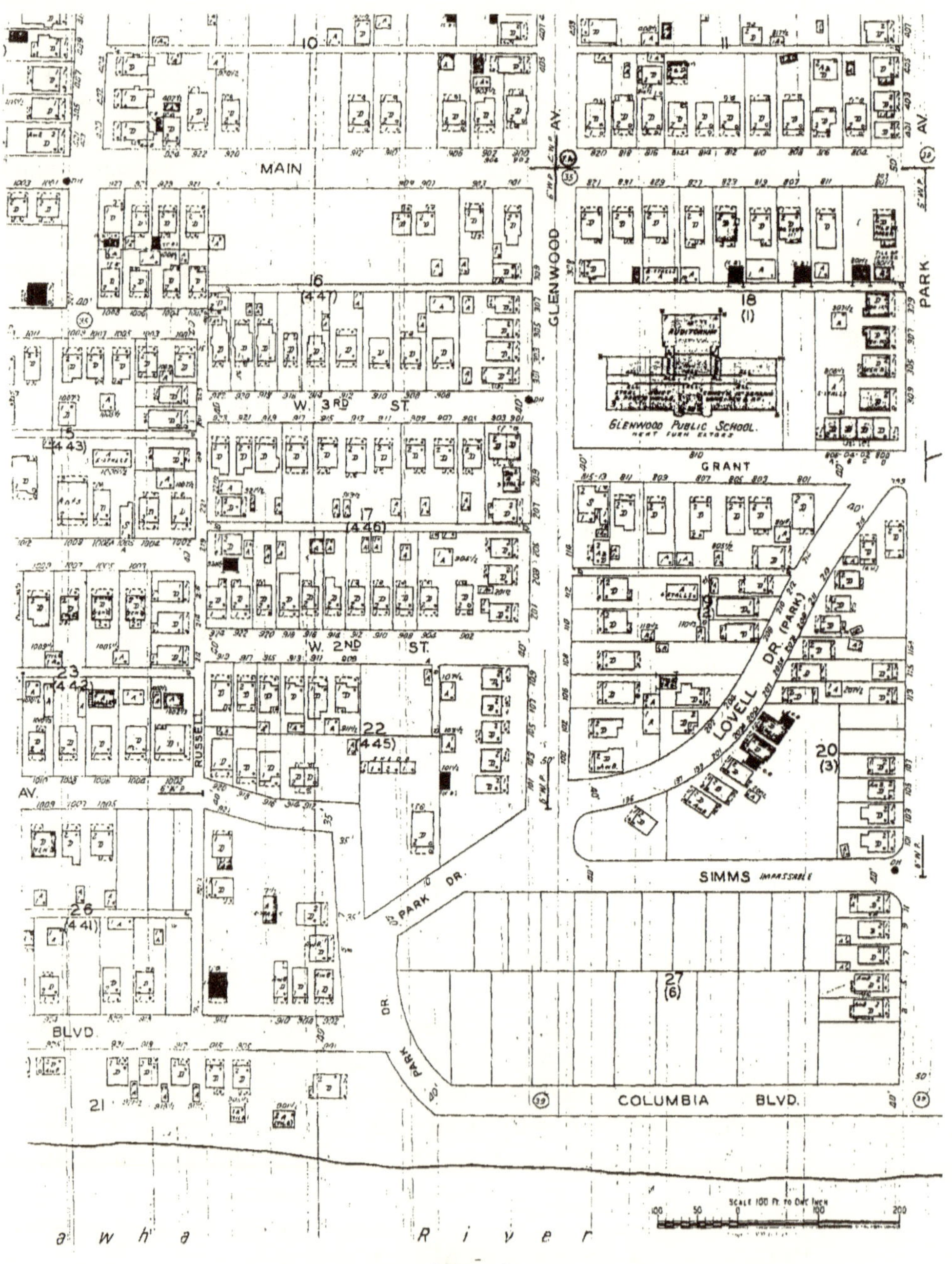
MAIN
GLENWOOD AV.
PARK AV.
W. 3RD ST.
W. 2ND ST.
GRANT
RUSSELL
AV.
LOVELL DR. (PARK)
GLENWOOD PUBLIC SCHOOL.
SIMMS
PARK DR.
BLVD.
COLUMBIA BLVD.
R i v e r

Map 1

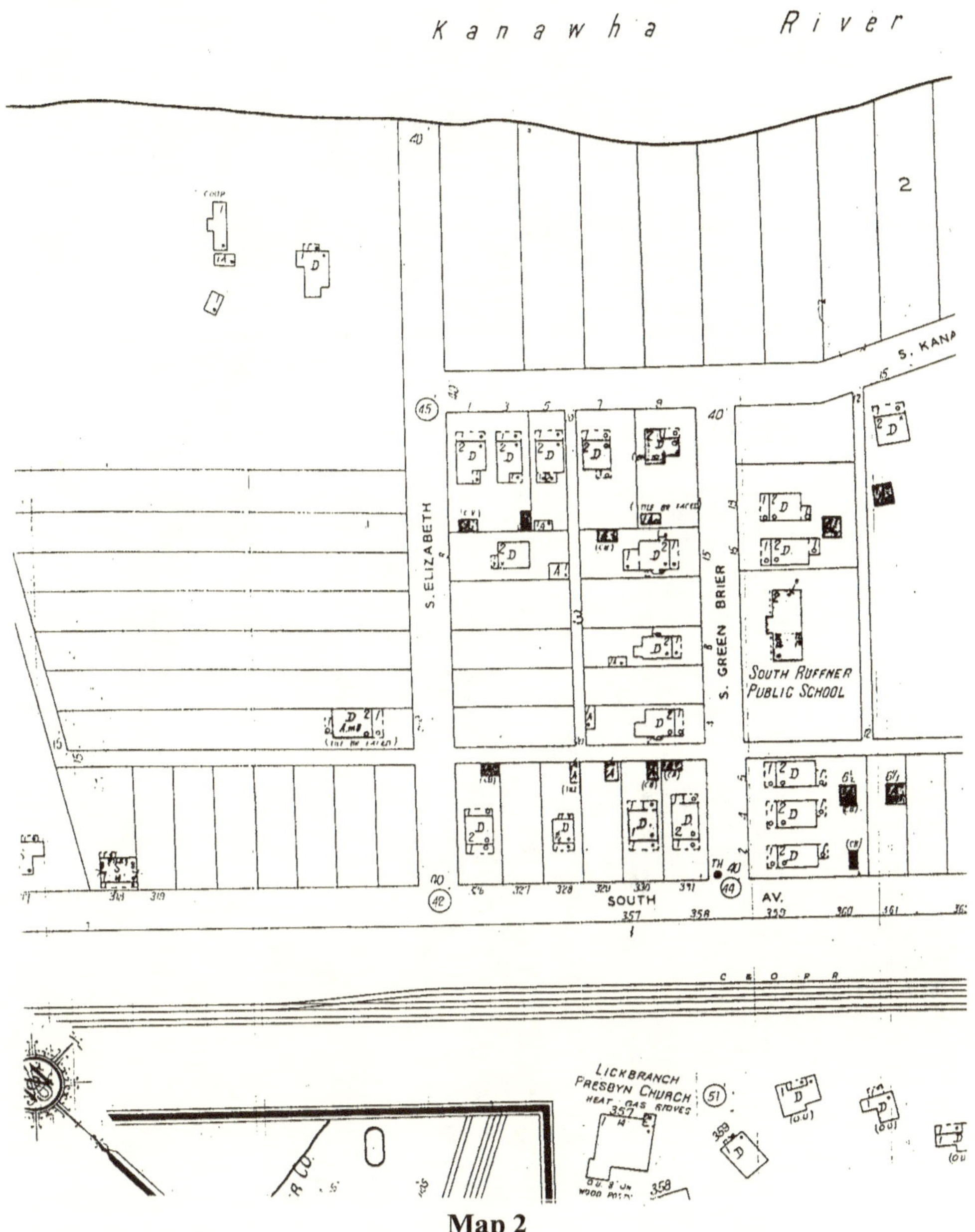
Kanawha River
S. KANA
S. ELIZABETH
S. GREEN BRIER
SOUTH RUFFNER
PUBLIC SCHOOL
SOUTH
AV.
LICKBRANCH
PRESBYN CHURCH
HEAT GAS STOVES
C & O R R

Map 2

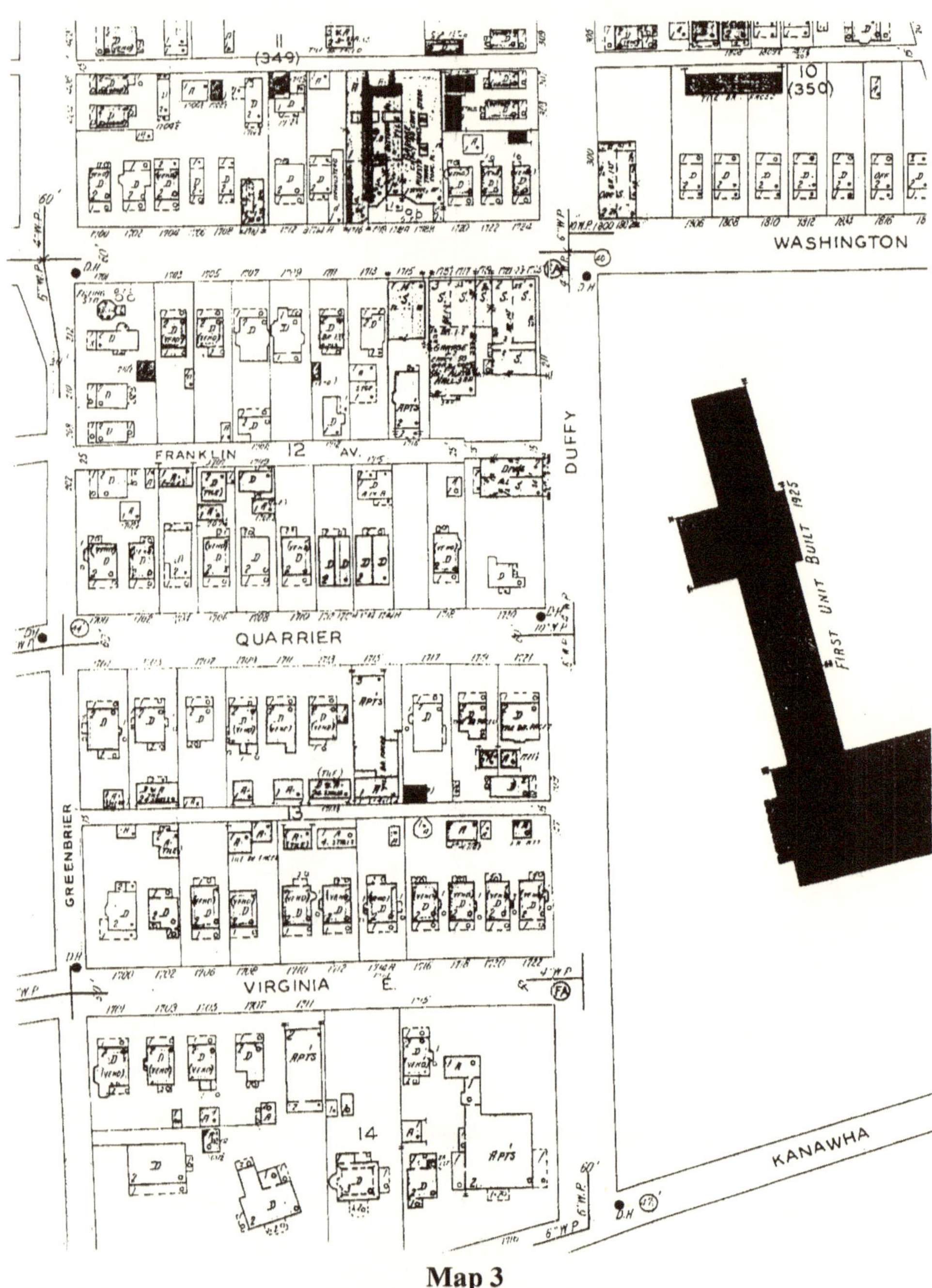
11
(349)
10
(350)
WASHINGTON
DUFFY
FRANKLIN
12
AV.
QUARRIER
FIRST UNIT BUILT 1925
GREENBRIER
VIRGINIA
E.
APTS
14
KANAWHA

Map 3

Population and the West Virginia Economy

Many observers have associated Charleston's early 20th Century prosperity with its thriving wholesale business. In 1898, J.C. Tipton wrote: "As a wholesale city Charleston, in proportion to her population, has scarcely a rival in the United States." [1] At this time and for the next several decades, the city's wholesalers were shipping out groceries, shoes, clothing, dry goods, furniture, stationary, hardware supplies, lumber, and more. Thirty years later, Charleston's Mayor Wertz in his book, City With a Future, called attention to the city's position as the focal point of wholesale trade in the center and southern part of the state. At this time, 1928, Wertz, reported that the volume of wholesale business was $50 million, which was about an eightfold increase from the time Tipton praised the city's wholesale volume. [2] In the next decade after Wertz's book appeared, Charleston's comprehensive plan called Charleston the trade center within a sixty-mile radius. In 1940, the Chamber of Commerce, in one its business surveys, reported that Charleston is a trade center serving twelve counties with a population of one-half million. The Chamber concluded: "Its wholesale and jobbing business is outstanding, being almost equal to its splendid retail business, which is easily the largest in the state." [3] The following year, the WPA Writers Project continued with the same refrain: "Wholesale houses here [Charleston] serve virtually every type of retail establishment in the southern part of the state."[4]

If Charleston prosperity is linked with the fortunes of nearby counties, a look at a few of them may provide some background for Charleston's increasing population to 1960 and its decline thereafter. Counties south of Charleston that fared well in the early part of the century were the coal producing counties of Fayette, Logan, McDowell, and Raleigh. While these counties grew, Charleston gained population, and when people began to leave the southern counties, Charleston's population shortly began to decline. Beginning in 1910, Fayette County's population increased with every decennial census until 1950 from 51.9 to 82.3 thousand. The pattern is identical for the other three counties. Logan in the same period grew from 18.4 in 1910 to 77.2 thousand in 1950; McDowell from 47.8 to 98.5 thousand; and Raleigh from 25.0 to 96.0 thousand. However, beginning with 1950, all four counties started to lose population and by 1970, the loss was significant. The amount of coal mined in these counties over the period from 1910 to 1970 followed the same curve as did the population. Coal tonnage increased to 1950, then declined between 1950 and 1970. Although some of the population loss may be explained by the decrease in coal tonnage mined, a more significant reason for the population decline in the coal counties may be found in the technological changes in coal mining that resulted in far fewer miners. Taking West Virginia as a whole, in 1950 nearly 120,000 miners extracted just over 145,000 million tons of coal. In 1970, the coal mined was nearly as great—143,000 million tons, but only 45,000 miners were needed to extract it, a threefold decrease in twenty years. This trend in the number of miners would be applicable to all counties, for the changing technology was industry and statewide. The falling population in the four coal counties was drastic. Fayette County's population decreased from 82.3 in 1950 to 49.3 thousand in 1970; Logan in the same twenty-year period from 77.2 to 46.3 thousand; McDowell from 98.5 to 50.6 thousand; and Raleigh declined from 96.0 to 49.3 thousand. For the four counties, the population decline was about 156,000. Because of the 1958 annexation that added 18,000 people to the city's population, Charleston's population showed an increase until 1960, but thereafter reflecting the southern coal counties, Charleston's population began a decade after decade decline. [5]

At the time that Charleston's population was following the decline of the southern counties, the capitol city was also being victimized by West Virginia' colonial economy. Civic boosters have seemingly been entranced by Charleston's proximity to large deposits of coal, natural gas, and oil, a fact that has caused the same boosters to conclude that economic and population growth would therefore accrue to Charleston. The infatuation with natural resources near to Charleston began well before the 20th Century. In the late 19th Century, John Hale wrote: "Within a circle described by radius of one hundred fifty miles around Charleston as a center of an embarrassment of riches which in variety, extent, and value is not equaled by any other locality of equal area in the continent.... With this vast storehouse of fuel and immense water power located so closely and conveniently surrounding Charleston, there is no reason why with proper development and adequate transportation facilities, the Kanawha Valley should not become the greatest manufacturing and chemical center in the world." [6] In 1926 the Charleston Chamber of Commerce was just as optimistic. The Chamber wrote: "The eyes of the industrial world are fixed on the great Kanawha Valley, and with the industrial development of this natural storehouse of energy [coal], greater Charleston is fast becoming in fact as well as name the Pittsburgh of the south." [7]

These predictions of industrial might of course were not realized and the reason is clear. The natural resources came to be owned by out of state corporations, which found it cheaper to transport the resources to out of state factories rather than to build the factories and develop the resources in the Valley. [8] The trend started early. The first report of the state inspector of mines in 1883 showed that about 1.4 tons of coal were mined in the Kanawha District and over 1.3 tons were shipped out of state. [9] A colonial economy of this sort cannot result in sustainable job growth, for it is in the processing of raw materials and not their extraction that creates long term employment. Processing has a broad meaning involving basic research, the continuous innovation of new products, and the creation of large organizations and management structures in order to get the products to market. Little of this was happening in the Kanawha Valley. The level of manufacturing employment in Charleston reflected the absence of materials processing. In 1909 manufacturing employees working in the city numbered 951. By 1935, manufacturing workers had increased to only 1056. True in 1929, the city had 2353 workers in manufacturing, but about one-half of this figure was accounted for by the Kelly Axe Handle plant on the West Side. As the Depression deepened, Kelly rapidly declined never to return as a major industrial player. In 1940, manufacturing employment was 1455, and by 1960, it had reached just over 3600. [10] (These are in-city figures only and do not include the chemical industries west of Charleston).

As the presence of natural resources resulted in misplaced boosterism for the city's future so the chemical plants as they began to appear in the World War I period also spawned undue optimism regarding Charleston's growth. Such optimism had little foundation because the chemical industry like the natural resources was also characterized by out of state ownership. However, at the time the location of corporate ownership was rarely considered. In this context, Mayor Wertz wrote in his book: "Charleston is growing very rapidly to become one of the great industrial centers of the United States, and its future in an industrial way is now assured." [11] In her study of Charleston and Valley industry from their beginnings to 1936, Elizabeth Goodall attributed Charleston's population growth from 1920 to 1930 to the expanding chemical industry. After detailing the expansion of the Valley's chemical plants to 1936, she concludes her study with these remarks: "Vast wealth has been invested in the development of the natural resources so abundant in the industrial area; outstanding civic improvements have been made.... To one who witnessed the phenomenal growth of the city, Charleston's future indeed looms bright." [12] This industrial optimism led to inflated population predictions. Mayor Dawson had the most inflated view. In his outlook for the city in December 1935, Dawson proposed a planning committee in order to "plan for the rapid growth of Charleston to a city of 200,000, which I think will be within ten years." [13] At the time Charleston's population was between sixty and sixty-seven thousand. Three years later, the more sober city comprehensive plan forecast the city's population to be 98,000 by 1960.

These rosy predictions reflected what John Williams in his book, West Virginia and the Captains of Industry, called the "development faith," [14] a very human expression of optimism but lacking any theoretical foundation. The remarks of Wertz and Dawson, both mayors, are statements of civic pride and boosterism characteristic of individuals in their position. The population forecast of the comprehensive plan, while more reflective than that of Dawson's, ignored the nature of West Virginia's economy, and was instead based on past population increases. Goodall's study also failed to consider the outside ownership of West Virginia's economy. Her study with respect to the chemical and other industries is entirely linear, and her reasoning is that since Charleston and the Valley grew in the Twenties and Thirties, their growth would continue. Goodall's optimism was justified to a limited extent for about twenty years. When she ended her study in 1936, chemical industry employment was about 7400. By 1960, Kanawha County employment in the industry was about 14,000, but by 1970, countywide chemical employment had fallen to 9800. By 1980, it was up to 10,300, but in 1990, the county's chemical employment had fallen to 5550. [15] Such zigzagging is hardly the stuff of sustainable employment growth. Williams, however, makes a point relevant to the long-term role of the chemical industry in the Valley. The industry, he points out consists of branch plants belonging to corporations based in places as New York, New Jersey, and Pittsburgh. Although unlike the coal industry, the chemical industry represented locally based manufacturing, its absentee ownership meant that Charleston would not be a headquarters city. [16] Thus the city would never achieve a large influx of private white collar and executive personnel. Failing to obtain such employment is of course detrimental in itself, but just as important, the absence of a high-income managerial class would mean that there would be few economic spin-offs resulting in additional employment. Thus, the lack of local ownership of manufacturing, the branch plant nature of the chemical industry, and the decrease in its wholesale market made it difficult for Charleston to sustain its early 20th Century growth.

As a final note regarding Charleston's population, it needs to be stressed that much of Charleston's population growth since 1930 has not been organic, that is, growth from within. It has come about largely because of annexation. The increase during the Thirties from 60,408 to 67,914 by 1940 was organic growth, because there was no annexation during the 1930's. But the decennial increase to 73,501 in 1950 can principally be attributed to the some 5000 people added by the 1948 annexation of North Charleston. Then by 1960, the city's population jumped to its highest point ever, 85,796 but, as was stated above, the large 1958 annexation and two minor boundary adjustment more than accounts for the increase. There were minor boundary adjustments during the 1970's and 1980's, but no significant annexations. With manufacturing stagnant, Charleston's population fell to 71,000 in 1980 and to less than 64,000 in 1980. Hence, since 1930, Charleston's population once annexations are factored out has showed no significant increase, and since 1960 a steady decline has been occurring.

Notes

Chapter 1

1. U.S. Department of Commerce, Bureau of Census, 12th Census of the United States, 1900: Population.

2. R.L. Polk & Co., Charleston Directory, Pittsburgh, PA, business section.

3. Ibid. and J.L. Tipton, Charleston and Its Resources, Charleston Business and Industrial Assn, Charleston, W. Va, 1898,p. 39.

4. Charleston Gazette, March 10, 1920, p.11 and April 20,1910, p.11. Also Daily Gazette, August 26, 1900.

5. Stan Cohen, Kanawha Valley Inmages, Pictorial Histories Publishing Co., Charleston, W.Va. 1987, p. 213.

6. Charleston Newspapers, About Your Company, self published, n.d. Also see Charleston Directory, ibid, 1901, and Tipton, ibid, pp. 35-37.

7. W.S. Laidley, History of Charleston and Kanawha County, West Virginia and Representative Citizens, Richmond-Arnold Publshing Co, Chicago, IL, 1911, pp. 243-48

8. Charleston Gazette, June 1, 1913 and Sept, 12, 1930. Also Frank Krebs, Where There is Faith:The Morris Harvey College Story, MHC Publications, 1974, p.251.

9. Laidley, p. 176 and Charleston Directory, 1901-1910.

10. Ibid., pp. 252-266 and Charleston Directory, 1901.

11. Simon Meyer, One Hundred Years: An Anthology of Charleston Jewry, Jones Printing Co., Charleston, W.Va 1972, pp. 101-110.

12. James Morton Callahan, Semi-Centennial History of West Virginia, Semi-Centennial Commission, 1913, pp. 317-18. Also Gazette, June 19.1949.

13. Mail-Tribune, July 21, 1900,p., 5.

14. Cohen, p. 180 and Laidley, p. 214.

15. George W. Hilton, ital, The Electric Interurban Railways in America, Stanford University Press, 1960, p. 305. Also West Virginia State Gazetteer and Business Directory, 1914-15.

16. Cohen, pp. 108-118 and Laidley, p. 209.

17. Laidley, pp. 201-2.

18. Gazette, May 17, 1900.

19. Charleston Directory, 1901,p. 291.

20. Laidley, pp., 183-92 and Charleston Directory, 1910, p.17.

21. Tipton, p, 9.

22. Ibid, pp.78-87.

23. Ibid, pp. 44-85 and Charleston Directory 1901.

24. Thirteen Census of United States, 1910: Vol. IX, Manufacturing.

25. Laidley, pp. 143-151 and Tipton, p. 92.

26. Gazette, March 23, 1960, p.18 and January 7, 1934, p.5 and Charleston Directory, business section of representative years.

27. See Gazette and Mail during December 1900 for display advertising.

28. Charles Amber & Fustus Summers, West Virginia, The Mountain State, 2d ed., Prentice-Hall, Inc., Englewood Cliffs, NJ, 1940, 1958, p. 545.

29. Charleston Directory, sections on business listings and individual addresses, 1901 and 1911.

30. Minutes, Charleston City Council, Sept 7, 1900, City Clerks Office, Charleston, WV. See also Julius deGruyter, Charleston, West Virginia, A Summery of the City Charter, Administrative Affairs, etc, Jarrett Printing Co., Charleston, W.Va., 1950, pp. 20-21.

31. Ibid., Minutes, October 4, 1900.

32. DeGruyter, pp. 40-45.

33. Charleston Directory, 1901 and Gazette, April 1, 1900, p. 1.

34. Minutes, Charleston City Council, January, 18, 1900.

35. Gazette, Sept 8, 1900, p. 12.

36. DeGruyter, pp. 47-49.

Chapter 2

1. Charleston Chamber of Commerce, Charleston West Virginia and Its Industrial Suburbs, Charleston, W. Va, 1921, p. 8.
2. Elizabeth J. Goodall, "The Charleston Industrial Area: Development, 1797-1937, West Virginia History, Vol XXX, October 1968, pp. 393-95. Also Gazette, June 23, 1923 and November 4, 1928. Also Charleston Chamber of Commerce, Illustrated and Descriptive Charleston, p. 12, n.d.
3. V. B. Harris, Great Kanawha, Jarrett Printing Company, Charleston, W.Va., 1974 and Cohen, ibid, p.151.
4. Charleston Chamber of Commerce, Charleston, West Virginia and Kanawha Valley Industries, 1926, p.23
5. Daily Mail, July 2, 1915, p. 1. Also see West Virginia State Gazetteer and Business Directory, 1917-18, section on Charleston.
6. Paul D. Marshall, Historical and Architectural Survey of Downtown, Charleston, West Virginia, Marshall & Associates, Inc., 1984.
7. Daily Mail, June 28, 1915, p. 2.
8. Daily Mail, December 28, 1935,p. 1.
9. Gazette, Sept 1, 1920, p.5 and December 22, 1920, p.5.
10. DeGruyter, pp. 45-55.

Chapter 3

1. Fifteenth Census of the United States, 1930, Manufacturers.

2. Municipal Planning Commission, City of Charleston, Comprehensive Plan, 1938.

3. Charleston, West Virginia and Kanawha Valley Industries, ibid, p.17.

4. Ibid, p. 5.

5. Charleston Directory, 1920, business section.

6. Fourteenth Census of the United States, 1920, Population.

7. Charleston and Industrial Suburbs, ibid, p.8

8. Gazette, November 11, 1923, p. 1 and Charleston Directory, 1925, business section.

9. Bernard Frieden, Downtown, Inc, MIT Press, Cambridge, MA, 1990, p. 9.

10. Gazette, March 24, 1921, p. 13

11. Sandy Wells, "Remembering The Diamond," Charleston Gazette, November 26, 1995, p. 21A.

12. Gazette, February, 6, 1927, p.2. sec 2.

13. Charleston Gazette, 1935, business section.

14. Gazette, December 9, 1923, p.1.

15. Self published promotion brochure by Daniel Boone Hotel. See W.Va Department of Archives and History clipping file, Cultural Center, Charleston, W.Va.

16. Gazette, May 9, 1926, p. 2

17. Gazette, April 24, 1927, Better Homes, p. 5; April 1, 1923, p. 9; April 22, 1923, p. 11.

18. Charleston Gazette, 1925, business section; Daily Mail, December 25, 1921, p.12. Also Gazette, October 4, 1991, p. 1C.

19. Gazette, June 16, 1963, p. H8 and July 28, 1971, p. 16. Also West Virginia Heritage Encyclopedia, Vol. 10 and 11, Supplemental Series, 1941, p. 157.

20. Unpublished article by Antonio Modarelle, June 2, 1947. See W. Va. Department of Archives and History clipping file, Cultural Center, Charleston, W.Va. Also see Gazette April 25, 1991, p. 1D.

21. Readers' Digest, June 1947. Also Gazette, October 22, 1989, p. 1E and Daily Mail, February 22, 1923, p. 9.

22. Addresses traced in Charleston Directory 1910 to 1923.

23. Gazette, May 13, 1926, p. 5; October 17, 1937, p. 2B; and October 24, 1964, p. 12. Also Daily Mail, June 1,1939.

24. Daily Mail, April 15, 1923, p. 1 and April 22, 1923, p. 4.

25. William W. Wertz, Charleston, City With A Future, self published, 1928, p. 12.

26. Council minutes, 1923 to 1931.

27. Daily Mail, January 1, 1922, p. 7.

28. Daily Mail, December 21, 1923, p. 1 and December 26, 1923, p. 1.

29. Council Minutes, 1925.

30. Council minutes, August 28, 1923.

31. Daily Mail, October, 20, 1923, p.1.

32. Daily Mail, February, 23, 1923, p. 1.

33. Gazette, January 3, 1926, sec 2, p. 1.

34. Daily Mail, January 19, 1926, p.1 and February 2, 1926, p. 1.

35. Daily Mail, December, 22, 1925, p. 1

36. Daily Mail, April 12, 1927 p. 1 and April 16, 1927, p. 1.

37. Daily Mail, October 22, 1929, p. 1.

38. Gazette, October 22, 1929, p. 1.

39. West Virginia Legislative Handbooks for the years concerned.

40. Charleston Directory, 1920, 1925, 1930, and 1935.

41. Daily Mail, May 3, 1930, p. 1.

42. Daily Mail, July 1, 1930, p. 1.

43. Council minutes, August 28, 1923.

44. Council minutes, August 27, 1929.

45. Council minutes, August, 1927.

46. Ibid.

47. Ibid.

48. Ibid.

Chapter 4

1. Charleston Chamber of Commerce, Economic Basis of Charleston and Its Environs, Charleston, W. Va. 1939.

2. Goodall, West Virginia Quarterly, ibid., p. 399.

3. Charleston Chamber of Commerce, Facts About Charleston, Charleston, W. Va., 1936. Also Gazette, October, 21, 1936 and Goodall, ibid., p. 398.

4. See Daily Mail for last Sunday in December for city building permits issued for all years. A summery for several years appear in Daily Mail, December 30, 1934, p. 4.

5. Goodall, ibid, p. 408. Also Charleston Chamber of Commerce, the Chemical City, Charleston, W. Va., 1929 and Facts About Charleston, ibid.

6. Daily Mail, March 29, 1929, p. 1 and Gazette, November 11, 1930.

7. Daily Mail, October 12, 1930, p. 1 and Gazette, November 21, 1930, p. 1.

8. Daily Mail, March 21, 1929, p. 1.and October 12, 1930, p. 1. Also Goodall, ibid., p. 401.

9. Daily Mail, December 4, 1932, Society, p. 1

10. Daily Mail, March 29, 1939, Society, p. 1.

11. Daily Mail, January 22, 1933, Society, p. 1.

12. Daily Mail, April 6, 1931, Society, p. 1.

13. Gazette, December 14, 1930, Society, p. 1.

14. Council minutes, August 1933.

15. Council minutes, August 12, 1930 and August 1933. Also Daily Mail, December 19, 1933, p. 6.

16. Constitution of West Virginia, Art X, Sec 1.

17. Daily Mail, October 24, 1934, p. 1 and December 30, 1934, p. 4.

18. Gazette, April 15, 1935, p. 1.

19. Council minutes, August 1935.

20. Daily Mail, August 20, 1935, p. 1.

21. Daily Mail, January 3, 1935, p. 5.

22. Daily Mail, January 3, 1937, p. 5.

23. Daily Mail, January 4, 1937, p. 3.

24. Daily Mail, December 30, 1936, p. 1 and January 3, 1937, p. 5

25. Gazette, January 8, 1937, p. 1.

26. Nomination Form, East End, National Register of Historic Places, State Preservation Office, Charleston, W. Va.

27. Ibid.

28. Harry Brawley, "Front Street Saturday Night," Goldenseal, Fall 1986, p. 8

29. Gazette, October 1, 1990, p. 9A.

30. Charleston Directory, 1936, street section. Also Charleston Chamber of Commerce, Charleston, Capitol City of West Virginia, 1940.

31. Daily Mail, September 20, 1938, p. 1.

32. Daily Mail, December 17, 1938, p. 1

33. Gazette, October 2, 1990, p. 2C.

34. Charleston, Capitol City of West Virginia, ibid. n.p.

35. Daily Mail, January 3, 1937, p. 11.

36. Ibid.

37. Facts About Charleston, ibid.

38. Ibid. Also Daily Mail, December 22, 1940, p. 1.

39. Gazette, January 1, 1937, p. 10.

40. Council minutes, August 31, 1937.

41. Daily Mail, April 18, 1939, p. 1.

42. Daily Mail, April 4, 1939, p. 5.

43. Daily Mail, August 31 1939, p. 1 and September 7, 1939, p. 1.

44. Daily Mail, December 21, 1939, p. 1.

45. Daily Mail, December 24, 1940, p. 3.

46. Daily Mail, June 7, 1942, p. 2 and November 15, 1942, p. 2.

47. Daily Mail, February 19, 1942, p. 2.

48. Gazette, September 8, 1940, p. 31.

49. Gazette, September 3, 1939, p. 1.

50. Gazette, September 8, 1940, p. 31.

Chapter 5

1. Gazette, April 2, 1950, p. 1.

2. Charleston Directory, 1950, business section.

3. Gazette, March 21, 1950, p. 8.

4. Charleston Directory, 1950, business section.

5. Gazette, May 25, 1950, p. 1.

6. Gazette, January 18, 1950, p.33.

7. Daily Mail, May 7, 1950, p. 18.

8. Seventeenth Census of the United States, 1950, Population.

9. Daily Mail, February 5, 1950, p.1

10. About Your Company, ibid.

11. Daily Mail, June 18, 1950, p. 20.

12. Gazette, April 18, 1950, p. 1.

13. Daily Mail, June 27, 1950, p. 8.

14. Gazette, June 20, 1950, p. 6.

15. Daily Mail, June 18, 1950, p. 20.

16. Council minutes, August 1950.

17. Daily Mail, August 24, 1950, p. 6

18. Gazette, December 25, 1949, p.1.

19. Gazette, December 5, 1949.

20. Gazette, July 28, 1967.

21. Daily Mail, February, 9, 1950, p. 8.

22. Gazette, August 6, 1950, p. 16.

23. Gazette, February 19, 1995 and June 12, 1996.

24. Daily Mail, May 16, 1950, p. 1.

25. Daily Mail, July 8, 1950.

26. Daily Mail, July 9, 1952

27. Gazette, March 23, 1950, p. 8.

28. Gazette, April 22, 1950, p. 8.

29. Seventeenth Census of the United States, Census on Housing, 1950.

30. Comprehensive Plan, ibid.

31. Daily Mail, June 20, 1950, p.6.

Chapter 6

1. City boundaries are given in the charters. See also deGruyter, ibid, pp. 40-49.

2. Charleston City Charter, Acts of Legislature of West Virginia, 1875, Sec., 21.

3. Charleston City Charter, 1915, Sec., 7.

4. For background material on Walker see West Virginia Heritage Encyclopedia, Vol. 22, Richwood, W. Va., 1976, p. 4830.

5. Quoted in D. H. Strother, The Capitol of West Virginia and the Great Kanawha Valley, Charleston Journal Office, 1872, p. 25.

6. Map Room, Kanawha County Courthouse, Book 1, p. 8.

7. DeGruyter, ibid., pp. 45-47.

8. Deed Books, Kanawha County Courthouse. See index of Grantor Deeds for Edgewood Land Company.

9. Nomination form, Edgewood Historic District, National Register of Historic Places, State Preservation Office, Charleston, W. Va. See also Gazette, January 3, 1990, p. 1D.

10. John P. Hale, Trans-Allegheny Pioneers, 3d. ed. Derreth Printing Co., Raleigh, North Carolina, 1886 and 1971, pp. 318-19.

11. Charleston City Engineer's maps, Engineer's Office, Charleston, W. Va.

12. Plat shown in Council minute book, October 1925, Clerk's Office, City Hall, Charleston, W. Va.

13. Eric Homberger, Historic Atlas of New York City, Henry Holt Co., New York, p. 67.

14. Gazette, November 11, 1923, p. 1.

15. DeGruyter, ibid., p. 26.

16. Comprehensive Plan, 1938, ibid., and Building Zone Map, 1939, Charleston, W. Va, 1939.

17. Daily Mail, December 17, 1936, p. 8.

18. Daily Mail, December 28, 1936, p. 7.

19. Municipal Planning Commission, Tentative Thoroughfare Plan, 1938 (This is a section of Comprehensive plan).

20. Daily Mail, December 20, 1936, p. 6.

21. Gazette, March 19, 1929, p. 1.

22. Gazette, November 11, 1923, p. 1.

23. Daily Mail, December 20, 1936, p. 7.

24. Council minutes, November 16, 1936.

25. Daily Mail, April 5, 1939, p. 1.

26. Municipal Planning Commission, Biennial Report, 1948-49, Charleston, W. Va, pp. 10-11.

27. Gazette, December 15, 1958, p. 12.

28. Daily Mail, March 22, 1960, p. 6.

29. Gazette, March 24, 1960, pp. 1 and 8.

30. Gazette, March 28, 1960, p. 20.

31. Gazette, March 23, 1960, p. 9.

32. Daily Mail, March 20, 1960, p. 6.

33. Daily Mail, March 29, 1960, p. 1.

34. Daily Mail, July 28, 1992, p. 1C.

35. DeGruyter, ibid. pp. 44-45.

36. Deed Books, Kanawha County Courthouse. See books 105-524, 106-103, and 414-389.

37. Daily Mail, June 26, 1975, p. 1B and Gazette-Mail, July 3, 1994, magazine.

38. Cohen, ibid. p. 246.

39. Deed Books, ibid. 273-207, 403-388, and 403-572.

40. Krebs, Where There is Faith, ibid. pp. 170-250.

41. Gazette, August 9, 1964, p. 20 and Daily Mail, May 20, 1951, p. 2.

42. West Virginia Code, annotated, Vol. 3, Sec. 8-6-5.

43. Daily Mail, April 6, 1948, p. 9.

44. Daily Mail, June 29, 1948, p. 1.

45. Municipal Planning Commission, Progress Report, Charleston, W. Va. 1960, pp. 3-4.

46. Gazette, December 11, 1958, p. 8.

47. Daily Mail, December 14, 1958, p. 1 and December 20, 1958, p. 1.

Chapter 7

1. West Virginia Constitution, 1972.

2. Joe William Trotter, Jr, Coal, Class, and Color, Blacks in Southern West Virginia 1915-1932, University of Illinois Press, 1990, p. 136.

3. James D. Randall and Anna Evans Gilmer, Black Past, Charleston, W. Va, 1989, p.37.

4. Trotter, ibid, p. 127.

5. For the headlines see the following front pages: Daily Mail, December 21, 1925 and January 2, 1926. Gazette April 3, 1921; March 16, 1922; and December 28, 1930.

6. Grantor Deed index. The deeds cited are found in Deed Books 285-130, 300-487, 776-123, and 795-452, Kanawha County Courthouse, Charleston, W. Va.

7. Bureau of Negro Welfare and Statistics (BNWS), Biennial Report, 1947-48, State of West Virginia, p. 146.

8. Ibid, 1951-52, pp. 105-7,

9. Gazette, December 8, 1958, p.2.

10. Gazette, November 27, 1995, p. 2C

11. Gazette-Mail, July 3, 1994, magazine, p. 34.

12. Daily Mail, November 9, 1989, p. 2B.

13. BNWS, ibid, 1947, p. 148.

14. Daily Mail, January 2, 1929, p. 1. Also Trotter, ibid, p. 253.

15. Gazette, June 2, 1984, p. 1C.

16. Code of Ordinances, City of Charleston, 1921, Sec. 318.

17. Charleston Directories, selected years 1925 – 1975. Also Randall, ibid, pp. 110-191.

18. Randall, ibid, p. 149.

19. Randall, ibid, p. 110

20. Charleston Directories, 1925 to 1965. Also Trotter, ibid, p. 156.

21. Randall, ibid, p. 115.

22. Ibid, p. 116.

23. James Randall, West Virginia Beacon Digest, September 7, 1988, p.3.

24. BNWS, ibid, 1947-48, p. 149.

25. Richard D. Hill, History of First Baptist Church of Charleston, West Virginia, self published, 1934.

26. BNWS, ibid, 1923-24, p. 60.

27. Randall, ibid, p. 16 and 241.

28. BNWS, ibid, 1937-38, p. 76.

29. Registration Form, Mattie V. Lee Home, National Register of Historic Places, State Preservation Office, Charleston, W. Va.

30. Randall, ibid, pp. 148, 163, 170-71.

31. Gazette-Mail, arch 2, 1966, p.6 and May 12, 1966.

32. Traced in Charleston Directories, 1960 to 1975, business sections.

33. Charleston Directories, 1970 and 1975.

34. Quoted in William Raspberry, Cincinnati Inquirer, October 29, 1993, p. 6.

35. Interview with Ben Starks, Gazette, March 12, 1980, p.6C.

36. West Virginia Beacon Journal, January 15, 1988 and Graffitti, March 1968, p. 4A.

37. Gazette, April 4, 1979, 1D.

38. Charleston Directory, 1936, street section.

39. Charleston Directory, 1955.

40. Gazette, February 25, 1966, p.8.

41. Gazette, August 8, 1968, p.29; March 11, 1969, p. 3; and July 11, 1970.

42. Friedan, ibid, pp. 23-24.

43. BNWS, ibid, 1921-22, pp. 46-47.

44. Gazette, August, 25, 1965, p. 1.

45. Code of Ordinances, City of Charleston, 1921, pp. 327-550. Also see Daily Mail, June 25, 1915, p. 1.

46. The four part series by K.W. Lee began August 25, 1965, p 1. Quote from August 27, 1965, p. 1.

47. Gazette, November 27, 1957, p. 15 and August 27, 1965, p.1.

48. Triangle clipping file, Kanawha County Public Library, Charleston, W. Va.

49. Gazette, December 15, 1958, p. 12.

50. Gazette, August 27, 1965, p.1.

51. Ibid.

52. Gazette, August 26, 1965, p. 1.

53. Gazette, December 25, 1965

54. Gazette, August 25, 1965, p. 1.

55. Martin Anderson, The Federal Bulldozer, MIT Press, Cambridge, Mass, 1964, chapters 1 and 12.

56. Gazette, February 22, 1970, p. 17A.

57. Gazette, August 22, 1968, p. 39.

58. Gazette, October 23, 1968, p. 4 and Daily Mail, February 18, 1969, p.5.

59. Gazette, October 23, 1968, p.4.

60. Gazette-Mail, August 15, 1965, p.8B.

61. Appraisals of Designated Parcels included in Triangle Urban Renewal Project, Number W. Va R-21, Charleston Urban Renewal Authority, Vol VII, April 1967. Located Kanawha County Public Library.

62. Randall, Ibid, pp. 105-09.

63. Gazette, February 18, 1969, Sec 2, p. 1.

64. Gazette, February 20, 1969, p.1and March 17, 1969, p. 13.

65. Gazette, February 19, 1969, p. 4.

66. Daily Mail, January 23, 1969, p.4.

67. Gazette, March 12, 1970, p.1.

68. Gazette, April 4, 1979, p.1D.

69. Ibid.

70. Daily Mail, December 9, 1983, p.1B and Gazette, April 12, 1986, p.16.

71. Daily Mail, November 6, 1980, p.1B.

72. Daily Mail, November 22, 1965, p.19.

73. Anderson, ibid, pp. 161-71.

74. Gazette, January 2, 1964

75. Biennial Report of Tax Commissioner of West Virginia, 1964-65, Charleston, W.Va. Also Reports of State Auditor of W. Va, State Capitol, Charleston, W.Va.

76. Daily Mail, March 1, 1968, p.1 and Gazette, April 24, 1968, p.17.

Chapter 8

1. Sanborn Insurance Maps show industry and housing along the rivers. See for Charleston, 1907 to 1950, Kanawha County Public Library.

2. Gazette, June 15, 1990, p. 1C and Daily Mail, April 24, 1992, p. 1C.
3. Daily Mail, July 17, 1984, p. 1B and February 27, 1990, p.1. Also Gazette, February 8, 1991, p.1C and June 4, 1995, p. 3C.
4. Daily Mail, September, 6, 2000, p.1.
5. Gazette, August 27, 1980, Today Sec, p. 1.
6. Gazette-Mail, July 3, 1994, magazine.
7. Gazette, October, 2. 1928, p. 2 and Daily Mail, October 9, 1928, p. 1. Also Council minutes, October 8, 1928.
8. Gazette, April 20, 1924, p. 1.
9. Daily Mail, December 31, 1933, p. 3.
10. Daily Mail, July 16, 1940, p. 3.
11. Daily Mail, August 11, 1966, p.4.
12. Daily Mail, January 11, 1966, p. 4.
13. Daily Mail, March 18, 1960, p. 13.
14. Gazette, March 9, 1966, p. 5.
15. Municipal Planning Commission, ibid, Biennial Report, 1938-39.
16. Parks Commission Bulletin, n.d., located in Clipping file, Charleston, Department of Archives and History, Cultural Center.
17. Daily Mail, November 10, 1981, Sec, 1B.
18. George S. Wallace, Huntington Through Seventy-Five Years, Huntington, W. Va, 1947, pp. 50-51.
19. Harris, ibid, p. 271.
20. Daily Mail, January 2, 1938, p. 12.

21. Daily Mail, April 9, 1939, Sec 3, p. 4.

22. Daily Mail, September 24, 1939, p. 1.

23. Municipal Planning Commission, Bridges to Tomorrow, Charleston, W, Va, 1996 (This is Charleston's latest comprehensive plan).

24. A Brief History of Oglebay Park, Wheeling, W.Va, a pamphlet in visitors' center at Oglebay.

25. Daily Mail, December 18, 1967, p. 19

26. Gazette, April 30, 1968, p. 8; November 8, 1969, p. 28; and February 16, 1972, p. 1B.

27. Gazette, October 7, 1994, p. 1C; June 8, 1997, p. 1C; and March 11, 1998, p.1C.

28. Ray Oldenburg, The Great Good Place:Cafes, Coffee Shops, Community Centers, Beauty Parlors, General Stores, Bars, Hangouts and How They Got You Through the Day, Paragon House, New York, 1989.

29. Andres Duary, etal, Suburban Nation, North Point Press, New York. 2000. Also Philip Langdon, A Better Place to Live, University of Massachusetts Press, Amhurst, Mass, 1994.

30. Charleston Directory, 1949 to 1955, business and street sections.

31. Municipal Planning Commission, Revised Zoning Ordinance, Charleston, W.Va, 1976.

32. Daily Mail, March 6, 1997, p.4B.

33. Nomination Form, Grosscup Road Historic District, National Register of Historic Places, State Preservation Office, Charleston, W.Va.

34. Gazette, April 28, 1978, p. 4B

35. Traced in Charleston Directories, 1925 to 1965, street section.

36. Gazette, January 4, 1972, p. 2B.

37. Nomination, East End Historic District, National Register of Historic Places, State Preservation Office, Charleston, W.Va.

38. Gazette, September 13, 1983, p. 2 and September 20, 1983, p. 1.

39. Craig Whitaker, Architecture and the American Dream, Clarkson Potter, New York, 1996, pp. 174-75.

40. A concise history of Charleston early landholdings is found in Marshall, ibid, pp. 4-10.

41. Gazette, September, 18, 1949, p.11.

42. Paul Marshall, Historic Structures Report: Kanawha County Courthouse, Marshall & Associates, Charleston, 1979, p.11.

43. Nomination Form, Kanawha County Courthouse, National Register of Historic Places, State Preservation Office, Charleston, W.Va.

44. Gazette, April 23, 1922, p. 3.

45. Daily Mail, August 31, 1923, p. 6.

46. This point is made by Whitaker, ibid, pp. 13-14, 209-13.

47. Quoted in The West Virginia Capitol: A Commemorative History, Legislature of West Virginia, 1982, p. 31.

48. Daily Mail, April 12, 1966, p. 1.

49. Gazette-Mail, July 11, 1976, p. 1C.

50. Daily Mail, January 8, 1969, p. 42.

51. Daily Mail, July 7, 1988

Chapter 9

1. Tipton, ibid, p.9

2. Wertz, ibid, p. 13.

3. Charleston Chamber of Commerce, Charleston, Capitol City of West Virginia, 1940, n.p.

4. West Virginia Heritage Encyclopedia, Vol. 10&11, supplemental series, Richwood, W.Va, 1974, p. 186.

5. West Virginia Legislative Handbook

6. John P. Hale, History of the Great Kanawha Valley, Gauley and New River Publishing Co, Gauley Bridge, W.Va, 1891, 1994, p. 210.

7. Charleston Chamber of Commerce, Charleston, West Virginia and the Kanawha Valley Industries, Charleston, W.Va, 1926, p.1.

8. Sources on the colonialism in Appalachia are ample. Concise statements of the West Virginia experience are John Alexander Williams, West Virginia and the Captains of Industry, WVU Foundation, 1976, chapter 5 and Williams, West Virginia: A Bicentennial History, W.W. Norton & Co, 1976, chapter 5.

9. Goodall, West Virginia Quarterly, Ibid, p. 376.

10. Comprehensive Plan, 1938, ibid. Also U.S. Census, Population, Social and Economic Characteristics, 1960.

11. Wertz, ibid, p. 13.

12. Goodall, ibid, p. 412.

13. Gazette, December 29, 1935, p. 12.

14. Williams, ibid, p. 193-74.

15. U.S. Census, Population, 1940 and 1960.

16. Williams, ibid, p. 185.

Bibliography

Books and Pamphlets

1. Amber, Charles and Summers, Festus. West Virginia, The Mountain State. 2d ed, Prentice-Hall, Englewood Cliffs, NJ, 1940.

2. Anderson, Martin. The Federal Bulldozer. MIT Press, Cambridge, MA, 1964.

3. Callahan, James Morton. Semi-Centennial History of West Virginia. Semi-Centennial Commission, 1913.

4. Charleston Area Medical Center Foundation. The Birth of a Medical Center: A History of CAMC. Pictorial Histories Publishing Co, Charleston, WV, 1988.

5. Charleston Chamber of Commerce. The Century Chronicle. 1901.

6. Charleston, West Virginia, The Sources and Evidences of its

7. Charleston, West Virginia and Its Industrial Suburbs. 1921.

8. Charleston, West Virginia and Kanawha Valley Industries. 1926.

9. The Chemical City, Charleston, WV. 1929.

10. Facts About Charleston. 1936.

11. Economic Base of Charleston and Its Environs. 1939.

12. Charleston, Capitol City of West Virginia. 1940.

13. Charleston Newspapers. About Your Company. self published, n.d.

14. Cohen, Stan. Kanawha Valley Images. Pictorial Histories Publishing Co, Charleston, WV, 1987.

15. De Gruyter, Julius A. Charleston, West Virginia, A Summery of the City Charter, Administrative Affairs, etc. Jarrett Printing Co, Charleston, WV, 1950.

16. Frieden, Bernard. Downtown, Inc. MIT Press, Cambridge, MA, 1990.

17. Hale, John p. Trans-Allegheny Pioneers. Derroth Printing Co, 3d ed, 1886, 1971.

18. Harris, V.B. Great Kanawha. Jarrett Printing Co, Charleston, WV, 1974.

19. Hill, Richard D. History of First Baptist Church of Charleston, West Virginia, self published, 1939.

20. Hilton, George W, etal. The Electric Interurban Railways in America, Stanford University Press, 1960.

21. Homberger, Eric. Historical Atlas of New York City, Henry Holt & Co, New York, 1994.

22. Krebs, Frank. Where There Is Faith: The Morris Harvey College Story. MHC Publications, 1974.

23. Laidlay, W.S. History of Charleston and Kanawha County. Richmond-Arnold Publishing Co, Chicago, IL, 1911.

24. Marshall, Paul. Historic Structure Report, Kanawha County Courthouse. Marshall and Associates, Inc, 1979.
25. Marshall, Paul. Historical and Architectural Survey of Downtown Charleston, West Virginia. Marshall and Associates, Inc, 1984.

26. Meyer, Simon, ed. One Hundred Years: An Anthology of Charleston Jewry. Jones Printing Co, Charleston, WV, 1972.

27. Morgan, John G. 175 Charleston. Charleston Gazette, 1970.

28. Randall, James D. and Gilmore, Anna Evans. Black Past. Charleston, WV, 1989.

29. Rice, Otis K. Charleston and the Kanawha Valley. Windsor Publications, Woodland Hills, CA, 1981.

30. Strother, David H. The Capitol of West Virginia and the Great Kanawha Valley, Charleston Journal Office, 1872.

31. Tipton, J.L. Charleston and Its Resources. Charleston Business and Industrial Association, Charleston, WV, 1898.

32. Trotter, Joe William Jr. Coal, Class, and Color: Blacks in Southern West Virginia 1915-1932, University of Illinois Press, Urbana, IL, 1990.

33. Wertz, William W. Charleston, City with a Future. self published, Charleston, WV, 1928.

34. Williams, John Alexander. West Virginia, A Bicentennial History. W.W. Norton &Co, New York, 1976.

35. Williams, John Alexander. West Virginia and the Captains of Industry. West Virginia University Foundation, Morgantown, 1976.

Documents

1. Appraisals of Designated Parcels, Triangle Urban Renewal Project, West Virginia, R-21, Charleston Urban Renewal Authority, Vol. XII, April 1967.

2. Bureau of Negro Welfare and Statistics, Biennial Reports, 1921-1952, State of West Virginia.

3. Charters of the City of Charleston, West Virginia, 1875, 1915 and 1919.

4. Code of General Ordinances of the Common Council of the City of Charleston, West Virginia, 1886. Compiled by J.D. Baines.

5. Code of Ordinances of the City of Charleston, West Virginia, 1921.Compiled by Uriah Barnes.

6. Council Minutes. City of Charleston, 1900-1980, City Clerk, Charleston, WV.

7. Deed Books, Kanawha County. Kanawha County Courthouse.

8. Land and Building Plats, Map Room, Kanawha County Courthouse.

9. Land Plats, City Engineer, Charleston, WV.

10. Municipal Planning Commission. Biennial Reports, 1948-49.

11. Municipal Planning Commission. Building Zone Ordinance and Map, City of Charleston, 1939.

12. Municipal Planning Commission. Building Zone Ordinance, Revised, City of Charleston, 1976

13. Municipal Planning Commission. Comprehensive Plans, City of Charleston, 1938, 1962, 1973,1996

14. Polk, R.L.Charleston Directory, Pittsburgh, PA, 1900-1980.

15. Polk, R.L. West Virginia State Gazetteer and Business Directory, Pittsburgh, PA, 1891-1924.

16. State Auditor Reports, State Capitol Office, Charleston, WV, 1980-90.

17. Tax Commissioner of West Virginia, Biennial Reports, 1964-65, Charleston, WV.

18. West Virginia Legislative Handbook, 1900-1934. Beginning 1935 title changed to West Virginia Blue Book, Clerk of the Senate, Charleston, WV.

19. Ward Maps, City Clerks Office, Charleston, WV.

Newspapers and Periodicals

1. Charleston Gazette, 1900 – current.

2. Charleston Daily Mail, 1900 – current.

3. West Virginia Beacon Digest, 1940 – 1980

4. Brawley, Harry. “Front Street Saturday Night.” Goldenseal, Fall 1986.

5. Goddall, Cecile R. Development of Municipal Government, Charleston, West Virginia, 1794-1936.” West Virginia History, Vol. XXX, January 1968.

6. Goodall, Elizabeth J. "The Charleston Industrial Area: Development, 1797-1937." West Virginia History, Vol. XXX, October 1968.

7. Trotter, Margaret G. "A Glimpse of Charleston in the 1890's: From a Contemporary Diary." West Virginia History, Vol. XXXV, January 1974.

8. Kanawha County Public Library, clipping file.

9. West Virginia Department of Archives and History, clipping file.

Maps

1. Sanborn Insurance Maps, Charleston, West Virginia, 1907-1950. On microfilm for intermittent years at the Kanawha County Public Library.

www.ingramcontent.com/pod-product-compliance
Lightning Source LLC
Chambersburg PA
CBHW030322290526
45785CB00001B/470

* 9 7 8 0 7 5 9 6 7 9 9 0 0 *